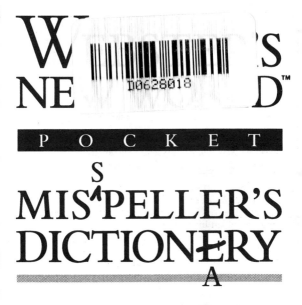

W   ' S
NE   D™

P O C K E T

MIS'PELLER'S
DICTIONERY

The Editors of
Webster's New World Dictionary

Michael Agnes
Editor-in-Chief

SECOND EDITION

Macmillan • USA

Webster's New World™
Pocket Misspeller's Dictionary, Second Edition

This book is a revised and enlarged edition of
Webster's New World™ Misspeller's Dictionary,
copyright © 1983 by Simon & Schuster, Inc.

Macmillan General Reference
A Simon & Schuster Macmillan Company
1633 Broadway
New York, NY 10019-6785

A Webster's New World™ Book
MACMILLAN is a registered trademark of Macmillan, Inc.
WEBSTER'S NEW WORLD DICTIONARY
is a registered trademark of Simon & Schuster, Inc.

Dictionary Editorial Offices:
New World Dictionaries
850 Euclid Avenue
Cleveland, OH 44114-3354

ISBN 0-02-861720-7
Manufactured in the United States of America
1 2 3 4 5 6 7   97 98 99 00 01 02

How to Use This Book

"How do I find it in the dictionary if I can't spell it?"

Most of us have been faced with the problem of looking up a word in the dictionary without really being sure how to spell it. Some people experience this more often than others. In preparing this special dictionary of more than 15,000 misspellings and 9,000 correct spellings, the editors have anticipated some of the typical miscalculations in spelling that users might make. While many words cause only minor confusion, some others cause serious difficulties. Though we have given only one or two possible misspellings for most words, we have supplied as many as four for a few others.

"How does a misspeller's dictionary work?"

- Each misspelling is given on the left side of the column, alphabetically. Opposite it is the correct spelling printed in boldface with small centered dots to show where the words are usually broken at the ends of lines.
- Some pairs or groups of words also have notes in italics and within parentheses following the correct spelling. These notes contain brief definitions or other information to assist you in identifying the correct spelling.
- For words having more than one acceptable spelling, only the first spelling given in *Webster's*

New World College Dictionary, Third Edition, is shown here.

"How do words come to be misspelled?"

In selecting possible misspellings for this dictionary we considered problems that writers often have, especially in the following general categories:

- uncertainty about whether a consonant is doubled, leading to misspellings, such as mispelling, Massachusets, or gallactic
- uncertainty about the order of vowels, such as siezure or seige
- errors resulting from mispronunciation, such as momento, dias, or mushmelon, or from dropping or slurring over a vowel or syllable, as menstrate or mathmatics
- homonyms, or words that have the same pronunciation but different spellings and different meanings, such as bore and boar, maze and maize, or flew, flue, and flu
- unrelated words with similar spellings that can be confused, such as dairy and diary
- addition of a vowel to a word, such as mayorality or athelete
- errors resulting from an incorrect understanding of a word's origin and development, such as cold slaw or hairbrained

We have also indicated pairings of words that often cause confusion:

- singulars and plurals, such as crisis and crises or basis and bases
- masculine and feminine forms, such as fiancé and fiancée or alumni and alumnae
- nouns and verbs, such as breath and breathe

"What do I do if I can't find the word in the misspelled words column?"

You may be able to determine the correct spelling of a word if you know how to pronounce it. The Word Finder Table below can help you to accomplish this. The table shows how the sounds of English consonants and vowels are represented in the spelling of various words. Try dividing the word into syllables and concentrating on the pronunciation of each syllable. By using the table to test various possible spellings, you may be able to determine the correct one.

WORD FINDER TABLE

Consonant Sounds

1. If the sound is like the letter or letters—	2. try spelling with letters—	3. as in the words—
b as in *bed*	b, bb	ru**b**, ru**bb**er
ch as in *chin*	ch, tch, t, ti, te, cz	**ch**air, ca**tch**, na**t**ure, ques**ti**on, righ**te**ous, **Cz**ech

(continued)

Consonant Sounds (cont.)

1. If the sound is like the letter or letters—	2. try spelling with letters—	3. as in the words—
d as in *dog*	d, dd, ed	no**d**, ri**dd**le, endanger**ed**
f as in *fall*	f, ff, gh, ph, lf	**f**ix, di**ff**erent, laug**h**, **ph**one, cal**f**
g as in *get*	g, gg, gh, gu, gue	**g**ive, e**gg**, **gh**ost, **gu**ard, catalo**gue**
h as in *help*	h, wh	**h**er, **wh**o
j as in *jump*	j, g, gg, d, di, dg, dj	**j**am, **g**em, exa**gg**erate, gra**d**uate, sol**di**er, ju**dg**ment, a**dj**ective
k as in *kiss*	k, lk, c, cc, ch, kh, ck, cqu, cu, qu, q, que	**k**ite, wa**lk**, **c**an, a**cc**ount, an**ch**or, **kh**aki, lu**ck**, la**cqu**er, bis**cu**it, li**qu**or, li**q**uid, uni**que**
l as in *leg*	l, ll, sl, ln	**l**eave, ca**ll**, i**sl**and, ki**ln**
m as in *meat*	m, mm, mb, mn, lm, gm	dru**m**, ha**mm**er, cli**mb**, hy**mn**, ca**lm**, diaphra**gm**
n as in *nose*	n, nn, gn, kn, pn	**n**ear, di**nn**er, **gn**ome, **kn**eel, **pn**eumonia

(continued)

Consonant Sounds (cont.)

1. If the sound is like the letter or letters—	2. try spelling with letters—	3. as in the words—
ng as in *ring*	ng, nk, ngue	lo**ng**, thi**nk**, to**ngue**
p as in *put*	p, pp, ph	ho**p**, di**pp**er, she**ph**erd
r as in *red*	r, rr, rh, wr	**r**iver, be**rr**y, **rh**yme, **wr**ong
s as in *see*	s, ss, sc, c, ps	**s**it, mi**ss**, **sc**ience, **c**ent, **ps**ychology
s as in *pleasure*	z, ge, s, si	a**z**ure, gara**ge**, lei**s**ure, confu**si**on
sh as in *she*	sh, s, ss, sch, sci, si, ssi, ce, ch, ci, ti	**sh**are, **s**ure, i**ss**ue, **sch**wa, con**sci**ence, man**si**on, mi**ssi**on, o**ce**an, ma**ch**ine, spe**ci**al, na**ti**on
t as in *top*	t, th, tt, ght, ed	**t**eam, **Th**omas, be**tt**er, bou**ght**, hook**ed**
v as in *vat*	v, lv, f	lo**v**e, sa**lv**e, o**f**
w as in *wish*	w, wh, o, u	**w**ait, **wh**ile, ch**o**ir, q**u**iet
y as in *yard*	y, i, j	**y**ellow, on**i**on, hallelu**j**ah
z as in *zebra*	z, zz, s, ss, x, cz	**z**one, bu**zz**ard, bu**s**y, sci**ss**ors, **x**ylophone, **cz**ar

Vowel Sounds

1. If the sound is like the letter or letters—	2. try spelling with letters—	3. as in the words—
a as in *cat*	a, ai, au	**a**sk, pl**ai**d, l**au**gh
a as in *cake*	a, ai, au, ay, ea, ei, eigh, ey, et	**a**te, r**ai**n, g**au**ge, p**ay**, br**ea**k, v**ei**l, w**eigh**, ob**ey**, bouqu**et**
a as in *car*	a, ah, ea, o	sw**a**n, **ah**, h**ea**rt, sp**o**t
a as in *fall*	a, au, aw, o, oa, oo, ou	**a**ll, **au**tumn, **aw**ful, l**o**ng, br**oa**d, d**oo**r, c**ou**gh
e as in *ten*	e, ea, ei, eo, ie, a, ae, ai, ay, aye, u	**e**very, h**ea**vy, th**ei**r, l**eo**pard, fri**e**nd, **a**ny, **ae**rosol, s**ai**d, s**ay**s, pr**ay**er, b**u**ry
e as in *me*	e, ea, ee, ei, eo, ey, i, ie, ae, oe	**e**qual, **ea**t, **ee**l, rec**ei**ve, p**eo**ple, k**ey**, mach**i**ne, f**ie**ld, alg**ae**, Ph**oe**nix
i as in *fit*	i, ie, ea, ee, ei, o, u, ui, y	**i**ll, p**ie**r, h**ea**r, b**ee**n, w**ei**rd, w**o**men, b**u**sy, b**ui**ld, h**y**mn
i as in *ice*	i, ie, igh, ei, ey,	k**i**te, t**ie**, s**igh**,

(*continued*)

Vowel Sounds (cont.)

1. If the sound is like the letter or letters—	2. try spelling with letters—	3. as in the words—
	ai, uy, y, ye	h**ei**ght, **eye**, **ai**sle, b**uy**, fl**y**, r**ye**
o as in *cot*	o, a, ah, ea	sp**o**t, sw**a**n, **ah**, h**ea**rt
o as in *for*	o, oa, oo, ou, aw, au, a	l**o**ng, br**oa**d, d**oo**r, c**ou**gh, **aw**ful, **au**tumn, **a**ll
o as in *go*	o, oa, oe, ou, ough, ow, ew, eau, au	**o**pen, **oa**t, t**oe**, s**ou**l, th**ough**, gr**ow**, s**ew**, plat**eau**, m**au**ve
u as in *up*	u, o, oo, oe, ou	s**u**mmer, s**o**n, fl**oo**d, d**oe**s, d**ou**ble
u as in *rule*	u, oo, o, oe, ou, ue, ui, eu, ew, ough	l**u**nar, t**oo**l, m**o**ve, sh**oe**, s**ou**p, bl**ue**, fr**ui**t, mane**u**ver, thr**ew**, thr**ough**
u as in *pull*	u, oo, o, oul	p**u**sh, w**oo**d, w**o**man, w**oul**d
u as in *fur*	u, e, ea, i, o, ou, y	t**u**rn, g**e**rm, h**ea**rd, b**i**rd, w**o**rm, c**ou**rage, m**y**rtle
a as in *about*	a, e, i, o, u	**a**go, **a**gent, penc**i**l, at**o**m, circ**u**s
oi as in *oil*	oi, oy, uoy	m**oi**st, b**oy**, b**uoy**
ou as in *out*	ou, ough, ow	m**ou**th, b**ough**, n**ow**

Sometimes certain letter combinations (rather than single sounds) cause problems when you are trying to find a word. Here are some common ones:

If you've tried...	then try...	If you've tried...	then try...	If you've tried...	then try...
pre	per, pro, pri, pra, pru	cks, gz	x	fiz	phys
		us	ous	ture	teur
per	pre, pir, pur, par, por	tion	sion, cion, cean, cian	tious	seous
				air	are
is	us, ace, ice	le	tle, el, al	ance	ence
ere	eir, ear, ier	kw	qu	ant	ent
wi	whi	cer	cre	able	ible
we	whe	ei	ie	sin	syn, cin, cyn
zi	xy	si	psy, ci		

The following abbreviations are used:

adj.	adjective	*pl.*	plural
adv.	adverb	*poss.*	possessive
aux.v.	auxiliary verb	*pp.*	past participle
conj.	conjunction	*prep.*	preposition
f.	feminine	*pron.*	pronoun
interj.	interjection	*prp.*	present participle
m.	masculine	*pt.*	past tense
n.	noun	*sing.*	singular
		v.	verb

A

| WRONG | RIGHT | WRONG | RIGHT |

WRONG	RIGHT	WRONG	RIGHT
abalish	**abol·ish**	abnormallity	
abaminable	**abom·i·na·ble**		**ab·nor·mal·i·ty**
abarigine	**ab·o·rig·i·ne**	abnormel	**ab·nor·mal**
abayance	**abey·ance**	abnoxious	**ob·nox·ious**
abbacus	**ab·a·cus**	abominible	**abom·i·na·ble**
abbandon	**aban·don**	abored	**aboard**
abbatement	**abate·ment**	aborrigine	**ab·o·rig·i·ne**
abberation	**ab·er·ra·tion**	abowt	**about**
abbolition	**ab·o·li·tion**	abrasieve	**ab·ra·sive**
abbortion	**abor·tion**	abrazion	**ab·ra·sion**
abbundant	**abun·dant**	abrest	**abreast**
abcence	**ab·sence**	abreviate	**ab·bre·vi·ate**
abcess	**ab·scess**	abriged	**abridged**
abdacate	**ab·di·cate**	abrup	**abrupt**
abdaminal	**ab·dom·i·nal**	absalutely	**ab·so·lute·ly**
abducktion	**ab·duc·tion**	absalve	**ab·solve**
abedience	**obe·di·ence**	abscand	**ab·scond**
abel	**able**	abscene	**ob·scene**
abelisk	**ob·e·lisk**	abscent	**ab·sent**
abhorent	**ab·hor·rent**	abscure	**ob·scure**
abillity	**abil·i·ty**	absense	**ab·sence**
abiss	**abyss**	absequious	**ob·se·qui·ous**
abjeck	**ab·ject**	abserd	**ab·surd**
abjective	**ob·jec·tive**	absess	**ab·scess**
abligation	**ob·li·ga·tion**	absession	**ob·ses·sion**
abligatory	**ob·lig·a·to·ry**	absidian	**ob·sid·i·an**
abliterate	**ob·lit·er·ate**	abskond	**ab·scond**
ablong	**ob·long**	absolete	**ob·so·lete**

WRONG	RIGHT	WRONG	RIGHT
absolutly	**ab·so·lute·ly**	accompanyment	
absorbant	**ab·sorb·ent**		**ac·com·pa·ni·ment**
absorbtion	**ab·sorp·tion**	accoustic	**acous·tic**
abstacle	**ob·sta·cle**	accrew	**ac·crue**
abstane	**ab·stain**	accross	**across**
abstanent	**ab·sti·nent**	accult	**oc·cult**
abstetrics	**ob·stet·rics**	accummulate	
abstinant	**ab·sti·nent**		**ac·cu·mu·late**
abstinense	**ab·sti·nence**	accupational	
abstrack	**ab·stract**		**oc·cu·pa·tion·al**
abtrusive	**ob·tru·sive**	accupressure	**acu·pres·sure**
abundent	**abun·dant**	accupuncture	
abusave	**abu·sive**		**acu·punc·ture**
abuze	**abuse**	accurasy	**ac·cu·ra·cy**
abzolve	**ab·solve**	accurrate	**ac·cu·rate**
abzorb	**ab·sorb** *(take in)*	accute	**acute**
abzurd	**ab·surd**	accuzation	**ac·cu·sa·tion**
academicly	**aca·dem·i·cal·ly**	acede	**ac·cede** *(agree)*
a capella	**a cap·pel·la**	acedemically	
accademy	**acad·e·my**		**aca·dem·i·cal·ly**
Accapulco	**Aca·pul·co**	acelerator	**ac·cel·er·a·tor**
accede	**ex·ceed** *(surpass)*	acent	**ac·cent** *(emphasis)*
accellerator	**ac·cel·er·a·tor**	acept	**ac·cept** *(receive)*
accept	**ex·cept** *(omit)*	aceptable	**ac·cept·a·ble**
accepted	**ex·cept·ed**	acepted	**ac·cept·ed**
	(left out)		*(approved)*
acceptible	**ac·cept·a·ble**	acerage	**acre·age**
access	**ex·cess** *(surplus)*	acess	**ac·cess** *(approach)*
accessable	**ac·ces·si·ble**	acetiline	**acet·y·lene**
accessary	**ac·ces·so·ry**	acetominofen	
accidently	**ac·ci·den·tal·ly**		**aceta·min·o·phen**
acclusion	**oc·clu·sion**	acheivement	
accollade	**ac·co·lade**		**achieve·ment**
accomodation		achord	**ac·cord**
	ac·com·mo·da·tion	acidentally	**ac·ci·den·tal·ly**

WRONG	RIGHT	WRONG	RIGHT
aclaim	**ac·claim**	acter	**ac·tor**
aclectic	**ec·lec·tic**	activety	**ac·tiv·i·ty**
aclimate	**ac·cli·mate**	actoress	**ac·tress**
a'clock	**o'clock**	actualy	**ac·tu·al·ly**
acme	**ac·ne** *(pimples)*	acuemen	**acu·men**
acne	**ac·me** *(peak)*	acumulate	**ac·cu·mu·late**
acolade	**ac·co·lade**	acurate	**ac·cu·rate**
acommodation		acurracy	**ac·cu·ra·cy**
......**ac·com·mo·da·tion**		acursed	**ac·curs·ed**
acompaniment		acusation	**ac·cu·sa·tion**
......**ac·com·pa·ni·ment**		acuse	**ac·cuse**
acomplice	**ac·com·plice**	acustic	**acous·tic**
acomplish	**ac·com·plish**	acustom	**ac·cus·tom**
acord	**ac·cord**	ad	**add** *(combine)*
acordion	**ac·cor·di·on**	adament	**ad·a·mant**
acost	**ac·cost**	adanoids	**ad·e·noids**
acount	**ac·count**	adapt	**ad·ept** *(expert)*
acquaintence		adapt	**adopt** *(choose)*
......**ac·quaint·ance**		adaptible	**adapt·a·ble**
Acquarius	**Aquar·i·us**	adaquate	**ad·e·quate**
acquiesence		add	**ad** *(advertisement)*
......**ac·qui·es·cence**		addage	**ad·age**
acrabat	**ac·ro·bat**	addative	**ad·di·tive**
acrage	**acre·age**	addept	**ad·ept** *(expert)*
acramonious		addick	**ad·dict**
......**acri·mo·ni·ous**		addition	**edi·tion**
acrilic	**acryl·ic**		*(book issue)*
acrue	**ac·crue**	additionaly	**ad·di·tion·al·ly**
acsend	**as·cend**	adeiu	**adieu** *(goodbye)*
acsent	**ac·cent** *(emphasis)*	adelweiss	**edel·weiss**
acsent	**as·cent** *(a rising)*	adendum	**ad·den·dum**
acsept	**ac·cept** *(receive)*	adep	**ad·ept** *(expert)*
acsertain	**as·cer·tain**	ader	**ad·der** *(snake)*
acsetic	**as·cet·ic** *(austere)*	adhear	**ad·here**
actavate	**ac·ti·vate**	adhezive	**ad·he·sive**

3

WRONG	RIGHT	WRONG	RIGHT
adict	**ad·dict**	advancment	
adige	**ad·age**		**ad·vance·ment**
adition	...**ad·di·tion** *(adding)*	advantagious	
aditive	**ad·di·tive**		**ad·van·ta·geous**
adjunck	**ad·junct**	adventureous	
adjurn	**ad·journ**		**ad·ven·tur·ous**
adjutent	**ad·ju·tant**	adverse	....**averse** *(unwilling)*
admanish	**ad·mon·ish**	adversery	**ad·ver·sary**
admeral	**ad·mi·ral**	advertisment	
admeration	....**ad·mi·ra·tion**		**ad·ver·tise·ment**
administer	**ad·min·is·ter**	advice	**ad·vise** *(v.)*
administration		advisary	**ad·vi·so·ry**
	..........**ad·min·is·tra·tion**	advise	**ad·vice** *(n.)*
administrater		adzorb	**ad·sorb**
	..........**ad·min·is·tra·tor**		*(collect on surface)*
admirible	**ad·mi·ra·ble**	Aegian	**Ae·ge·an**
admision	**ad·mis·sion**	aeresol	**aer·o·sol**
admissable	**ad·mis·si·ble**	aeronatical	
admitance	**ad·mit·tance**		**aer·o·nau·ti·cal**
ad nauzeam		afable	**af·fa·ble**
	................**ad nau·se·am**	afair	**af·fair**
adnoids	**ad·e·noids**	afasia	**apha·sia**
ado	**adieu** *(goodbye)*	afect	....**af·fect** *(to influence)*
adolescant	**ad·o·les·cent**	afectionate	....**af·fec·tion·ate**
adom	**at·om**	afective	**af·fec·tive**
adoo	**ado** *(fuss)*		*(emotional)*
adopt	**adapt** *(adjust)*	affadavit	**af·fi·da·vit**
adorible	**ador·a·ble**	affare	**af·fair**
adrennalin	**ad·ren·al·in**	affect	**ef·fect** *(result)*
adress	**ad·dress**	affective	**ef·fec·tive**
adressible	**ad·dress·a·ble**		*(having effect)*
adue	**ado** *(fuss)*	affend	**of·fend**
adultarate	**adul·ter·ate**	affible	**af·fa·ble**
adultry	**adul·tery**	afficionado	**afi·cio·nado**
advacate	**ad·vo·cate**	affilliate	**af·fil·i·ate**

WRONG	RIGHT
affirmitive	af·firm·a·tive
affluent	ef·flu·ent *(flowing)*
affraid	afraid
affusive	ef·fu·sive
Afganistan	Afghan·i·stan
aficcionado	afi·cio·na·do
afid	aphid
afidavit	af·fi·da·vit
afiliate	af·fil·i·ate
afinity	af·fin·i·ty
afirm	af·firm
afirmative	af·firm·a·tive
afix	af·fix
afliction	af·flic·tion
afluent	af·flu·ent *(rich)*
aford	af·ford
aforism	aph·o·rism
aformentioned	afore·men·tioned
afrayed	afraid
Afreca	Af·ri·ca
afrodisiac	aph·ro·dis·i·ac
afront	af·front
afterward	af·ter·word *(epilogue)*
afterword	af·ter·ward *(later)*
aganize	ag·o·nize
agast	aghast
agensy	agen·cy
agetate	ag·i·tate
aggresion	ag·gres·sion
aggrivate	ag·gra·vate
agitater	ag·i·ta·tor

WRONG	RIGHT
agled	ogled
agnastic	ag·nos·tic
agraculture	agri·cul·ture
agravate	ag·gra·vate
agreegious	egre·gious
agreeible	agree·a·ble
agregate	ag·gre·gate
agrerian	agrar·i·an
agression	ag·gres·sion
ahed	ahead
aid	aide *(assistant)*
aide	aid *(help)*
ail	ale *(a drink)*
ailmint	ail·ment
air	err *(be wrong)*
air	heir *(inheritor)*
airate	aer·ate
airess	heir·ess
airial	aer·i·al
airid	ar·id
airie	aer·ie *(nest)*
airobic	aer·o·bic
airodynamics	aer·o·dy·nam·ics
aironautical	aer·o·nau·ti·cal
airosol	aer·o·sol
airospace	aer·o·space
airplain	air·plane
aisle	isle *(island)*
ajacent	ad·ja·cent
ajective	ad·jec·tive
ajenda	agen·da
ajoining	ad·join·ing
ajourn	ad·journ

WRONG	RIGHT
ajulation	**ad·u·la·tion**
ajunct	**ad·junct**
ajust	**ad·just**
ajutant	**ad·ju·tant**
ake	**ache**
aknowledge	**ac·knowl·edge**
akorn	**acorn**
akrid	**ac·rid**
a la cart	**a la carte**
alamony	**al·i·mo·ny**
alay	**al·lay** *(relieve)*
Albaquerque	**Albu·quer·que**
albem	**al·bum**
albetross	**al·ba·tross**
albinoes	**al·bi·nos**
albumen	**al·bu·min** *(class of proteins)*
albumin	**al·bu·men** *(egg white)*
alchoholic	**al·co·hol·ic**
ale	**ail** *(be ill)*
aleet	**elite** *(best)*
alege	**al·lege**
alegiance	**al·le·giance**
alegory	**al·le·go·ry**
alegro	**al·le·gro**
alergy	**al·ler·gy**
aleviate	**al·le·vi·ate**
alfactory	**ol·fac·to·ry**
algabra	**al·ge·bra**
algie	**al·gae**
Algiria	**Al·ge·ria**
alian	**al·ien**

WRONG	RIGHT
aliance	**al·li·ance**
alied	**al·lied**
aligator	**al·li·ga·tor**
alimentary	**ele·men·ta·ry** *(basic)*
alinement	**align·ment**
alius	**ali·as**
alkaholic	**al·co·hol·ic**
alkeline	**al·ka·line**
all	**awl** *(tool)*
Allabama	**Al·a·bama**
allabaster	**al·a·bas·ter**
allacation	**al·lo·ca·tion**
allbatross	**al·ba·tross**
allderman	**al·der·man**
alledge	**al·lege**
allegience	**al·le·giance**
allert	**alert**
alley	**al·ly** *(join; partner)*
allibi	**al·i·bi**
allience	**al·li·ance**
allies	**al·leys** *(pl.; narrow lanes)*
alligater	**al·li·ga·tor**
allignment	**align·ment**
allimentary	**ali·men·ta·ry** *(nourishing)*
allimony	**al·i·mo·ny**
allive	**ol·ive**
allmanac	**al·ma·nac**
allmighty	**al·mighty**
allmost	**al·most**
alloting	**al·lot·ting**
alloud	**aloud** *(loudly)*
allowence	**al·low·ance**

WRONG	RIGHT	WRONG	RIGHT
allready	**al·ready**	alumni	**alum·nae** *(f., pl.)*
allthough	**al·though**	alure	**al·lure**
alltogether	**al·to·geth·er**	alusion	**al·lu·sion**
allude	**elude** *(escape)*		*(reference)*
alluminum	**alu·mi·num**	alusive	**al·lu·sive**
allusion	**elu·sion**		*(referring to)*
	(an escape)	amature	**am·a·teur**
allusion	**il·lu·sion**	amazment	**amaze·ment**
	(false idea)	ambaguity	**am·bi·gu·i·ty**
allusive	**elu·sive**	ambasador	**ambas·sa·dor**
	(hard to grasp)	ambeance	**am·bi·ance**
allusive	**il·lu·sive**	ambedextrous	
	(deceptive)		**am·bi·dex·trous**
allways	**al·ways**	ambiant	**am·bi·ent**
ally	**al·ley**	ambitous	**am·bi·tious**
	(sing.; narrow lane)	ambivalance	
almend	**al·mond**		**am·biv·a·lence**
alocation	**al·lo·ca·tion**	ambudsman	
alotting	**al·lot·ting**		**om·buds·man**
aloud	**al·lowed** *(permitted)*	ambulence	**am·bu·lance**
alowance	**al·low·ance**	ameanable	**ame·na·ble**
alowed	**al·lowed**	amego	**ami·go**
	(permitted)	ameible	**ami·a·ble**
aloy	**al·loy**	amelet	**om·e·let**
alphebet	**al·pha·bet**	amelliorate	**amel·io·rate**
altar	**al·ter** *(to change)*	amend	**emend** *(correct)*
altatude	**al·ti·tude**	amenible	**ame·na·ble**
alter	**al·tar**	ameno	**ami·no**
	(table for worship)	amfetamine	
alterior	**ul·te·ri·or**		**amphet·a·mine**
alterration	**alter·a·tion**	amfibian	**am·phib·i·an**
Altseimer's	**Alz·hei·mer's**	amicible	**am·i·ca·ble**
alturnate	**al·ter·nate**	ammareto	**ama·ret·to**
alude	**al·lude** *(refer to)*	ammendment	
alumnae	**alum·ni** *(m., pl.)*		**amend·ment**

WRONG	RIGHT
ammends	amends
ammoral	amor·al
ammorous	am·o·rous
ammorphous	amor·phous
ammortize	am·or·tize
ammount	amount
ammulet	am·u·let
amnezia	am·ne·sia
amnibus	om·ni·bus
amnisty	am·nes·ty
amond	al·mond
amonia	am·mo·nia
amore	amour
ampear	am·pere
ampitheater	am·phi·the·a·ter
amplefy	am·pli·fy
ampletude	am·pli·tude
amuk	amok
amunition	ammu·ni·tion
anackronism	anach·ro·nism
analisis	anal·y·sis (sing.)
analitic	an·a·lyt·ic
analize	an·a·lyze
anallogy	anal·o·gy
anals	an·nals (records)
analysis	anal·y·ses (pl.)
analyst	an·nal·ist
	(writer of annals)
anamation	an·i·ma·tion
anamosity	an·i·mos·i·ty
anasthetic	an·es·thet·ic
anatamy	anat·o·my
anceint	an·cient

WRONG	RIGHT
ancester	an·ces·tor
ancilary	an·cil·lary
ancor	an·chor
anecdote	an·ti·dote
	(remedy)
aneckdote	an·ec·dote
	(story)
anemal	an·i·mal
anex	an·nex
angel	an·gle
	(corner; aspect)
angenue	in·gé·nue
angeoplasty	
	an·gio·plas·ty
angery	an·gry
angle	an·gel (spirit)
angwish	an·guish
anice	an·ise (plant)
anigma	enig·ma
anihilate	an·ni·hi·late
animasity	an·i·mos·i·ty
aniss	anus (fundament)
aniversary	anni·ver·sa·ry
anjina	an·gi·na
anjiogram	an·gio·gram
ankel	an·kle
anker	an·chor
annal	anal (of the anus)
annalgesic	an·al·ge·sic
annalist	an·a·lyst
	(one who analyzes)
annalog	an·a·log
annalogy	anal·o·gy
annalysis	anal·y·sis (sing.)
annarchist	an·ar·chist

8

WRONG	RIGHT
annatation	**an·no·ta·tion**
annewity	**an·nu·i·ty**
annialate	**an·ni·hi·late**
anniversory	
	anni·ver·sa·ry
annix	**an·nex**
annoint	**anoint**
annomaly	**anom·a·ly**
annonymous	
	anon·y·mous
annorexia	**an·o·rex·ia**
announcment	
	an·nounce·ment
annualy	**an·nu·al·ly**
annule	**an·nu·al**
annull	**an·nul**
annunciate	**enun·ci·ate**
	(pronounce)
anomally	**anom·a·ly**
anonemous	**anon·y·mous**
anorrexia	**an·o·rex·ia**
anotation	**an·no·ta·tion**
anouncement	
	an·nounce·ment
anoy	**an·noy**
anser	**an·swer**
ansestor	**an·ces·tor**
ansillary	**an·cil·lary**
ant	**aunt** *(relative)*
antadote	**an·ti·dote**
	(remedy)
antaginistic	
	an·tag·o·nis·tic
antalope	**an·te·lope**
antanym	**an·to·nym**

WRONG	RIGHT
antartic	**ant·arc·tic**
antasid	**ant·ac·id**
antchovy	**an·cho·vy**
ante	**an·ti** *(opposed)*
anteak	**an·tique**
antebiotic	**an·ti·bi·ot·ic**
antecedant	**an·te·ced·ent**
anteclimax	**an·ti·cli·max**
antedepressant	
	an·ti·de·pres·sant
antefreeze	**an·ti·freeze**
antehistamine	
	an·ti·his·ta·mine
antena	**an·ten·na**
antepasto	**an·ti·pas·to**
anteperspirant	
	an·ti·per·spir·ant
antequated	**an·ti·quat·ed**
anteseedent	**an·te·ced·ent**
anteseptic	**an·ti·sep·tic**
anthalogy	**an·thol·o·gy**
anthrapology	
	an·thro·pol·o·gy
anti	**an·te** *(stake; share)*
antibiatic	**an·ti·bi·ot·ic**
anticapate	**an·tic·i·pate**
anticedent	**an·te·ced·ent**
antidate	**an·te·date**
antidepressent	
	an·ti·de·pres·sant
antidote	**an·ec·dote** *(story)*
antihistamean	
	an·ti·his·ta·mine
antiperspirent	
	an·ti·per·spir·ant

WRONG	**RIGHT**	WRONG	**RIGHT**
antisipate	**an·tic·i·pate**	apeasement	
antithasis	**an·tith·e·sis**		**ap·pease·ment**
	(sing.)	apecks	**apex**
antithesis		apellate	**ap·pel·late**
	an·tith·e·ses *(pl.)*	apendage	**ap·pend·age**
antlur	**ant·ler**	apendicitis	
antonim	**an·to·nym**		**ap·pen·di·ci·tis**
antrepreneur		apendix	**ap·pen·dix**
	en·tre·pre·neur	apethetic	**ap·a·thet·ic**
anual	**an·nu·al**	apetite	**ap·pe·tite**
anuity	**an·nu·i·ty**		*(hunger)*
anull	**an·nul**	apharism	**aph·o·rism**
anullment	**an·nul·ment**	aphradisiac	**aph·ro·dis·i·ac**
anunceate	**enun·ci·ate**	aplaud	**ap·plaud**
anunciate	**an·nun·ci·ate**	aplause	**ap·plause**
	(announce)	aple	**ap·ple**
anvel	**an·vil**	apliance	**ap·pli·ance**
anxeity	**anx·i·e·ty**	aplication	**ap·pli·ca·tion**
anxous	**anx·ious**	aplom	**aplomb**
anywere	**an·y·where**	aply	**ap·ply**
anyx	**on·yx**	apocalipse	**apoc·a·lypse**
anziety	**anx·i·e·ty**	apocrephal	**apoc·ry·phal**
apacalypse	**apoc·a·lypse**	apointment	
apacryphal	**apoc·ry·phal**		**ap·point·ment**
Apalachia	**Appa·la·chia**	apology	**apol·o·gy**
apall	**ap·pall**	apollogetic	**apol·o·get·ic**
aparatus	**ap·pa·ra·tus**	Apolo	**Apol·lo**
aparel	**ap·par·el**	aportionment	
aparently	**ap·par·ent·ly**		**ap·por·tion·ment**
aparition	**ap·pa·ri·tion**	apossum	**opos·sum**
apartmint	**apart·ment**	apostrophies	
apastle	**apos·tle**		**apos·tro·phes** *(pl.)*
apature	**ap·er·ture**	apostrophy	**apos·tro·phe**
apeal	**ap·peal**		*(sing.)*
apearance	**ap·pear·ance**	appathetic	**ap·a·thet·ic**

10

WRONG	RIGHT	WRONG	RIGHT
appatite	**ap·pe·tite** *(hunger)*	appricot	**apri·cot**
appeerence	**ap·pear·ance**	apprise	**ap·praise** *(estimate)*
appeasment	**ap·pease·ment**	approachible	**ap·proach·a·ble**
appeel	**ap·peal**	appropos	**ap·ro·pos**
appel	**ap·ple**	appropreate	**ap·pro·pri·ate**
Appelachia	**Appa·la·chia**	approvel	**ap·prov·al**
appelate	**ap·pel·late**	apracot	**apri·cot**
appendacitis	**ap·pen·di·ci·tis**	apraisal	**ap·prais·al**
appendege	**ap·pend·age**	apraise	**ap·praise** *(estimate)*
appendicks	**ap·pen·dix**	apreciate	**ap·pre·ci·ate**
apperatus	**ap·pa·ra·tus**	aprehend	**ap·pre·hend**
apperel	**ap·par·el**	aprentice	**ap·pren·tice**
apperently	**ap·par·ent·ly**	aprise	**ap·prise** *(inform)*
apperture	**ap·er·ture**	aproachable	**ap·proach·a·ble**
applacation	**ap·pli·ca·tion**	apropoe	**ap·ro·pos**
applaws	**ap·plause**	apropriate	**ap·pro·pri·ate**
applie	**ap·ply**	aproval	**ap·prov·al**
applience	**ap·pli·ance**	aprove	**ap·prove**
applomb	**aplomb**	aproximate	**ap·prox·i·mate**
apploud	**ap·plaud**	aptatude	**ap·ti·tude**
appocalypse	**apoc·a·lypse**	aptic	**op·tic**
appocryphal	**apoc·ry·phal**	aquaduct	**aq·ue·duct**
Appolo	**Apol·lo**	aquaintance	**ac·quaint·ance**
appologetic	**apol·o·get·ic**	aquamurine	**aq·ua·ma·rine**
appology	**apol·o·gy**	aquareum	**aquar·i·um**
appostle	**apos·tle**	Aquerius	**Aquar·i·us**
appostrophe	**apos·tro·phe** *(sing.)*	aquiduct	**aq·ue·duct**
apprahend	**ap·pre·hend**	aquiescence	**ac·qui·es·cence**
appraise	**ap·prise** *(inform)*	aquire	**ac·quire**
appraximate	**ap·prox·i·mate**		

11

WRONG	RIGHT	WRONG	RIGHT
aquitted	**ac·quit·ted**	arkives	**ar·chives**
araign	**ar·raign**	armachure	**ar·ma·ture**
arange	**or·ange**	armadilo	**ar·ma·dil·lo**
arangement		armastice	**ar·mi·stice**
	ar·range·ment	armement	**ar·ma·ment**
arangutan	**orang·u·tan**	armer	**ar·mor**
aray	**ar·ray**	armery	**ar·mory**
arbatrate	**ar·bi·trate**	arogance	**ar·ro·gance**
arbitrery	**ar·bi·trary**	arouze	**arouse**
arc	**ark** *(enclosure)*	arow	**ar·row**
archangle	**arch·an·gel**	arrain	**ar·raign**
archary	**arch·ery**	arrangment	
archipellago			**ar·range·ment**
	ar·chi·pel·ago	arrogence	**ar·ro·gance**
architechure		arromatic	**ar·o·mat·ic**
	ar·chi·tec·ture	arrouse	**arouse**
arduos	**ar·du·ous**	arsenel	**ar·se·nal**
ardvark	**aard·vark**	arsinic	**ar·se·nic**
area	**aria** *(melody)*	arsinist	**ar·son·ist**
arears	**ar·rears**	artachoke	**ar·ti·choke**
Arees	**Ar·i·es**	artacle	**ar·ti·cle**
aregano	**oreg·a·no**	artafact	**ar·ti·fact**
arest	**ar·rest**	artaficial	**arti·fi·cial**
arguement	**ar·gu·ment**	artary	**ar·tery**
aria	**ar·ea** *(region)*	artfull	**art·ful**
aristacratic	**aris·to·crat·ic**	artheritis	**ar·thri·tis**
arithmatic	**arith·me·tic**	arthrascopic	
arival	**ar·riv·al**		**ar·thro·scop·ic**
arizing	**aris·ing**	artic	**arc·tic**
ark	**arc** *(curve)*	artickle	**ar·ti·cle**
arkade	**ar·cade**	artifack	**ar·ti·fact**
arkaic	**ar·cha·ic**	artilery	**ar·til·lery**
arkangel	**arch·an·gel**	artirial	**ar·te·ri·al**
Arkensaw	**Ar·kan·sas**	artisticly	**artis·ti·cal·ly**
arkeology	**ar·chae·ol·o·gy**	arye	**awry**

WRONG	RIGHT
asailant	**as·sail·ant**
asassin	**as·sas·sin**
asassinate	**assas·si·nate**
asault	**as·sault**
asay	**as·say** *(analyze)*
ascent	**as·sent** *(consent)*
ascent	**ac·cent** *(emphasis)*
ascertane	**as·cer·tain**
ase	**ace**
asembly	**as·sem·bly**
asent	**as·sent** *(consent)*
aserbic	**acer·bic**
asert	**as·sert**
asess	**as·sess**
asetate	**ac·e·tate**
asetic	**as·cet·ic** *(austere)*
asett	**as·set**
asetylene	**acet·y·lene**
asfault	**as·phalt**
asfixiate	**as·phyx·i·ate**
asidic	**acid·ic**
asignment	**as·sign·ment**
asilum	**asy·lum**
asimilation	**as·sim·i·la·tion**
asistance	**as·sist·ance**
asociation	**as·so·ci·a·tion**
asorted	**as·sort·ed**
aspeck	**as·pect**
asperagus	**as·par·a·gus**
asperin	**as·pi·rin**
aspholt	**as·phalt**
aspin	**as·pen**
asprin	**as·pi·rin**
aspyre	**as·pire**
assailent	**as·sail·ant**

WRONG	RIGHT
assalt	**as·sault**
assasanate	**assas·si·nate**
assasin	**as·sas·sin**
assay	**es·say** *(try; composition)*
assembley	**as·sem·bly**
assent	**as·cent** *(a rising)*
assimulation	**as·sim·i·la·tion**
assinement	**as·sign·ment**
assinine	**as·i·nine**
assistence	**as·sist·ance**
assparagus	**as·par·a·gus**
assurence	**as·sur·ance**
assurt	**as·sert**
asswage	**as·suage**
astanish	**as·ton·ish**
astarisk	**as·ter·isk**
astaroid	**as·ter·oid**
astensible	**os·ten·si·ble**
astigmatism	**stig·ma·tism** *(condition of normal lens)*
astoot	**as·tute**
astralogy	**as·trol·o·gy**
astranaut	**as·tro·naut**
astrangement	**es·trange·ment**
astranomy	**as·tron·o·my**
astringint	**as·trin·gent**
astronot	**as·tro·naut**
asuage	**as·suage**
asume	**as·sume**
asumption	**as·sump·tion**
asurance	**as·sur·ance**

WRONG	RIGHT
ataché	**at·ta·ché**
atachment	**at·tach·ment**
atack	**at·tack**
atainment	**at·tain·ment**
atamic	**atom·ic**
atempt	**at·tempt**
atendance	**at·tend·ance**
atention	**at·ten·tion**
atest	**at·test**
athaletics	**ath·let·ics**
athelete	**ath·lete**
athiestic	**athe·is·tic**
athoritarian	**author·i·tar·i·an**
athority	**au·thor·i·ty**
atic	**at·tic**
atire	**at·tire**
atitude	**at·ti·tude**
atlus	**at·las**
atmaspheric	**atmos·pher·ic**
atonment	**atone·ment**
atorney	**at·tor·ney**
atract	**at·tract**
atraphy	**at·ro·phy**
atrasity	**atroc·i·ty**
atribution	**at·tri·bu·tion**
atrition	**at·tri·tion**
atrocous	**atro·cious**
atrofy	**at·ro·phy**
atrotious	**atro·cious**
attanement	**at·tain·ment**
attashay	**at·ta·ché**
attemp	**at·tempt**
attendence	**at·tend·ance**

WRONG	RIGHT
attension	**at·ten·tion**
attentave	**at·ten·tive**
atter	**ot·ter**
attonement	**atone·ment**
attorny	**at·tor·ney**
atum	**at·om**
atune	**at·tune**
audable	**au·di·ble**
audasity	**au·dac·i·ty**
audatorium	**au·di·to·ri·um**
audeo	**au·dio**
audiance	**au·di·ence**
Augist	**Au·gust**
aukward	**awk·ward**
aul	**awl** *(tool)*
auning	**awn·ing**
aunt	**ant** *(insect)*
aural	**oral** *(of the mouth)*
aurel	**au·ral** *(of the ear)*
auspaces	**aus·pi·ces**
auspitious	**aus·pi·cious**
austairity	**aus·ter·i·ty**
austeer	**aus·tere**
autagraph	**au·to·graph**
autamatic	**au·to·mat·ic**
autamobile	**au·to·mo·bile**
autanamous	**au·ton·o·mous**
autapsy	**au·top·sy**
auther	**au·thor**
autherize	**au·thor·ize**
authoratarian	**author·i·tar·i·an**
autockracy	**au·toc·ra·cy**
autoes	**au·tos**

14

WRONG	RIGHT	WRONG	RIGHT
automabile	**au·to·mo·bile**	awdience	**au·di·ence**
autonomos		awdio	**au·dio**
	au·ton·o·mous	awdition	**au·di·tion**
autum	**au·tumn**	awditorium	**au·di·to·ri·um**
auxilary	**aux·il·ia·ry**	awear	**aware**
avacado	**av·o·ca·do**	awefully	**aw·ful·ly**
availible	**avail·a·ble**	awesum	**awe·some**
avalanch	**av·a·lanche**	awfuly	**aw·ful·ly**
avanue	**av·e·nue**	awile	**awhile**
avarage	**av·er·age**	awktion	**auc·tion**
avaricous	**ava·ri·cious**	awkword	**awk·ward**
avaunt-guarde		aword	**award**
	avant-garde	awsome	**awe·some**
aveation	**avi·a·tion**	awthentic	**au·then·tic**
avelanche	**av·a·lanche**	awthor	**au·thor**
avericious	**ava·ri·cious**	awthorize	**au·thor·ize**
averse	**ad·verse** *(opposed)*	awtistic	**au·tis·tic**
avinue	**av·e·nue**	awtocracy	**au·toc·ra·cy**
avoidible	**avoid·a·ble**	awtopsy	**au·top·sy**
avrage	**av·er·age**	awtumn	**au·tumn**
avud	**av·id**	axel	**ax·le**
avursion	**aver·sion**	axes	**ax·is** *(sing.)*
awate	**await**	axis	**ax·es** *(pl.)*
awburn	**au·burn**	ayatolah	**aya·tol·lah**
awdacity	**au·dac·i·ty**	azbestos	**as·bes·tos**
awdible	**au·di·ble**	azthma	**asth·ma**

B

WRONG	RIGHT
babboon	**ba·boon**
Babelonian	**Bab·y·lo·ni·an**
babled	**bab·bled**
babling	**bab·bling**
babooshka	**ba·bush·ka**
babtism	**bap·tism**
babtist	**bap·tist**
babtize	**bap·tize**
babyed	**ba·bied**
Babyllonian	**Bab·y·lo·ni·an**
bacallaureate	**bac·ca·lau·re·ate**
baccanal	**bac·cha·nal**
bacchanallean	**bac·cha·na·li·an**
baccilus	**ba·cil·lus**
Baccus	**Bac·chus**
bach	**batch** (quantity)
bachalor	**bach·e·lor**
bachannal	**bac·cha·nal**
Bachus	**Bac·chus**
backake	**back·ache**
backalaureate	**bac·ca·lau·re·ate**
backammon	**back·gam·mon**
backanal	**bac·cha·nal**

WRONG	RIGHT
backanalian	**bac·cha·na·li·an**
backbord	**back·board**
backbraking	**back·break·ing**
backgamen	**back·gam·mon**
backloged	**back·logged**
backpak	**back·pack**
backround	**back·ground**
backword	**back·ward**
bactiria	**bac·te·ria**
badder	**bat·ter**
baddering	**bat·ter·ing**
baddery	**bat·tery**
bade	**bayed** (howled)
badjer	**badg·er**
badminten	**bad·min·ton**
badmitten	**bad·min·ton**
baffeling	**baf·fling**
bafling	**baf·fling**
bafoon	**buf·foon**
bagage	**bag·gage**
bagammon	**back·gam·mon**
bager	**badg·er**
bagle	**ba·gel**
baid	**bade**

16

WRONG	RIGHT	WRONG	RIGHT
baige	**beige**	ballistik	**bal·lis·tic**
bail	**bale** *(bundle)*	ballsa	**bal·sa**
bailful	**bale·ful**	ballsam	**bal·sam**
bait	**bate** *(lessen)*	ballust	**bal·last**
bakrey	**bak·ery**	balogna	**bo·lo·gna**
bakteria	**bac·te·ria**	balona	**bo·lo·gna**
balad	**bal·lad**	baloon	**bal·loon**
balancable	**bal·ance·a·ble**	balot	**bal·lot** *(voting slip)*
balancible	**bal·ance·a·ble**	balroom	**ball·room**
balast	**bal·last**	balsom	**bal·sam**
balcany	**bal·co·ny**	Baltamore	**Bal·ti·more**
bale	**bail** *(money)*	bambu	**bam·boo**
bale bond	**bail bond**	banall	**ba·nal**
balefull	**bale·ful**	bananza	**bo·nan·za**
balence	**bal·ance**	banaster	**ban·is·ter**
balerina	**bal·le·ri·na**	banbon	**bon·bon**
balero	**bo·le·ro**	banbox	**band·box**
balet	**bal·let** *(dance)*	band	**banned** *(forbidden)*
baliff	**bai·liff**	bandade	**Band-Aid**
balister	**bal·us·ter**	bandet	**ban·dit**
balistic	**bal·lis·tic**	bandie	**ban·dy**
Balivia	**Bo·liv·ia**	bandige	**band·age**
Balken	**Bal·kan**	bandjo	**ban·jo**
balkony	**bal·co·ny**	bands	**banns**
ball	**bawl** *(cry)*		*(marriage announcement)*
ballance	**bal·ance**	bandwagen	**band·wag·on**
ballarina	**bal·le·ri·na**	banel	**ba·nal**
ballay	**bal·let** *(dance)*	baner	**ban·ner**
ballcony	**bal·co·ny**	banign	**be·nign**
ballderdash	**bal·der·dash**	banjoe	**ban·jo**
ballet	**bal·lot** *(voting slip)*	bankett	**ban·quette**
ballid	**bal·lad**		*(bench)*
balligerance		bankrupcy	**bank·rupt·cy**
	bel·lig·er·ence	bankwet	**ban·quet** *(feast)*
ballister	**bal·us·ter**	bannana	**ba·nana**

17

WRONG	RIGHT
bannish	**ban·ish**
bannister	**ban·is·ter**
banns	**bans** *(forbids)*
banquit	**ban·quet** *(feast)*
bans	**banns**
	(marriage announcement)
bansai	**bon·sai**
	(tree shaping)
banstand	**band·stand**
bantom	**ban·tam**
banwagon	**band·wag·on**
baptest	**bap·tist**
baptizm	**bap·tism**
baracks	**bar·racks**
baracuda	**bar·ra·cu·da**
barage	**bar·rage**
barbacue	**bar·be·cue**
barbarrian	**bar·bar·i·an**
barbel	**bar·bell** *(weights)*
barbell	**bar·bel**
	(hairlike growth)
barberian	**bar·bar·i·an**
barberous	**bar·ba·rous**
barbery	**bar·ber·ry**
barbichurate	
	bar·bi·tu·rate
barble	**bar·bel**
	(hairlike growth)
Barcilona	**Bar·ce·lo·na**
bare	**bear** *(animal; carry)*
bared	**barred** *(excluded)*
ba-relief	**bas-re·lief**
baren	**bar·on** *(noble)*
baren	**bar·ren** *(sterile)*
baret	**bar·rette** *(hair clasp)*

WRONG	RIGHT
barfoot	**bare·foot**
bargan	**bar·gain**
baricade	**bar·ri·cade**
barier	**bar·ri·er**
bariness	**bar·on·ess**
baring	**bar·ring**
	(preventing)
bario	**bar·rio**
barister	**bar·ris·ter**
barly	**bar·ley**
barnicle	**bar·na·cle**
baroke	**ba·roque**
baron	**bar·ren** *(sterile)*
baronness	**bar·on·ess**
baroom	**bar·room**
barracade	**bar·ri·cade**
barred	**bard** *(poet)*
barren	**bar·on** *(noble)*
barreo	**bar·rio**
barret	**bar·rette**
	(hair clasp)
barricks	**bar·racks**
barricuda	**bar·ra·cu·da**
barristor	**bar·ris·ter**
barritone	**bar·i·tone**
barrol	**bar·rel**
barrometer	**ba·rom·e·ter**
barron	**bar·ren** *(sterile)*
barroque	**ba·roque**
barrow	**bor·row**
	(take temporarily)
Barsilona	**Bar·ce·lo·na**
bartendor	**bar·tend·er**
basanet	**bas·si·net**
	(baby bed)

18

basanet ....**bas·i·net** *(helmet)*

baschion ....**bas·tion**

base ....**bass** *(voice)*

based ...**baste** *(sew; moisten)*

basel..................**bas·il** *(herb)*

basel..................**bas·al** *(basic)*

basemint ....**base·ment**

basen ....**ba·sin**

base-relief............**bas·re·lief**

baserk......................**ber·serk**

bases ....**ba·sis** *(sing.)*

bashfull ....**bash·ful**

basicly ....**bas·i·cal·ly**

basil ....**bas·al** *(basic)*

basillica ....**ba·sil·i·ca**

basillus ....**ba·cil·lus**

basinet ....**bas·si·net**
(baby bed)

basis ......**ba·ses** *(pl. of basis)*

baskit ....**bas·ket**

baskitball ....**bas·ket·ball**

basment ....**base·ment**

basoon ....**bas·soon**

basque ....**bask** *(warm)*

basquet ....**bas·ket**

bass ....**base** *(foundation)*

bassanet ....**bas·si·net**
(baby bed)

bassilica ....**ba·sil·i·ca**

bassit......................**bas·set**

bass-relief ....**bas·re·lief**

basterd ....**bas·tard**

bata ....**be·ta**

bata carotene ....
............**be·ta car·o·tene**

batallion ....**bat·tal·ion**

batchelor............**bach·e·lor**

bate ....**bait** *(lure)*

bateak ....**ba·tik**

bated...............**bat·ted** *(hit)*

batery ....**bat·tery**

bath ....**bathe** *(v.)*

bathas ....**ba·thos**

bathe ....**bath** *(n.)*

bathouse ....**bath·house**

bating ....**bat·ting** *(hitting)*

battallion............**bat·tal·ion**

batton ....**bat·ten** *(fasten)*

batton ....**ba·ton** *(stick)*

baud ....**bawd** *(prostitute)*

baudy ....**bawdy**

baught................**bought**
(purchased)

bauk ....**balk**

baul ....**bawl** *(cry)*

Baveria ....**Ba·var·ia**

bawble....................**bau·ble**

bawd....**baud** *(measurement)*

bawk............................**balk**

bawl..................**ball** *(sphere)*

bawxite ....**baux·ite**

bayanet ....**bay·o·net**

bayliff ....**bai·liff**

baynal ....**ba·nal**

bayonnet ....**bay·o·net**

bayoo ....**bay·ou**

bazaar ....**bi·zarre** *(odd)*

bazare ....**ba·zaar** *(market)*

bazil ....**bas·il** *(herb)*

be ....**bee** *(insect)*

WRONG	RIGHT	WRONG	RIGHT
beach	**beech** *(tree)*	beet	**beat** *(strike)*
beachead	**beach·head**	beever	**bea·ver**
beachnut	**beech·nut**	befudle	**be·fud·dle**
beakon	**bea·con**	begger	**beg·gar**
beanary	**bean·ery**	beggin	**be·gin**
bear	**beer** *(drink)*	beggining	**be·gin·ning**
bear	**bare** *(naked)*	begile	**be·guile**
bearfoot	**bare·foot**	begining	**be·gin·ning**
bearly	**bare·ly**	behaf	**be·half**
beastial	**bes·tial**	behavor	**be·hav·ior**
beastiary	**bes·ti·ary**	behemuth	**be·he·moth**
beat	**beet** *(vegetable)*	belaber	**be·la·bor**
beateous	**beau·te·ous**	beleif	**be·lief** *(n.)*
beatle	**bee·tle**	beleive	**be·lieve** *(v.)*
beattitude	**be·at·i·tude**	Belgiam	**Bel·gium**
beaudacious	**bo·da·cious**	belicose	**bel·li·cose**
beautey	**beau·ty**	belief	**be·lieve** *(v.)*
beautious	**beau·te·ous**	believe	**be·lief** *(n.)*
beauttitian	**beau·ti·cian**	believeable	**be·liev·a·ble**
becken	**beck·on**	beliggerance	
becom	**be·calm**		**bel·lig·er·ence**
bedazle	**be·daz·zle**	bell	**belle** *(woman)*
bedclose	**bed·clothes**	bellacose	**bel·li·cose**
bedlum	**bed·lam**	belles-letters	
bedsted	**bed·stead**		**belles-let·tres**
beech	**beach** *(shore)*	bellfry	**bel·fry**
beecon	**bea·con**	Bellgium	**Bel·gium**
beed	**bead**	bell-lettres	**belles-let·tres**
beefstake	**beef·steak**	bellow	**be·low** *(down)*
beegle	**bea·gle**	below	**bel·low** *(roar)*
beeker	**beak·er**	ben	**been** *(pp. of be)*
beem	**beam**	benadiction	
been	**bean** *(legume)*		**ben·e·dic·tion**
beenery	**bean·ery**	benaficial	**ben·e·fi·cial**
beer	**bier** *(coffin platform)*	beneeth	**be·neath**

WRONG	RIGHT
benefacter	**ben·e·fac·tor**
benefficial	**ben·e·fi·cial**
beneficiery	**ben·e·fi·ci·ary**
benefitted	**ben·e·fit·ed**
benevolance	
	be·nev·o·lence
benevolant	**be·nev·o·lent**
Bengel	**Ben·gal**
benidiction	**ben·e·dic·tion**
benifactor	**ben·e·fac·tor**
benificiary	**ben·e·fi·ci·ary**
benifited	**ben·e·fit·ed**
benine	**be·nign**
bennevolent	
	be·nev·o·lent
benzene	**ben·zine**
	(cleaning fluid)
benzine	**ben·zene**
	(chemistry)
bequeathe	**be·queath**
berch	**birch**
bereev	**be·reave**
berg	**burg** *(town)*
berger	**burgh·er** *(citizen)*
berger	**bur·ger** *(hamburger)*
berglar	**bur·glar**
Bergundy	**Bur·gun·dy**
berial	**bur·i·al**
beritone	**bar·i·tone**
berl	**burl**
berlap	**bur·lap**
berlesque	**bur·lesque**
berly	**bur·ley** *(tobacco)*
berly	**bur·ly** *(rough)*
berometer	**ba·rom·e·ter**

WRONG	RIGHT
beroque	**ba·roque**
berp	**burp**
berray	**be·ret** *(cap)*
berrel	**bar·rel**
berrier	**bar·ri·er**
berrow	**bar·row**
berry	**bury** *(cover)*
bersitis	**bur·si·tis**
bersurk	**ber·serk**
berth	**birth** *(origin)*
bery	**ber·ry** *(fruit)*
beschial	**bes·tial**
beseige	**be·siege**
beserk	**ber·serk**
bestiery	**bes·ti·ary**
bestro	**bis·tro**
beta carotine	
	be·ta car·o·tene
Bethleham	**Beth·le·hem**
betrothe	**be·troth**
betwene	**be·tween**
beuty	**beau·ty**
beval	**bev·el**
beverege	**bev·er·age**
bevvel	**bev·el**
bewillder	**be·wil·der**
bewt	**butte** *(hill)*
bewteous	**beau·te·ous**
bewtician	**beau·ti·cian**
bewty	**beau·ty**
biagraphy	**bi·og·ra·phy**
bialogical	**bi·o·log·i·cal**
biasses	**bi·as·es**
bibleography	
	bib·li·og·ra·phy

WRONG	RIGHT
bibliofile	**bib·li·o·phile**
bicalm	**be·calm**
bicarbanate	**bi·car·bon·ate**
bicentenial	
	bi·cen·ten·ni·al
bich	**bitch**
bicicle	**bi·cy·cle**
bicusped	**bi·cus·pid**
bidazzle	**be·daz·zle**
bideck	**be·deck**
biding	**bid·ding** *(offering)*
biege	**beige**
bigatry	**big·ot·ry**
biggamy	**big·a·my**
biggot	**big·ot**
biggotry	**big·ot·ry**
bight	**byte** *(string of bits)*
bigomy	**big·a·my**
bigonia	**be·gon·ia**
biguile	**be·guile**
bihemoth	**be·he·moth**
biker	**bick·er** *(squabble)*
bilabor	**be·la·bor**
bilatteral	**bi·lat·er·al**
bilboard	**bill·board**
bild	**build**
bilding	**build·ing**
biliards	**bil·liards**
bilion	**bil·lion**
bilje	**bilge**
billay	**be·lay**
billingual	**bi·lin·gual**
billionnnaire	**bil·lion·aire**
billious	**bil·ious**
billon	**bil·lion**

WRONG	RIGHT
bindary	**bind·ery**
bineath	**be·neath**
binery	**bi·na·ry**
binevolent	**be·nev·o·lent**
binnocular	**bin·oc·u·lar**
biochemistry	
	bi·o·chem·is·try
biodegradible	
	bi·o·de·grad·a·ble
bioengeneering	
	bi·o·en·gi·neer·ing
biogerphy	**bi·og·ra·phy**
biolegy	**bi·ol·o·gy**
biorythm	**bi·o·rhythm**
biotecnology	
	bi·o·tech·nol·o·gy
bipartesan	**bi·par·ti·san**
bipass	**by·pass**
bipassed	**by·passed**
biproduct	**by·prod·uct**
bireave	**be·reave**
biret	**be·ret** *(cap)*
birth	**berth** *(space)*
bisalt	**ba·salt**
biscut	**bis·cuit**
biseech	**be·seech**
bisen	**bi·son**
bisentennial	
	bi·cen·ten·ni·al
biseps	**bi·ceps**
bisexule	**bi·sex·u·al**
bisiege	**be·siege**
bisk	**bisque**
biskit	**bis·cuit**
bisness	**busi·ness**

WRONG	RIGHT	WRONG	RIGHT
bissexual	**bi·sex·u·al**	blasfeme	**blas·pheme**
bissoon	**bas·soon**	blasphamy	**blas·phe·my**
bistander	**by·stand·er**	blatency	**bla·tan·cy**
bit	**bitt** *(post)*	blatent	**bla·tant**
bit	**bite** *(chomp)*	blatter	**blad·der**
bit	**byte** *(string of bits)*	blazen	**bla·zon**
bite	**bight** *(curve)*	blead	**bleed**
bite	**byte** *(string of bits)*	bleap	**bleep**
bitern	**bit·tern**	bleechers	**bleach·ers**
bitoominous	**bi·tu·mi·nous**	bleek	**bleak**
bitray	**be·tray**	bleery	**bleary**
bitt	**bit** *(binary digit)*	blemesh	**blem·ish**
bitumenous	**bi·tu·mi·nous**	blend	**blende** *(ore)*
biuld	**build**	blende	**blend** *(mix)*
biulding	**build·ing**	blesed	**bless·ed**
bivouaced	**biv·ou·acked**	blew	**blue** *(color)*
bivouac	**biv·ou·ac**	blisful	**bliss·ful**
biway	**by·way**	blisster	**blis·ter**
biwilder	**be·wil·der**	blite	**blight**
biyou	**bay·ou**	blith	**blithe**
bizaar	**bi·zarre** *(odd)*	blithly	**blithe·ly**
Bizantine	**By·zan·tine**	blits	**blitz**
bizarre	**ba·zaar** *(marked)*	blizard	**bliz·zard**
bizness	**busi·ness**	bloc	**block** *(mass)*
bizooka	**ba·zoo·ka**	blochy	**blotchy**
blackmale	**black·mail**	block	**bloc** *(group)*
blair	**blare**	blockadge	**block·age**
blamless	**blame·less**	blockaid	**block·ade**
blanche	**blanch**	blodily	**blood·i·ly**
blandeshment	**blan·dish·ment**	blody	**bloody**
blankit	**blan·ket**	blokade	**block·ade**
blarny	**blar·ney**	bloodally	**blood·i·ly**
		bloodey	**bloody**
		bloored	**blurred**
		blosome	**blos·som**

WRONG	RIGHT
blossum	**blos·som**
blotchey	**blotchy**
blote	**bloat**
blowse	**blouse**
blubbry	**blub·bery**
bluberry	**blue·ber·ry**
blubonnet	**blue·bon·net**
blud	**blood**
bluddy	**bloody**
blue	**blew** *(gusted)*
bluebonet	**blue·bon·net**
blugeon	**bludg·eon**
blume	**bloom**
blured	**blurred**
blurr	**blur**
bo	**beau** *(boyfriend)*
boar	**boor** *(rude person)*
boar	**bore** *(dull person)*
boarish	**boor·ish**
bobalink	**bob·o·link**
bobben	**bob·bin**
bobbie pin	**bob·by pin**
bobed	**bobbed**
bobin	**bob·bin**
bobushka	**ba·bush·ka**
bobwite	**bob·white**
boch	**botch**
bochulism	**bot·u·lism**
boddice	**bod·ice**
boddy	**bawdy**
boddy	**body**
bodess	**bod·ice**
boggey	**bog·gy** *(marshy)*
bogy	**bo·gey** *(golf term)*
bohemean	**bo·he·mi·an**

WRONG	RIGHT
boicott	**boy·cott**
boistrous	**bois·ter·ous**
bokay	**bou·quet**
bolder	**boul·der** *(rock)*
bole	**boll** *(pod)*
bole	**bowl** *(round container)*
boll	**bole** *(tree trunk)*
bolla	**bo·la**
bollder	**bold·er** *(more daring)*
bollder	**bould·er** *(rock)*
bollero	**bo·le·ro**
Bollivia	**Bo·liv·i·a**
bollster	**bol·ster**
bolony	**bo·lo·gna**
bom	**bomb** *(explosive)*
bom	**balm** *(ointment)*
bomb	**balm** *(ointment)*
bombadier	**bom·bar·dier**
bommy	**balmy** *(mild)*
bomshell	**bomb·shell**
bonana	**ba·nana**
bondege	**bond·age**
bondfire	**bon·fire**
boney	**bony**
bonnbonn	**bon·bon**
bonnfire	**bon·fire**
bonsai	**ban·zai** *(cry)*
bonusses	**bo·nus·es**
bonyness	**bon·i·ness**
bonzai	**ban·zai** *(cry)*
bonzai	**bon·sai** *(tree shaping)*
Boodist	**Bud·dhist**

WRONG	RIGHT	WRONG	RIGHT
boodoir	**bou·doir**	botten	**but·ton**
boofant	**bouf·fant**	bottum	**bot·tom**
bookeeper	**book·keep·er**	boudwar	**bou·doir**
boolevard	**boul·e·vard**	boufont	**bouf·fant**
boollabaisse		bough	**bow** (bend)
	bouil·la·baisse	bought	**bout** (fight)
boollion	**bul·lion** (metal)	bouillebais	**bouil·la·baisse**
boomarang	**boom·er·ang**	bouillon	**bul·lion** (metal)
booquet	**bou·quet**	boulavard	**boul·e·vard**
boor	**bore** (dull person)	boullibase	**bouil·la·baisse**
boor	**boar** (hog)	boullion	**bouil·lon** (broth)
boorgeois	**bour·geois**	boullion	**bul·lion** (metal)
bootcher	**butch·er**	boundry	**bound·a·ry**
bootee	**boo·ty** (loot)	bounse	**bounce**
bootique	**bou·tique**	bounteful	**boun·ti·ful**
booty	**boot·ee** (shoe)	bountey	**boun·ty**
borch	**borsch**	bountious	**boun·te·ous**
bord	**bored** (weary)	bourben	**bour·bon**
bord	**board** (wood)	bourden	**bur·den** (load)
Bordeau	**Bor·deaux**	bourgen	**bur·geon**
bore	**boor** (rude person)	bourgeosie	**bour·geoi·sie**
bore	**boar** (hog)	bourgois	**bour·geois**
bored	**board** (wood)	boursar	**bur·sar**
borish	**boor·ish**	bout	**bought** (purchased)
born	**borne** (carried)	bouteak	**bou·tique**
borow	**bor·row**	bouttoniere	
	(take temporarily)		**bou·ton·niere**
borron	**bo·ron**	bouy	**buoy** (floater)
borrough	**bor·ough** (town)	bouyancy	**buoy·an·cy**
borrow	**bor·ough** (town)	boveen	**bo·vine**
borsh	**borsch**	bow	**beau** (boyfriend)
bosum	**bos·om**	bow	**bough** (branch)
botannical	**bo·tan·i·cal**	bowel	**bowl**
botanny	**bot·a·ny**		(round container)
botchulism	**bot·u·lism**	bowl	**bole** (tree trunk)

WRONG	RIGHT	WRONG	RIGHT
bowl	**boll** *(pod)*	brazier	**bras·siere** *(bra)*
bowl	**bow·el** *(intestine)*	brazure	**bra·zier** *(grill)*
bowla	**bo·la**	breach	**breech** *(bottom)*
bowlder	**boul·der** *(rock)*	bread	**breed** *(produce)*
bowlderize	**bowd·ler·ize**	bread	**bred** *(produced)*
bowllegged	**bow·leg·ged**	break	**brake** *(stop)*
bowndary	**bound·a·ry**	breakible	**break·a·ble**
bownteous	**boun·te·ous**	breath	**breadth** *(width)*
bowntiful	**boun·ti·ful**	breath	**breathe** *(v.)*
bownty	**boun·ty**	breathe	**breath** *(n.)*
bowt	**bout** *(fight)*	breaze	**breeze**
bowvine	**bo·vine**	bred	**bread** *(loaf)*
boxite	**baux·ite**	bredfruit	**bread·fruit**
boy	**buoy** *(floater)*	bredth	**breadth** *(width)*
boycot	**boy·cott**	breech	**breach** *(break)*
boysterous	**bois·ter·ous**	breezally	**breez·i·ly**
bozum	**bos·om**	breezey	**breezy**
brackin	**brack·en**	breif	**brief**
braggard	**brag·gart**	breth	**breath** *(n.)*
Braile	**Braille**	brethern	**breth·ren**
braise	**braze** *(solder)*	Breton	**Brit·on** *(Celt)*
braize	**braise** *(cook)*	brevery	**bre·vi·a·ry**
braize	**braze** *(solder)*	brevety	**brev·i·ty**
braizen	**bra·zen**	breviery	**bre·vi·a·ry**
brake	**break** *(burst)*	brewnet	**bru·nette**
braker	**break·er** *(wave)*	brewry	**brew·ery**
braselet	**brace·let**	bribary	**brib·ery**
brasen	**bra·zen**	brickette	**bri·quette**
brasier	**bra·zier** *(grill)*	bridal	**bri·dle** *(of a horse)*
brasiere	**bras·siere** *(bra)*	bridle	**brid·al** *(of a bride)*
brasure	**bra·zier** *(grill)*	brieviary	**bre·vi·a·ry**
brauth	**broth**	brigadeer	**brig·a·dier**
Braylle	**Braille**	brige	**bridge**
braze	**braise** *(cook)*	brik-a-brak	**bric-a-brac**
brazeness	**bra·zen·ness**	brillience	**bril·liance**

WRONG	RIGHT	WRONG	RIGHT
brillient	**bril·liant**	brontasaurus	
briney	**briny**		**bron·to·saurus**
briquett	**bri·quette**	broo	**brew**
brisle	**bris·tle**	brooch	**broach** *(introduce)*
Britain	**Brit·on** *(Celt)*	Brooklin	**Brook·lyn**
Britainy	**Brit·ta·ny**	broom	**brougham**
Britania	**Bri·tan·nia**		*(carriage)*
Brittain	**Brit·ain**	broom	**brume** *(mist)*
	(Great Britain)	broonet	**bru·nette**
Brittainy	**Brit·ta·ny**	broose	**bruise**
Brittania	**Bri·tan·nia**	broot	**brut** *(champagne)*
Brittanica	**Bri·tan·nica**	broot	**brute** *(beast)*
Brittony	**Brit·ta·ny**	broshure	**bro·chure**
broach	**brooch** *(jewelry)*	broughm	**brougham**
broague	**brogue**		*(carriage)*
brocaid	**bro·cade**	brouse	**browse**
broche	**brooch** *(jewelry)*	browny	**brown·ie**
broche	**broach**	browth	**broth**
	(introduce)	browze	**browse**
brocolli	**broc·co·li**	bruit	**brut** *(champagne)*
broge	**brogue**	bruit	**brute** *(beast)*
brokade	**bro·cade**	bruitish	**brut·ish**
brokerege	**bro·ker·age**	bruize	**bruise**
brokoli	**broc·co·li**	brume	**brougham**
brokrage	**bro·ker·age**		*(carriage)*
broncheal	**bron·chi·al**	brume	**broom** *(sweeper)*
	(adj.)	bruse	**bruise**
bronchial		Brussle sprouts	
	bron·chi·ole *(n.)*		**Brus·sels sprouts**
bronchitus	**bron·chi·tis**	brut	**bruit** *(rumor)*
bronkial	**bron·chi·al** *(adj.)*	brutallity	**bru·tal·i·ty**
bronkiole		brutallize	**bru·tal·ize**
	bron·chi·ole *(n.)*	brute	**bruit** *(rumor)*
bronkitis	**bron·chi·tis**	brute	**brut** *(champagne)*
Bronks	**Bronx**	bubbley	**bub·bly**

WRONG	RIGHT	WRONG	RIGHT
bucanneer	**buc·ca·neer**	bullrush	**bul·rush**
buccolic	**bu·col·ic**	bullwark	**bul·wark**
bucher	**butch·er**	bullwip	**bull·whip**
buckaneer	**buc·ca·neer**	bulwork	**bul·wark**
bucksome	**bux·om**	bumlebee	**bum·ble·bee**
bucollic	**bu·col·ic**	bungelow	**bun·ga·low**
bucskin	**buck·skin**	bunyon	**bun·ion**
Budda	**Bud·dha**	buoyency	**buoy·an·cy**
budder	**but·ter**	burbon	**bour·bon**
budderfly	**but·ter·fly**	burch	**birch**
buddie	**bud·dy**	burdgeon	**bur·geon**
Buddist	**Bud·dhist**	bureaukrat	**bureau·crat**
budgit	**budg·et**	bureucracy	
budgitery	**budg·et·ary**		**bureau·cra·cy**
budoir	**bou·doir**	burg	**berg** *(iceberg)*
bufay	**buf·fet**	Burgandy	**Bur·gun·dy**
buffelo	**buf·fa·lo**	burgeler	**bur·glar**
bufoon	**buf·foon**	burgeoisie	**bour·geoi·sie**
buget	**budg·et**	burger	**burgh·er** *(citizen)*
bugetary	**budg·et·ary**	burgh	**burg** *(town)*
buggey	**bug·gy**	burgher	**bur·ger**
buiscut	**bis·cuit**		*(hamburger)*
bukolic	**bu·col·ic**	burgler	**bur·glar**
bukskin	**buck·skin**	burlesk	**bur·lesque**
buldog	**bull·dog**	burley	**bur·ly** *(rough)*
buldozer	**bull·doz·er**	Burlin	**Ber·lin**
bulet	**bul·let**	burly	**bur·ley** *(tobacco)*
buletin	**bul·le·tin**	burm	**berm**
bulevard	**boul·e·vard**	Burmuda	**Ber·mu·da**
bullbous	**bul·bous**	burocracy	**bureau·cra·cy**
bullegged	**bow·leg·ged**	burow	**bur·row** *(dig)*
bullie	**bul·ly**	burrage	**bar·rage**
bullion	**bouil·lon** *(broth)*	burrial	**bur·i·al**
bullit	**bul·let**	burro	**bur·row** *(dig)*
bulliten	**bul·le·tin**	burrow	**bor·ough** *(town)*

WRONG	RIGHT
burrow	**bor·row**
	(take temporarily)
burrow	**bur·ro** *(donkey)*
burrsitis	**bur·si·tis**
burry	**bury** *(cover)*
burser	**bur·sar**
burserk	**ber·serk**
bus	**buss** *(kiss)*
busness	**busi·ness**
busom	**bos·om**
buss	**bus** *(coach)*
bussle	**bus·tle**
but	**butt** *(end)*
butain	**bu·tane**
butchary	**butch·ery**
bute	**butte** *(hill)*
buter	**but·ter**
buterfly	**but·ter·fly**
butlar	**but·ler**
butress	**but·tress**
butt	**butte** *(hill)*
buttary	**but·tery**
butte	**butt** *(end)*
butten	**but·ton**
buttoneer	**bou·ton·niere**

WRONG	RIGHT
buttox	**but·tocks**
buttrass	**but·tress**
buttuck	**but·tock**
buxem	**bux·om**
buy	**bye** *(secondary)*
buzom	**bos·om**
buzzar	**ba·zaar** *(market)*
buzzar	**bi·zarre** *(odd)*
buzzerd	**buz·zard**
by	**buy** *(purchase)*
by	**bye** *(secondary)*
byases	**bi·as·es**
bycicle	**bi·cy·cle**
bye	**buy** *(purchase)*
byfocals	**bi·fo·cals**
byle	**bile**
bynary	**bi·na·ry**
byological	**bi·o·log·i·cal**
byology	**bi·ol·o·gy**
byprodduct	**by·prod·uct**
bystanderd	**by·stand·er**
byte	**bit** *(binary digit)*
byte	**bight** *(curve)*
bywey	**by·way**
Byzentine	**By·zan·tine**

C

WRONG	RIGHT
cabage	**cab·bage**
cabaray	**cab·a·ret**
cabboose	**ca·boose**
cabel	**ca·ble** *(thick rope)*
cabenet	**cab·i·net**
caberet	**cab·a·ret**
cable	**ca·bal** *(secret group)*
caburnet	**ca·ber·net**
cacao	**co·coa** *(chocolate)*
cacaphony	**ca·coph·o·ny**
Cacasian	**Cau·ca·sian**
caccus	**cau·cus**
cacky	**kha·ki**
cacoon	**co·coon**
cactis	**cac·tus**
caddaver	**ca·dav·er**
caddie	**cad·dy** *(tea tray)*
cadette	**ca·det**
cadie	**cad·die** *(golfer)*
cadry	**ca·dre**
cady	**cad·dy** *(tea tray)*
Caeser	**Cae·sar**
Caezarean	**Cae·sar·e·an**
cafateria	**caf·e·te·ria**
cafeine	**caf·feine**
cafe latte	**caf·fe lat·te**
caffe	**ca·fé**
caffee	**cof·fee**

WRONG	RIGHT
caffeteria	**caf·e·te·ria**
caffiene	**caf·feine**
caften	**caf·tan**
Cajin	**Ca·jun**
cajoll	**ca·jole**
caktus	**cac·tus**
calaber	**cal·i·ber**
Calafornia	**Cal·i·for·nia**
calammity	**ca·lam·i·ty**
calandar	**cal·en·dar** *(table of dates)*
calarie	**cal·o·rie**
calasthenics	**cal·is·then·ics**
calcalate	**cal·cu·late**
calculater	**cal·cu·la·tor**
cale	**kale**
caleidoscope	**ka·lei·do·scope**
calendar	**col·an·der** *(strainer)*
caligraphy	**cal·lig·ra·phy**
calipso	**ca·lyp·so**
calistenics	**cal·is·then·ics**
callamari	**ca·la·mari**
callamine	**cal·a·mine**
callamity	**ca·lam·i·ty**
calldron	**cal·dron**

WRONG	RIGHT
callendar	**cal·en·dar**
	(table of dates)
calliber	**cal·i·ber**
callico	**cal·i·co**
calliflower	**cau·li·flower**
callorie	**cal·o·rie**
callous	**cal·lus**
	(hardened skin)
callus	**cal·lous** *(insensitive)*
calsium	**cal·ci·um**
calvary	**cav·al·ry** *(troops)*
Calvery	**Cal·va·ry**
	(Biblical place)
camaflage	**cam·ou·flage**
camasole	**cam·i·sole**
cameleon	**cha·me·le·on**
camfor	**cam·phor**
camio	**cam·eo**
cammel	**cam·el**
cammera	**cam·era**
cammomile	**cham·o·mile**
cammouflage	
	cam·ou·flage
campane	**cam·paign**
campas	**cam·pus**
campound	**com·pound**
camra	**cam·era**
Canadien	**Ca·na·di·an**
canapé	**can·o·py** *(awning)*
canapée	**ca·na·pé**
	(appetizer)
canaster	**can·is·ter**
cancelation	
	can·cel·la·tion
cancker	**can·ker**

WRONG	RIGHT
candadate	**can·di·date**
canded	**can·did**
candedacy	**can·di·da·cy**
candel	**can·dle**
candellabrum	
	can·de·la·brum
cander	**can·dor**
candyed	**can·died**
canen	**can·on** *(church law)*
canery	**ca·nary**
canibal	**can·ni·bal**
caning	**can·ning**
	(preserving)
cannal	**ca·nal**
cannapé	**ca·na·pé**
	(appetizer)
cannary	**ca·nary**
cannasta	**ca·nas·ta**
cannen	**can·non**
	(large gun)
cannidate	**can·di·date**
cannine	**ca·nine**
canning	**can·ing** *(flogging)*
cannister	**can·is·ter**
cannola	**ca·no·la**
cannon	**can·on**
	(church law)
canon	**can·non**
	(large gun)
canopy	**ca·na·pé**
	(appetizer)
cansel	**can·cel**
canser	**can·cer**
cant	**can't** *(cannot)*
cantalever	**can·ti·le·ver**

WRONG	RIGHT	WRONG	RIGHT
cantalope	**can·ta·loupe**	carachteristic	
cantene	**can·teen**		**char·ac·ter·is·tic**
canter	**can·tor** *(singer)*	caracter	**char·ac·ter**
cantor	**can·ter** *(gallop)*		*(personality)*
canue	**ca·noe**	Caralina	**Car·o·li·na**
canvas	**can·vass** *(poll)*	carat	**car·et**
canvass	**can·vas** *(cloth)*		*(proofreader's mark)*
canyun	**can·yon**	carat	**car·rot** *(vegetable)*
capabel	**ca·pa·ble**	carban	**car·bon**
capasity	**ca·pac·i·ty**	carbanated	**car·bon·at·ed**
capatal	**cap·i·tal**	carbarater	**car·bu·ret·or**
	(city; chief)	carbene	**car·bine**
capchure	**cap·ture**	carberetor	**car·bu·ret·or**
capeble	**ca·pa·ble**	carbind	**car·bine**
capichulate	**capit·u·late**	carbond	**car·bon**
capilary	**cap·il·lary**	carburator	**car·bu·ret·or**
capital	**cap·i·tol** *(building)*	carcanoma	**car·ci·no·ma**
capitol	**cap·i·tal**	carcus	**car·cass**
	(city; chief)	cardagan	**car·di·gan**
capitolism	**cap·i·tal·ism**	cardbord	**card·board**
capitualate	**capit·u·late**	cardeac	**car·di·ac**
cappaccino	**cap·puc·cino**	cardeology	**car·di·ol·o·gy**
cappillary	**cap·il·lary**	cardeovascular	
cappitulate	**capit·u·late**		**car·di·o·vas·cu·lar**
Capracorn	**Cap·ri·corn**	cardiak	**car·di·ac**
caprise	**ca·price**	cardialogy	**car·di·ol·o·gy**
capsle	**cap·sule**	cardinel	**car·di·nal**
captan	**cap·tain**	cardiovasclar	
captavate	**cap·ti·vate**		**car·di·o·vas·cu·lar**
captave	**cap·tive**	cardnal	**car·di·nal**
capter	**cap·tor**	carear	**ca·reer**
capter	**cap·ture**	carefull	**care·ful**
captian	**cap·tion**	carefuly	**care·ful·ly**
capuccino	**cap·puc·cino**	carel	**car·rel** *(study desk)*
Carabbean	**Car·ib·be·an**	caremel	**car·a·mel**

WRONG	RIGHT
caret	**car·at** *(gem weight)*
caret	**car·rot** *(vegetable)*
caret	**kar·at** *(1/24)*
carfully	**care·ful·ly**
cariage	**car·riage**
caricature	**char·ac·ter** *(personality)*
caricture	**car·i·ca·ture** *(picture)*
carier	**car·ri·er**
caries	**car·ries** *(form of carry)*
carion	**car·ri·on**
carisma	**cha·ris·ma**
carivan	**car·a·van**
carma	**kar·ma**
carmel	**car·a·mel**
carnaval	**car·ni·val**
carnavore	**car·ni·vore**
carnege	**car·nage**
carnel	**car·nal**
carniverous	**car·niv·o·rous**
carol	**car·rel** *(study desk)*
carosene	**ker·o·sene**
carot	**car·rot** *(vegetable)*
carotted	**ca·rot·id**
carouze	**ca·rouse**
carpel tunnel syndrome	**car·pal tun·nel syn·drome**
carpetting	**car·pet·ing**
carpinter	**car·pen·ter**
carpit	**car·pet**
carrafe	**ca·rafe**
carrage	**car·riage**

WRONG	RIGHT
carrasel	**car·ou·sel**
carravan	**car·a·van**
carrel	**car·ol** *(song)*
carress	**ca·ress**
Carribbean	**Car·ib·be·an**
carricature	**car·i·ca·ture** *(picture)*
carridge	**car·riage**
carrien	**car·ri·on**
carries	**car·ies** *(decay)*
carring	**car·ry·ing**
carrob	**car·ob**
carrol	**car·ol** *(song)*
carrot	**car·at** *(gem weight)*
carrot	**car·et** *(proofreader's mark)*
carrotene	**car·o·tene**
carrouse	**ca·rouse**
carsinogen	**car·cin·o·gen**
carsinoma	**car·ci·no·ma**
cartalage	**car·ti·lage**
cart blanche	**carte blanche**
cartell	**car·tel**
carten	**car·ton**
cartillage	**car·ti·lage**
cartrige	**car·tridge**
cartune	**car·toon**
casally	**cas·u·al·ly**
caseing	**cas·ing**
caseno	**ca·si·no** *(gambling room)*
caserole	**cas·se·role**
casette	**cas·sette**
cashe	**cache** *(hiding place)*

WRONG	RIGHT
casheer	**cash·ier**
cashmeer	**cash·mere**
cashou	**cash·ew**
cashually	**cas·u·al·ly**
cashualty	**cas·u·al·ty**
casino	**cas·si·no**
	(card game)
caskade	**cas·cade**
caskit	**cas·ket**
casment	**case·ment**
casock	**cas·sock**
cassarole	**cas·se·role**
casscade	**cas·cade**
cassel	**cas·tle**
casseno	**cas·si·no**
	(card game)
casset	**cas·sette**
cassino	**ca·si·no**
	(gambling room)
casstanets	**cas·ta·nets**
cast	**caste** *(social rank)*
castagate	**cas·ti·gate**
caster	**cas·tor** *(oil)*
castor	**cast·er** *(wheel)*
castrait	**cas·trate**
casulty	**cas·u·al·ty**
catachism	**cat·e·chism**
cataclism	**cat·a·clysm**
catacome	**cat·a·comb**
catagory	**cat·e·go·ry**
catalist	**cat·a·lyst**
catalitic	**cat·a·lyt·ic**
catapalt	**cat·a·pult**
catapillar	**cat·er·pil·lar**
catarack	**cat·a·ract**

WRONG	RIGHT
catastrophies	
	ca·tas·tro·phes *(pl.)*
catastrophy	**ca·tas·tro·phe**
catchew	**cash·ew**
cateclism	**cat·a·clysm**
catelog	**cat·a·log**
Cathalic	**Cath·o·lic**
cathater	**cath·e·ter**
cathedrel	**ca·the·dral**
Cathlic	**Cath·o·lic**
cattalog	**cat·a·log**
cattegory	**cat·e·go·ry**
cattel	**cat·tle**
catterpillar	**cat·er·pil·lar**
caulaflower	**cau·li·flower**
cautius	**cau·tious**
cavaleir	**cav·a·lier**
Cavalry	**Cal·va·ry**
	(Biblical place)
cavaty	**cav·i·ty**
cavear	**cav·i·ar**
cavelcade	**cav·al·cade**
cavelier	**cav·a·lier**
cavelry	**cav·al·ry** *(troops)*
cavurn	**cav·ern**
cawk	**caulk**
cayak	**kayak**
cayote	**coy·o·te**
Ceasarean	**Cae·sar·e·an**
cecada	**ci·ca·da**
ceder	**ce·dar**
ceese	**cease**
ceiling	**seal·ing** *(fastening)*
celabrate	**cel·e·brate**
celantro	**ci·lan·tro**

celebrety	**ce·leb·ri·ty**
celery	**sal·a·ry** *(pay)*
celesstial	**ce·les·tial**
cell	**sell** *(trade for money)*
cellar	**sell·er** *(vendor)*
cellebrate	**cel·e·brate**
cellebrity	**ce·leb·ri·ty**
celler	**cel·lar** *(basement)*
cellery	**cel·e·ry** *(vegetable)*
cellestial	**ce·les·tial**
cellibacy	**cel·i·ba·cy**
cellofane	**cel·lo·phane**
celophane	**cel·lo·phane**
celp	**kelp**
Celsus	**Cel·si·us**
celulite	**cel·lu·lite**
celullite	**cel·lu·lite**
celuloid	**cel·lu·loid**
cematery	**cem·e·tery**
cemical	**chem·i·cal**
cemint	**ce·ment**
cemotherapy	**chem·o·ther·a·py**
censer	**cen·sor** *(prohibiter)*
censor	**cen·sure** *(blame)*
censor	**cen·ser** *(incense box)*
censor	**sen·sor** *(detection device)*
censure	**cen·sor** *(prohibiter)*
cent	**sent** *(pt. of send)*
cent	**scent** *(smell)*
centagrade	**cen·ti·grade**
centameter	**cen·ti·me·ter**

centapede	**cen·ti·pede**
centenial	**cen·ten·ni·al**
centerpeice	**cen·ter·piece**
centery	**cen·tu·ry**
centrel	**cen·tral**
centrifagle	**cen·trif·u·gal**
centrifical	**cen·trif·u·gal**
cepter	**scep·ter**
ceptic	**sep·tic**
cerafe	**ca·rafe**
ceramik	**ce·ram·ic**
ceramony	**cer·e·mo·ny**
cercumstance	**cir·cum·stance**
cerdential	**cre·den·tial**
cereal	**se·ri·al** *(in a series)*
cerebrel	**cer·e·bral**
ceriel	**ce·re·al** *(grain)*
cerramic	**ce·ram·ic**
cerrebral	**cer·e·bral**
cerremony	**cer·e·mo·ny**
certan	**cer·tain**
certifacate	**cer·tif·i·cate**
certifyable	**cer·ti·fi·a·ble**
cervex	**cer·vix**
Cesar	**Cae·sar**
cession	**ses·sion** *(meeting)*
Chabley	**Cha·blis**
chairiot	**char·i·ot**
chairwoman	**char·wom·an** *(cleaning person)*
chalay	**cha·let**
chalenge	**chal·lenge**
challet	**cha·let**

WRONG	RIGHT
challice	**chal·ice**
chammeleon	
	cha·me·le·on
chammy	**cham·ois**
champaign	**cham·pagne**
	(wine)
champeon	**cham·pi·on**
chancelor	**chan·cel·lor**
chandalier	**chan·de·lier**
chane	**chain**
chanel	**chan·nel**
changable	**change·a·ble**
changeing	**chang·ing**
chansellor	**chan·cel·lor**
chaparone	**chap·er·on**
chaplin	**chap·lain**
chappel	**chap·el**
chaptor	**chap·ter**
character	**car·i·ca·ture**
	(picture)
charactoristic	
	char·ac·ter·is·tic
charaty	**char·i·ty**
charcole	**char·coal**
chariat	**char·i·ot**
charish	**cher·ish**
charizma	**cha·ris·ma**
charrade	**cha·rade**
chartreuze	**char·treuse**
charwoman	
	chair·wom·an
	(person in charge)
chase longue	
	chaise longue
chasen	**chas·ten**

WRONG	RIGHT
chasim	**chasm**
chassy	**chas·sis**
chastaty	**chas·ti·ty**
chastize	**chas·tise**
Chatanooga	
	Chat·ta·noo·ga
chatel	**chat·tel**
chater	**chat·ter**
chateu	**châ·teau**
chaufer	**chauf·feur** *(driver)*
chauvanism	**chau·vin·ism**
cheap	**cheep** *(chirp)*
chearful	**cheer·ful**
cheatah	**chee·tah**
checanery	**chi·can·ery**
Checkoslovakia	
	Czech·o·slo·va·kia
Chedar	**Ched·dar**
cheek	**chic** *(fashionable)*
cheep	**cheap** *(inexpensive)*
cheeze	**cheese**
cheif	**chief** *(leader)*
cheif	**chef** *(cook)*
chello	**cel·lo**
chematherapy	
	chem·o·ther·a·py
chemestry	**chem·is·try**
chemize	**che·mise**
chennille	**che·nille**
cherade	**cha·rade**
cherisma	**cha·ris·ma**
cherity	**char·i·ty**
chern	**churn**
cherrish	**cher·ish**
cherrubic	**che·ru·bic**

WRONG	RIGHT	WRONG	RIGHT
chessnut	**chest·nut**	chow main	**chow mein**
chic	**sheik**	chozen	**cho·sen**
	(Arab chief)	chranic	**chron·ic**
Chicanno	**Chi·ca·no**	chranological	
chicery	**chic·o·ry**		**chron·o·log·i·cal**
chickory	**chic·o·ry**	chrisanthemum	
chieftan	**chief·tain**		**chrys·an·the·mum**
chiken	**chick·en**	chrissen	**chris·ten**
chilli	**chili** *(pepper)*	Christanity	**Chris·ti·an·i·ty**
chily	**chilly** *(cold)*	chromasome	
chiminey	**chim·ney**		**chro·mo·some**
chinchila	**chin·chilla**	chronacle	**chron·i·cle**
chintsy	**chintzy**	chuckel	**chuck·le**
chior	**choir**	cianide	**cy·a·nide**
chipmonk	**chip·munk**	Cianti	**Chi·an·ti**
chirapractor		ciberpunk	**cy·ber·punk**
	chi·ro·prac·tor	ciberspace	**cy·ber·space**
chire	**choir**	cicle	**cy·cle**
chisle	**chis·el**	ciclone	**cy·clone**
chivallry	**chiv·al·ry**	cieling	**ceil·ing**
Chiwawa	**Chi·hua·hua**		*(overhead covering)*
chloranate	**chlo·ri·nate**	cigerette	**cig·a·rette**
chloraphyl	**chlo·ro·phyll**	cilinder	**cyl·in·der**
chlorene	**chlo·rine**	cillia	**cil·ia**
chocalate	**choc·o·late**	cinama	**cin·e·ma**
chock	**chalk** *(white powder)*	cinammon	**cin·na·mon**
choise	**choice**	Cinncinnati	**Cin·cin·nati**
cholestrol	**cho·les·ter·ol**	circalate	**cir·cu·late**
chollera	**chol·era**	circas	**cir·cus**
choosen	**cho·sen**	circeler	**cir·cu·lar**
choral	**cor·al** *(shell)*	circiut	**cir·cuit**
chord	**cord** *(string)*	circomscribe	
chorreography			**cir·cum·scribe**
	chor·e·og·ra·phy	circomstantial	
chouder	**chow·der**		**cir·cum·stan·tial**

WRONG	RIGHT	WRONG	RIGHT

WRONG	RIGHT
circuler	**cir·cu·lar**
circumfrence	**cir·cum·fer·ence**
circumsize	**cir·cum·cise**
circumspeck	**cir·cum·spect**
circumstanse	**cir·cum·stance**
circumstansial	**cir·cum·stan·tial**
cirhosis	**cir·rho·sis**
ciropractor	**chi·ro·prac·tor**
cirrosis	**cir·rho·sis**
cist	**cyst** *(sac)*
cisturn	**cis·tern**
citazen	**cit·i·zen**
cite	**sight** *(vision)*
cite	**site** *(location)*
cittadel	**cit·a·del**
civilazation	**civ·i·li·za·tion**
civillian	**ci·vil·ian**
clairavoyance	**clair·voy·ance**
clame	**claim**
clammor	**clam·or**
claranet	**clar·i·net**
claraty	**clar·i·ty**
clarefy	**clar·i·fy**
clarical	**cler·i·cal**
clarinnet	**clar·i·net**
clarvoyance	**clair·voy·ance**
classafication	**clas·si·fi·ca·tion**

WRONG	RIGHT
clastrophobia	**claus·tro·pho·bia**
claws	**clause** *(grammar)*
clearence	**clear·ance**
cleavedge	**cleav·age**
cleaver	**clev·er** *(sly)*
cleche	**cli·ché**
cleek	**clique** *(group of people)*
cleerance	**clear·ance**
cleet	**cleat**
cleevage	**cleav·age**
clemmency	**clem·en·cy**
clenser	**cleans·er**
cleptomaniac	**klep·to·ma·ni·ac**
clever	**cleav·er** *(large knife)*
cliantele	**cli·en·tele**
click	**clique** *(group of people)*
clientell	**cli·en·tele**
climactic	**cli·mat·ic** *(of a climate)*
climatic	**cli·mac·tic** *(of a climax)*
climet	**cli·mate**
clinicly	**clin·i·cal·ly**
clishay	**cli·ché**
cloke	**cloak**
clorinate	**chlo·ri·nate**
clorophyl	**chlo·ro·phyll**
close	**clothes** *(apparel)*
clostrophobia	**claus·tro·pho·bia**

38

WRONG	RIGHT
cloth	**clothe** *(v.)*
clothe	**cloth** *(n.)*
clotheing	**cloth·ing**
clothes	**close** *(shut)*
cloyster	**clois·ter**
cluch	**clutch**
clumsey	**clum·sy**
clurgy	**cler·gy**
coagalate	**co·ag·u·late**
coaless	**co·a·lesce**
coallition	**co·a·li·tion**
coarse	**course**
	(way; class)
cobolt	**co·balt**
cocane	**co·caine**
cocanut	**co·co·nut**
cocao	**ca·cao** *(tree)*
coccoon	**co·coon**
coch	**coach**
cockaroach	**cock·roach**
cocoa	**ca·cao** *(tree)*
cocoe	**co·coa** *(chocolate)*
codefy	**cod·i·fy**
codependant	
	co·de·pend·ent
codiene	**co·deine**
codle	**cod·dle**
coersion	**co·er·cion**
cofee	**cof·fee**
coffen	**cof·fin**
cogatate	**cog·i·tate**
cogenital	**con·gen·i·tal**
cognizent	**cog·ni·zant**
coherense	**co·her·ence**
cohesave	**co·he·sive**

WRONG	RIGHT
coifure	**coif·fure**
	(hair style)
coincidance	
	co·in·ci·dence
coinside	**co·in·cide**
colaborate	**col·lab·o·rate**
colage	**col·lage** *(art form)*
colander	**cal·en·dar**
	(table of dates)
colapse	**col·lapse**
colar	**col·lar** *(neck band)*
colateral	**col·lat·er·al**
cold slaw	**cole·slaw**
cole	**coal** *(mineral)*
coleague	**col·league**
colector	**col·lec·tor**
colege	**col·lege** *(school)*
colegiate	**col·le·giate**
colen	**co·lon**
coler	**col·or**
colera	**chol·era**
colesce	**co·a·lesce**
colesterol	**cho·les·ter·ol**
colide	**col·lide**
colision	**col·li·sion**
colition	**co·a·li·tion**
collage	**col·lege** *(school)*
collander	**col·an·der**
	(strainer)
collapseable	**col·laps·i·ble**
collecter	**col·lec·tor**
college	**col·lage** *(art form)*
collegue	**col·league**
coller	**col·lar** *(neck band)*
collerd	**col·lard** *(kale)*

WRONG	RIGHT
collic	**col·ic**
colliseum	**col·i·se·um**
collitis	**co·li·tis**
collogne	**co·logne**
collonial	**co·lo·ni·al**
collonnade	**col·on·nade**
Collorado	**Col·o·rado**
collossal	**co·los·sal**
collum	**col·umn**
collumnist	**col·um·nist**
colonade	**col·on·nade**
colone	**co·logne**
coloquial	**col·lo·qui·al**
colosal	**co·los·sal**
columist	**col·um·nist**
columm	**col·umn**
coma	**com·ma**
	(punctuation mark)
comand	**com·mand**
combatave	**com·bat·ive**
combustable	
	com·bus·ti·ble
comedianne	
	co·me·di·enne *(f.)*
comedien	
	co·me·di·an *(m.)*
comedien	**co·me·di·enne** *(f.)*
comeing	**com·ing**
comemorative	
	com·mem·o·ra tive
comencement	
	com·mence·ment
comend	**com·mend**
comentary	**com·men·tary**
comerce	**com·merce**

WRONG	RIGHT
comfert	**com·fort**
comfiscate	**con·fis·cate**
comfortible	**com·fort·a·ble**
comidy	**com·e·dy**
comiserate	**com·mis·er·ate**
comissary	**com·mis·sary**
comission	**com·mis·sion**
comitment	**com·mit·ment**
comitted	**com·mit·ted**
comittee	**com·mit·tee**
comm	**comb**
comma	**co·ma** *(stupor)*
commadore	**com·mo·dore**
comman	**com·mon**
commatose	**co·ma·tose**
commemrative	
	com·mem·o·ra·tive
commensement	
	com·mence·ment
commentater	
	com·men·ta·tor
commerse	**com·merce**
commisary	**com·mis·sary**
commision	**com·mis·sion**
commited	**com·mit·ted**
commitee	**com·mit·tee**
committment	
	com·mit·ment
commizerate	
	com·mis·er·ate
commodaty	**com·mod·i·ty**
commonist	**com·mu·nist**
communacible	
	com·mu·ni·ca·ble
comode	**com·mode**

WRONG	RIGHT	WRONG	RIGHT
comodity	**com·mod·i·ty**	complane	**com·plain**
comon	**com·mon**	complecated	
comotion	**com·mo·tion**		**com·pli·cat·ed**
compack	**com·pact**	complection	
compackor	**com·pac·tor**		**com·plex·ion**
compacter	**com·pac·tor**	complement	
compannion	**com·pan·ion**		**com·pli·ment**
compareable	**com·pa·ra·ble**		*(praise)*
comparitively		complementry	
	com·par·a·tive·ly		**com·ple·men·ta·ry**
compas	**com·pass**	completly	**com·plete·ly**
compasionate		complient	**com·pli·ant**
	com·pas·sion·ate	compliment	
compasition			**com·ple·ment**
	com·po·si·tion		*(part of a whole)*
compatable	**com·pat·i·ble**	complimentry	
compatence	**com·pe·tence**		**com·pli·men·ta·ry**
compatition		complisity	**com·plic·i·ty**
	com·pe·ti·tion	componant	**com·po·nent**
compell	**com·pel**	composet	**com·pos·ite**
compeny	**com·pa·ny**	composor	**com·pos·er**
competance		comprable	**com·pa·ra·ble**
	com·pe·tence	compramise	
competative			**com·pro·mise**
	com·pet·i·tive	comprehensable	
competeing	**com·pet·ing**		**com·pre·hen·si·ble**
compettiter	**com·pet·i·tor**	comprize	**com·prise**
compinsation		compulsery	**com·pul·so·ry**
	com·pen·sa·tion	comrad	**com·rade**
complacation		comunal	**com·mu·nal**
	com·pli·ca·tion	comunicable	
complacent	**com·plai·sant**		**com·mu·ni·ca·ble**
	(obliging)	comunication	
complaisant	**com·pla·cent**		**com·mu·ni·ca·tion**
	(smug)	comunion	**com·mun·ion**

41

WRONG	RIGHT
comunist	**com·mu·nist**
comunity	**com·mu·ni·ty**
comuter	**com·mut·er**
conbine	**com·bine**
conceed	**con·cede**
conceivible	**con·ceiv·a·ble**
concensus	**con·sen·sus**
concherto	**con·cer·to**
concideration	**con·sid·er·a·tion**
conciet	**con·ceit**
concievable	**con·ceiv·a·ble**
concommitant	**con·com·i·tant**
concordence	**con·cord·ance**
concorse	**con·course**
concreet	**con·crete**
concurent	**con·cur·rent**
concusion	**con·cus·sion**
condament	**con·di·ment**
condaminium	**con·do·min·i·um**
condansation	**con·den·sa·tion**
condascend	**con·de·scend**
condem	**con·demn** *(censure)*
condem	**con·dom** *(prophylactic)*
condence	**con·dense**
condesend	**con·de·scend**
condimint	**con·di·ment**
condit	**con·duit**

WRONG	RIGHT
condolance	**con·do·lence**
condominimum	**con·do·min·i·um**
conducter	**con·duc·tor**
condusive	**con·du·cive**
Conecticut	**Con·nect·i·cut**
conection	**con·nec·tion**
confascate	**con·fis·cate**
confecktion	**con·fec·tion**
confedence	**con·fi·dence**
confedercy	**con·fed·er·a·cy**
confered	**con·ferred**
conferrence	**con·fer·ence**
confesion	**con·fes·sion**
confeti	**con·fet·ti**
confidance	**con·fi·dence**
confidensial	**con·fi·den·tial**
confinment	**con·fine·ment**
confirmation	**con·for·ma·tion** *(shape)*
conflick	**con·flict**
conformation	**con·fir·ma·tion** *(ceremony; verification)*
confrence	**con·fer·ence**
conglommerate	**con·glom·er·ate**
congradulate	**con·grat·u·late**
congragation	**con·gre·ga·tion**
congruance	**con·gru·ence**

WRONG	RIGHT	WRONG	RIGHT
conivance	con·niv·ance	consiliatory	con·cil·i·a·to·ry
conjagate	con·ju·gate	consious	con·scious
conjenial	con·gen·ial		*(aware)*
conjenital	con·gen·i·tal	consise	con·cise
conjer	con·jure	consistancy	con·sis·ten·cy
conjestion	con·ges·tion	consoladation	con·sol·i·da·tion
conklave	con·clave	consome	con·som·mé
Conneticut	Con·nect·i·cut	consonent	con·so·nant
connivence	con·niv·ance	conspirecy	con·spir·a·cy
connoiseur	con·nois·seur	constapation	con·sti·pa·tion
conotation	con·no·ta·tion	constatution	con·sti·tu·tion
conquerer	con·quer·or	constelation	con·stel·la·tion
consaquence	con·se·quence	constent	con·stant
consceince	con·science	construcktion	con·struc·tion
	(morals)	consul	coun·sel *(advice)*
consceintious	con·sci·en·tious	consul	coun·cil *(legislature)*
conscience	con·scious	consultent	con·sult·ant
	(aware)	consumate	con·sum·mate
conscious	con·science	consummé	con·som·mé
	(morals)	contack	con·tact
conseal	con·ceal	contageous	con·ta·gious
consede	con·cede	contamanate	con·tam·i·nate
conseit	con·ceit	contane	con·tain
consentrate	con·cen·trate	contemparary	con·tem·po·rary
consentric	con·cen·tric		
conseptual	con·cep·tu·al		
conserned	con·cerned		
consert	con·cert		
conservitave	con·ser·va·tive		
consession	con·ces·sion		
consicrate	con·se·crate		

43

WRONG	RIGHT	WRONG	RIGHT

contemptable......................
..............**con·tempt·i·ble**
contenental ...**con·ti·nen·tal**
conterdiction ....
..............**con·tra·dic·tion**
contestent........**con·test·ant**
continnuation ....
..............**con·tin·u·a·tion**
continous.......**con·tin·u·ous**
continuence.......................
..............**con·tin·u·ance**
contoor ....**con·tour**
contrabution......................
..............**con·tri·bu·tion**
contrack ....**con·tract**
contraseption....................
..............**con·tra·cep·tion**
contraversial ....
..............**con·tro·ver·sial**
contrery................**con·trary**
contrivence ....**con·triv·ance**
controling ....**con·trol·ling**
conubial...........**con·nu·bi·al**
convalesence......................
...........**con·va·les·cence**
conveneince........................
.................**con·ven·ience**
conversent ......**con·ver·sant**
convertable ....**con·vert·i·ble**
convienience.......................
.................**con·ven·ience**
conyac ....**cogn·ac**
coo.................**coup** (revolt)
coolent.................**cool·ant**
coopon.................**cou·pon**

coordenation ....
..............**co·or·di·na·tion**
coparison ......**com·par·i·son**
coper.....................**cop·per**
copyer ....**cop·i·er**
corageous ....**cou·ra·geous**
coral............**cho·ral** (music)
coral ....**cor·ral** (pen)
cord ....**chord** (music)
cordaroy ....**cor·du·roy**
cordgial ....**cor·dial**
cordination ....
..............**co·or·di·na·tion**
coreck ....**cor·rect**
corection ....**cor·rec·tion**
corelation ......**cor·re·la·tion**
corenary ....**cor·o·nary**
coreography ....
............**chor·e·og·ra·phy**
corespondence ....
.........**cor·re·spond·ence**
corespondent ....
............**cor·re·spond·ent**
(writer)
coridor ....**cor·ri·dor**
coroborate.........................
................**cor·rob·o·rate**
coronery ....**cor·o·nary**
corosion.............**cor·ro·sion**
corparation ....
..............**cor·po·ra·tion**
corperal ....**cor·po·ral**
corps ......**corpse** (dead body)
corpse ....**corps**
(group of people)

WRONG	RIGHT
corpusle	**cor·pus·cle**
correspondance	**cor·re·spond·ence**
correspondent	**co·re·spond·ent** *(legal term)*
corrollary	**cor·ol·lary**
corruptable	**cor·rupt·i·ble**
cortizone	**cor·ti·sone**
corugated	**cor·ru·gat·ed**
coruptible	**cor·rupt·i·ble**
corus	**cho·rus**
cosign	**co·sine** *(mathematics term)*
cosine	**co·sign** *(sign jointly)*
cosmapolitan	**cos·mo·pol·i·tan**
costic	**caus·tic**
cotage	**cot·tage**
cotemtible	**con·tempt·i·ble**
coterize	**cau·ter·ize**
coton	**cot·ton**
council	**coun·sel** *(advice)*
counsel	**con·sul** *(government representative)*
counsel	**coun·cil** *(legislature)*
countenence	**coun·te·nance**
counterevolutionary	**coun·ter·rev·o·lu·tion·ary**
counterfit	**coun·ter·feit**

WRONG	RIGHT
countrey	**coun·try**
coup	**coupe** *(car)*
coupe	**coup** *(revolt)*
coupel	**cou·ple**
couragious	**cou·ra·geous**
courrage	**cour·age**
courrier	**cou·ri·er**
course	**coarse** *(rough)*
courtecy	**cour·te·sy**
courtious	**cour·te·ous**
court-marshall	**court-mar·tial**
covalant	**co·va·lent**
covanant	**cov·e·nant**
cowardace	**cow·ard·ice**
cowerdly	**cow·ard·ly**
coxe	**coax**
cozmetic	**cos·met·ic**
cozmic	**cos·mic**
craby	**crab·by**
crayen	**cray·on**
creachure	**crea·ture** *(animal)*
creak	**creek** *(stream)*
creap	**creep**
creater	**cre·a·tor** *(one who creates)*
creater	**crea·ture** *(animal)*
credance	**cre·dence**
creditible	**cred·it·a·ble**
creek	**creak** *(squeak)*
cressant	**crois·sant** *(roll)*
cressent	**cres·cent**
crevasse	**crev·ice** *(narrow cleft)*

WRONG	RIGHT	WRONG	RIGHT
crevice	**cre·vasse** *(deep fissure)*	crusible	**cru·ci·ble**
crewel	**cru·el** *(mean)*	crusifix	**cru·ci·fix**
crickit	**crick·et**	crusify	**cru·ci·fy**
criminel	**crim·i·nal**	crysanthemum	**chrys·an·the·mum**
criple	**crip·ple**	crystalize	**crys·tal·lize**
criptic	**cryp·tic**	cubberd	**cup·board**
crises	**cri·sis** *(sing.)*	cubical	**cu·bi·cle** *(small room)*
crisis	**cri·ses** *(pl.)*		
cristal	**crys·tal**	cubicle	**cu·bi·cal** *(cube-shaped)*
Cristianity	**Chris·ti·an·i·ty**		
criticizm	**crit·i·cism**	cuboard	**cup·board**
critisize	**crit·i·cize**	cudly	**cud·dly**
crocadile	**croc·o·dile**	cudos	**ku·dos**
croche	**cro·chet**	cue	**queue** *(line)*
crochety	**crotch·ety**	cuepon	**cou·pon**
croisant	**crois·sant** *(roll)*	cugel	**cudg·el**
crokay	**cro·quet** *(game)*	cuizine	**cui·sine**
crokette	**cro·quette** *(food)*	cullinary	**cu·li·nary**
crome	**chrome**	culmanate	**cul·mi·nate**
cromosome	**chro·mo·some**	culpible	**cul·pa·ble**
cronic	**chron·ic**	culpret	**cul·prit**
cronicle	**chron·i·cle**	cultavate	**cul·ti·vate**
cronological	**chron·o·log·i·cal**	cultureal	**cul·tur·al**
crooton	**crou·ton**	cummulative	**cumu·la·tive**
croquet	**cro·quette** *(food)*	cumpass	**com·pass**
croquette	**cro·quet** *(game)*	cumquot	**kum·quat**
croshet	**cro·chet**	cuning	**cun·ning**
crucefy	**cru·ci·fy**	cupbord	**cup·board**
cruel	**crew·el** *(needlework)*	curage	**cour·age**
crulty	**cru·el·ty**	curant	**cur·rant** *(raisin)*
crum	**crumb**	curater	**cu·ra·tor**
crusial	**cru·cial**	curcuit	**cir·cuit**
		curent	**cur·rent** *(stream)*

46

WRONG	RIGHT
curiculum	**cur·ric·u·lum**
curiousity	**cu·ri·os·i·ty**
curius	**cu·ri·ous**
curlycue	**curl·i·cue**
curmugeon	**cur·mudg·eon**
curnel	**ker·nel** *(grain)*
currant	**cur·rent** *(stream)*
current	**cur·rant** *(raisin)*
curricullum	**cur·ric·u·lum**
cursury	**cur·so·ry**
curtale	**cur·tail**
curteous	**cour·te·ous**
curtesy	**cour·te·sy**
curtin	**cur·tain**

WRONG	RIGHT
cushon	**cush·ion**
cusine	**cui·sine**
custady	**cus·to·dy**
custamer	**cus·tom·er** *(patron)*
custem	**cus·tom**
custerd	**cus·tard**
customery	**cus·tom·ary**
cutacle	**cut·i·cle**
cuting	**cut·ting**
cymbal	**sym·bol** *(mark)*
cynecal	**cyn·i·cal**
cypras	**cy·press**
Czechaslovakia	**Czech·o·slo·va·kia**

D

WRONG	RIGHT
dabris	**de·bris**
dacore	**dé·cor**
dacorum	**de·cor·um**
dacquiri	**dai·qui·ri**
daes	**da·is**
dafodil	**daf·fo·dil**
dager	**dag·ger**
dairey	**dairy** (*milk farm*)
daja vu	**dé·jà vu**
dalfin	**dol·phin**
dalia	**dahl·ia**
dalight	**day·light**
dalying	**dal·ly·ing**
dam	**damn** (*condemn*)
damedge	**dam·age**
damestic	**do·mes·tic**
dammable	**dam·na·ble**
dammage	**dam·age**
damn	**dam**
	(*animal; barrier*)
dandrif	**dan·druff**
dandylion	**dan·de·li·on**
dane	**deign** (*condescend*)
dangel	**dan·gle**
dangrous	**dan·ger·ous**
dannilion	**dan·de·li·on**
danse	**dance**
danty	**dain·ty**

WRONG	RIGHT
daper	**dap·per**
dappeled	**dap·pled**
dappreciate	**de·pre·ci·ate**
daquiri	**dai·qui·ri**
dareing	**dar·ing**
darey	**dairy** (*milk farm*)
darlling	**dar·ling**
dashbord	**dash·board**
dashhound	**dachs·hund**
dasturdly	**das·tard·ly**
dasy	**dai·sy**
dateing	**dat·ing**
datente	**dé·tente**
datta	**da·ta**
daudle	**daw·dle**
dauter	**daugh·ter**
davinity	**di·vin·i·ty**
davinport	**dav·en·port**
dawb	**daub**
dawntless	**daunt·less**
daylite	**day·light**
dayly	**dai·ly**
days	**daze** (*stun*)
daze	**days** (*pl. of day*)
dazle	**daz·zle**
dazy	**dai·sy**
deactavate	**de·ac·ti·vate**
deadlyer	**dead·li·er**

48

WRONG	RIGHT	WRONG	RIGHT
deadning	**dead·en·ing**	decleration	**dec·la·ra·tion**
deaffen	**deaf·en**	decmal	**dec·i·mal**
dealling	**deal·ing**	decon	**dea·con**
dealor	**deal·er**	deconjestant	
dear	**deer** *(animal)*		**de·con·gest·ant**
debackle	**de·ba·cle**	decoopage	**de·cou·page**
debanair	**deb·o·nair**	decrepet	**de·crep·it**
debass	**de·base**	decriminilize	
debatible	**de·bat·a·ble**		**de·crim·i·nal·ize**
debbit	**deb·it**	ded	**dead**
debillitate	**de·bil·i·tate**	dedacate	**ded·i·cate**
debochery	**de·bauch·ery**	deductable	**de·duct·i·ble**
deboner	**deb·o·nair**	deel	**deal**
debreif	**de·brief**	deen	**dean**
debrie	**de·bris**	deer	**dear** *(beloved)*
debter	**debt·or**	defacate	**def·e·cate**
debue	**de·but**	defacit	**def·i·cit**
decadance	**dec·a·dence**	defalt	**de·fault**
decadant	**dec·a·dent**	defammation	
decafeinated			**def·a·ma·tion**
	de·caf·fein·ated	defanitely	**def·i·nite·ly**
decapatate	**de·cap·i·tate**	defase	**de·face**
decarate	**dec·o·rate**	defecit	**def·i·cit**
decathalon	**de·cath·lon**	defeck	**de·fect**
decendant	**de·scend·ant**	defectave	**de·fec·tive**
decent	**de·scent**	defeet	**de·feat**
	(going down)	defendent	**de·fend·ant**
decent	**dis·sent**	deference	**dif·fer·ence**
	(disagreement)		*(being different)*
decible	**dec·i·bel**	deferrment	**de·fer·ment**
decietful	**de·ceit·ful**	deffend	**de·fend**
decieve	**de·ceive**	deffensive	**de·fen·sive**
decimel	**dec·i·mal**	deffinition	**def·i·ni·tion**
deckade	**dec·ade**	deffrost	**de·frost**
deckadence	**dec·a·dence**	deficeincy	**de·fi·cien·cy**

WRONG	RIGHT
defience	**de·fi·ance**
defind	**de·fined**
definitly	**def·i·nite·ly**
deformaty	**de·form·i·ty**
defrawd	**de·fraud**
degridation	**deg·ra·da·tion**
dehidrated	**de·hy·drat·ed**
dehumidafy	**de·hu·mid·i·fy**
dein	**deign** (condescend)
deisel	**die·sel**
dejeckted	**de·ject·ed**
dejenerate	**de·gen·er·ate**
de jour	**du jour** (of the day)
dekay	**de·cay**
delacatessen	**del·i·ca·tes·sen**
delagate	**del·e·gate**
delectible	**de·lec·ta·ble**
deleet	**de·lete**
delektable	**de·lec·ta·ble**
delerious	**de·lir·i·ous**
delicous	**de·li·cious**
delinquancy	**de·lin·quen·cy**
delite	**de·light**
deliverence	**de·liv·er·ance**
delivry	**de·liv·ery**
Dellaware	**Del·a·ware**
dellicacy	**del·i·ca·cy**
dellicatessen	**del·i·ca·tes·sen**
dellta	**del·ta**

WRONG	RIGHT
dellude	**de·lude**
delluge	**del·uge**
delt	**dealt**
delux	**de·luxe**
demacracy	**de·moc·ra·cy**
demacratic	**dem·o·crat·ic**
demagraphic	**demo·graph·ic**
demalition	**dem·o·li·tion**
deman	**de·mon**
demanstrable	**de·mon·stra·ble**
demeaner	**de·mean·or**
demension	**di·men·sion**
demigog	**dem·a·gogue**
deminish	**di·min·ish**
demize	**de·mise**
demmitasse	**dem·i·tasse**
democricy	**de·moc·ra·cy**
demollish	**de·mol·ish**
demollition	**dem·o·li·tion**
demonstrater	**dem·on·stra·tor**
demur	**de·mure** (coy)
demure	**de·mur** (object)
denamination	**de·nom·i·na·tion**
dence	**dense**
denchers	**den·tures**
denem	**den·im**
deniel	**de·ni·al**
denomonater	**de·nom·i·na·tor**
denounciation	**de·nun·ci·a·tion**

WRONG	RIGHT	WRONG	RIGHT
denounse	**de·nounce**	derregulate	**de·reg·u·late**
densaty	**den·si·ty**	derrelict	**der·e·lict**
dentel	**den·tal**	desacrate	**des·e·crate**
dentest	**den·tist**	desalate	**des·o·late**
denyed	**de·nied**	desastrous	**dis·as·trous**
deoderant	**de·o·dor·ant**	descendent	**de·scend·ant**
departmentallize		descent	**de·cent** *(proper)*
	de·part·men·tal·ize	descent	**dis·sent**
dependance			*(disagreement)*
	de·pend·ence	desciple	**dis·ci·ple**
dependible	**de·pend·a·ble**	deseased	**de·ceased**
depick	**de·pict**		*(dead)*
depillatory	**de·pil·a·to·ry**	deseased	**dis·eased** *(ill)*
depleet	**de·plete**	desegragate	
deplorible	**de·plor·a·ble**		**de·seg·re·gate**
deposatory	**de·pos·i·to·ry**	Desember	**De·cem·ber**
deposet	**de·pos·it**	desency	**de·cen·cy**
deppo	**de·pot**	desent	**de·cent** *(proper)*
depravation		desent	**de·scent**
	dep·ri·va·tion *(loss)*		*(going down)*
depravaty	**de·prav·i·ty**	desent	**dis·sent**
depreshiate	**de·pre·ci·ate**		*(disagreement)*
depresion	**de·pres·sion**	deseption	**de·cep·tion**
depressent	**de·pres·sant**	desert	**des·sert** *(food)*
deprivation		deserveing	**de·serv·ing**
	dep·ra·va·tion	desibel	**dec·i·bel**
	(a corrupting)	deside	**de·cide**
depriveing	**de·priv·ing**	desiduous	**de·cid·u·ous**
deputey	**dep·u·ty**	desimal	**dec·i·mal**
deragatory	**de·rog·a·to·ry**	desine	**de·sign**
deravation	**der·i·va·tion**	desipher	**de·ci·pher**
deregalate	**de·reg·u·late**	desireable	**de·sir·a·ble**
derelick	**der·e·lict**	desizion	**de·ci·sion**
derick	**der·rick**	despach	**dis·patch**
derigible	**dir·i·gi·ble**	despare	**de·spair**

51

WRONG	RIGHT	WRONG	RIGHT
despensable	**dis·pen·sa·ble**	dettonate	**det·o·nate**
desperate	**dis·pa·rate** *(not alike)*	dettor	**debt·or**
despicible	**des·pi·ca·ble**	deuse	**deuce**
despize	**de·spise**	devalluation	**de·val·u·a·tion**
despondant	**de·spond·ent**	deveant	**de·vi·ant**
desprate	**des·per·ate** *(hopeless)*	develope	**de·vel·op**
dessegergation	**de·seg·re·ga·tion**	developement	**de·vel·op·ment**
dessert	**des·ert** *(dry area)*	device	**de·vise** *(invent)*
dessert	**de·sert** *(abandon)*	devide	**di·vide**
desserts	**de·serts** *(rewards)*	devient	**de·vi·ant**
desserving	**de·serv·ing**	devillish	**dev·il·ish**
dessignated	**des·ig·nat·ed**	devine	**di·vine**
destany	**des·tiny**	devisable	**di·vis·i·ble** *(dividable)*
destatute	**des·ti·tute**	devise	**de·vice** *(mechanism)*
destenation	**des·ti·na·tion**	division	**di·vi·sion**
destructave	**de·struc·tive**	devistation	**dev·as·ta·tion**
detale	**de·tail**	devius	**de·vi·ous**
detane	**de·tain**	devulge	**di·vulge**
detant	**dé·tente**	dew	**due** *(owed)*
detatched	**de·tached**	dexteraty	**dex·ter·i·ty**
detektive	**de·tec·tive**	dextrus	**dex·ter·ous**
deterent	**de·ter·rent**	diabeetis	**di·a·be·tes**
detergant	**de·ter·gent**	diabollic	**di·a·bol·ic**
deterierate	**de·te·ri·o·rate**	diacese	**di·o·cese**
detestible	**de·test·a·ble**	diafram	**di·a·phragm**
deth	**death**	diaganal	**di·ag·o·nal**
detnate	**det·o·nate**	diagnoses	**di·ag·no·sis** *(sing.)*
detoor	**de·tour**	diagnosis	**di·ag·no·ses** *(pl.)*
detrack	**de·tract**	dialeck	**di·a·lect**
detramental	**det·ri·men·tal**	dialisis	**di·al·y·sis**

WRONG	RIGHT	WRONG	RIGHT
diamater	**di·am·e·ter**	diel	**di·al**
diaphram	**di·a·phragm**	dielect	**di·a·lect**
diarey	**di·a·ry** *(journal)*	dierhea	**di·ar·rhea**
diarrea	**di·ar·rhea**	diery	**di·a·ry** *(journal)*
dias	**da·is**	diesle	**die·sel**
diatetic	**di·e·tet·ic**	dietician	**di·e·ti·tian**
diatitian	**di·e·ti·tian**	diety	**de·i·ty**
dibacle	**de·ba·cle**	difault	**de·fault**
dibark	**de·bark**	difective	**de·fec·tive**
dibase	**de·base**	diferent	**dif·fer·ent**
dibatable	**de·bat·a·ble**	diferment	**de·fer·ment**
dibilitate	**de·bil·i·tate**	differance	**dif·fer·ence**
dicanter	**de·cant·er**		*(being different)*
dicapitate	**de·cap·i·tate**	difference	**def·er·ence**
dicathlon	**de·cath·lon**		*(yielding)*
diceased	**de·ceased** *(dead)*	diffrent	**dif·fer·ent**
diceitful	**de·ceit·ful**	diffuzion	**dif·fu·sion**
diceive	**de·ceive**	difiance	**de·fi·ance**
Dicember	**De·cem·ber**	dificiency	**de·fi·cien·cy**
diception	**de·cep·tion**	dificulty	**dif·fi·cul·ty**
dich	**ditch**	difile	**de·file**
dicide	**de·cide**	diflect	**de·flect**
dicipher	**de·ci·pher**	diformity	**de·form·i·ty**
dicision	**de·ci·sion**	difraud	**de·fraud**
diclension	**de·clen·sion**	difrost	**de·frost**
dicline	**de·cline**	diftheria	**diph·the·ria**
dicorum	**de·co·rum**	difuse	**dif·fuse**
dicrease	**de·crease**	difusion	**dif·fu·sion**
dicrepit	**de·crep·it**	digatal	**dig·it·al**
dicriminalize		digestable	**di·gest·i·ble**
	de·crim·i·nal·ize	digetal	**dig·it·al**
dictater	**dic·ta·tor**	digings	**dig·gings**
dictionery	**dic·tion·ary**	dignafied	**dig·ni·fied**
die	**dye** *(tint)*	dignatary	**dig·ni·tary**
diefy	**de·i·fy**	dignaty	**dig·ni·ty**

WRONG	RIGHT	WRONG	RIGHT
dignifyed	**dig·ni·fied**	dimure	**de·mure** *(coy)*
digree	**de·gree**	dinamic	**dy·nam·ic**
diktator	**dic·ta·tor**	dinamite	**dy·na·mite**
diktionary	**dic·tion·ary**	dinasaur	**di·no·saur**
dilay	**de·lay**	dinasty	**dy·nas·ty**
dilema	**di·lem·ma**	diner	**din·ner** *(meal)*
diletante	**dil·et·tante**	dinghy	**din·gy** *(grimy)*
dilete	**de·lete**	dingy	**din·ghy** *(boat)*
diliberation	**de·lib·er·a·tion**	dinial	**de·ni·al**
dilicious	**de·li·cious**	dining	**din·ning** *(repeating noisily)*
dilight	**de·light**	dinner	**din·er** *(small restaurant)*
dilinquency	**de·lin·quen·cy**	dinning	**din·ing** *(eating)*
dilirious	**de·lir·i·ous**	dinomination	**de·nom·i·na·tion**
diliver	**de·liv·er**	dinominator	**de·nom·i·na·tor**
dillapidated	**di·lap·i·dat·ed**	dinosor	**di·no·saur**
dillema	**di·lem·ma**	dinote	**de·note**
dilletante	**dil·et·tante**	dinounce	**de·nounce**
dilligence	**dil·i·gence**	dint	**dent**
dillusion	**de·lu·sion**	dinunciation	**de·nun·ci·a·tion**
dillute	**di·lute**	diosese	**di·o·cese**
dilude	**de·lude**	dipart	**de·part**
diluxe	**de·luxe**	dipendable	**de·pend·a·ble**
dimand	**de·mand** *(order)*	diper	**di·a·per**
dimeanor	**de·mean·or**	diplamat	**dip·lo·mat**
dimented	**de·ment·ed**	diplete	**de·plete**
dimention	**di·men·sion**	diplomasy	**di·plo·ma·cy**
dimise	**de·mise**	diplorable	**de·plor·a·ble**
dimminish	**di·min·ish**	dipresant	**de·pres·sant**
dimolish	**de·mol·ish**	diptheria	**diph·the·ria**
dimond	**di·a·mond** *(gem)*	diranged	**de·ranged**
dimoralize	**de·mor·al·ize**		
dimur	**de·mur** *(object)*		

WRONG	RIGHT
direck	**di·rect**
directer	**di·rec·tor**
directery	**di·rec·to·ry**
dirigable	**dir·i·gi·ble**
dirisive	**de·ri·sive**
dirth	**dearth**
disagrement	**dis·a·gree·ment**
disallusion	**dis·il·lu·sion**
disapear	**dis·ap·pear**
disapointment	**dis·ap·point·ment**
disaray	**dis·ar·ray**
disarmement	**dis·ar·ma·ment**
disasterous	**dis·as·trous**
disatisfied	**dis·sat·is·fied**
disbeleif	**dis·be·lief**
disberse	**dis·burse** *(pay out)*
disburse	**dis·perse** *(scatter)*
discapline	**dis·ci·pline**
descendant	**de·scend·ant**
discipal	**dis·ci·ple**
disclozure	**dis·clo·sure**
discourageing	**dis·cour·ag·ing**
discovry	**dis·cov·ery**
discreet	**dis·crete** *(separate)*
discression	**dis·cre·tion**
discrete	**dis·creet** *(prudent)*
discribe	**de·scribe**
discrimanation	**dis·crim·i·na·tion**

WRONG	RIGHT
discription	**de·scrip·tion**
discus	**dis·cuss** *(talk about)*
discusion	**dis·cus·sion**
discuss	**dis·cus** *(heavy disk)*
disdaneful	**dis·dain·ful**
disdressed	**dis·tressed**
dise	**dice**
disect	**dis·sect**
diseminate	**dis·sem·i·nate**
disenfectant	**dis·in·fect·ant**
disengagment	**dis·en·gage·ment**
disent	**dis·sent** *(disagreement)*
disentery	**dys·en·tery**
disert	**de·sert** *(abandon)*
disesed	**dis·eased** *(ill)*
disfigurment	**dis·fig·ure·ment**
disgise	**dis·guise**
disgrase	**dis·grace**
disign	**de·sign**
disilusion	**dis·il·lu·sion**
disimbark	**dis·em·bark**
disimilar	**dis·sim·i·lar**
disinfectent	**dis·in·fect·ant**
disintagrate	**dis·in·te·grate**
disipate	**dis·si·pate**
disiple	**dis·ci·ple**
disipline	**dis·ci·pline**
dislexia	**dys·lex·ia**
dislexic	**dys·lex·ic**

WRONG	RIGHT	WRONG	RIGHT
dismantel	**dis·man·tle**	disscount	**dis·count**
dismissle	**dis·miss·al**	dissemanate	
disobediance			**dis·sem·i·nate**
	dis·o·be·di·ence	dissent	**de·cent** *(proper)*
disolve	**dis·solve**	dissent	**de·scent**
disonant	**dis·so·nant**		*(going down)*
disonest	**dis·hon·est**	dissert	**des·sert** *(food)*
disorderley	**dis·or·der·ly**	disserts	**de·serts** *(rewards)*
dispach	**dis·patch**	dissinfectant	
dispair	**de·spair**		**dis·in·fect·ant**
disparate	**des·per·ate**	dissintegrate	
	(hopeless)		**dis·in·te·grate**
dispensible	**dis·pen·sa·ble**	dissmay	**dis·may**
disperaging	**dis·par·ag·ing**	dissonent	**dis·so·nant**
disperate	**dis·pa·rate**	disstiled	**dis·tilled**
	(not alike)	distence	**dis·tance**
disperse	**dis·burse**	disterb	**dis·turb**
	(pay out)	distinguash	**dis·tin·guish**
dispicable	**des·pi·ca·ble**	distink	**dis·tinct**
dispise	**de·spise**	distrabution	
dispite	**de·spite**		**dis·tri·bu·tion**
dispondent	**de·spond·ent**	distrack	**dis·tract**
disposible	**dis·pos·a·ble**	distraut	**dis·traught**
dispurse	**dis·perse** *(scatter)*	districk	**dis·trict**
disreguard	**dis·re·gard**	distrophy	**dys·tro·phy**
disreputible		distroy	**de·stroy**
	dis·rep·u·ta·ble	disuade	**dis·suade**
dissagree	**dis·a·gree**	ditergent	**de·ter·gent**
dissapate	**dis·si·pate**	ditermine	**de·ter·mine**
dissappear	**dis·ap·pear**	dity	**dit·ty**
dissappointment		divadend	**div·i·dend**
	dis·ap·point·ment	divaluation	
dissarmament			**de·val·u·a·tion**
	dis·ar·ma·ment	divelopment	
disscord	**dis·cord**		**de·vel·op·ment**

WRONG	RIGHT
divergance	**di·ver·gence**
diversafy	**di·ver·si·fy**
diversaty	**di·ver·si·ty**
divinety	**di·vin·i·ty**
divisable	**di·vis·i·ble**
	(dividable)
divizion	**di·vi·sion**
divoid	**de·void**
divorse	**di·vorce**
divour	**de·vour**
divout	**de·vout**
dizalve	**dis·solve**
dob	**daub**
dochshund	**dachs·hund**
docter	**doc·tor**
doctran	**doc·trine**
doctrinare	**doc·tri·naire**
documentery	
	doc·u·men·ta·ry
dodle	**daw·dle** *(loiter)*
dodle	**doo·dle** *(scribble)*
doe	**dough** *(flour)*
doller	**dol·lar**
dolphen	**dol·phin**
domane	**do·main**
dominent	**dom·i·nant**
dominoe	**dom·i·no**
domminate	**dom·i·nate**
doner	**do·nor**
donky	**don·key**
dontless	**daunt·less**
doosh	**douche**
dormatory	**dor·mi·to·ry**
dosege	**dos·age**
dosn't	**doesn't**

WRONG	RIGHT
dotter	**daugh·ter**
doury	**dow·ry**
doutful	**doubt·ful**
dowdey	**dow·dy**
dowery	**dow·ry**
dragatory	**de·rog·a·to·ry**
draggon	**drag·on**
drainege	**drain·age**
draipry	**drap·ery**
drammatic	**dra·mat·ic**
draneage	**drain·age**
dredful	**dread·ful**
dreery	**dreary**
drible	**drib·ble**
driping	**drip·ping**
driveing	**driv·ing**
drousy	**drow·sy**
drout	**drought**
drowsey	**drow·sy**
drugery	**drudg·ery**
drugist	**drug·gist**
dual	**du·el** *(fight)*
dubble	**dou·ble**
dubeous	**du·bi·ous**
due	**dew** *(moisture)*
duece	**deuce**
duel	**du·al** *(two)*
du jure	**de jure** *(by law)*
dum	**dumb**
dumbell	**dumb·bell**
dunkey	**don·key**
duplacate	**du·pli·cate**
durible	**du·ra·ble**
durress	**du·ress**
durring	**dur·ing**

WRONG	RIGHT	WRONG	RIGHT
durth	**dearth**	dying	**dye·ing** *(tinting)*
dutyful	**du·ti·ful**	dynamec	**dy·nam·ic**
dwindel	**dwin·dle**	dynesty	**dy·nas·ty**
dworf	**dwarf**	dynomite	**dy·na·mite**
dye	**die** *(stop living)*	dysintery	**dys·en·tery**
dyeing	**dy·ing**	dysleksia	**dys·lex·ia**
	(ending life)	dysleksic	**dys·lex·ic**

E

WRONG	RIGHT
eagel	**ea·gle**
eal	**eel**
ean	**eon** *(time period)*
earake	**ear·ache**
earfull	**ear·ful**
earie	**ee·rie** *(weird)*
earing	**ear·ring**
earn	**urn** *(vase)*
easally	**eas·i·ly**
easle	**ea·sel**
eastword	**east·ward**
eather	**ei·ther** *(each)*
eatible	**eat·a·ble**
eau de colone	
	eau de Co·logne
eavening	**eve·ning**
eaves	**eves** *(nights)*
eb	**ebb**
ebbony	**eb·ony**
ebulient	**ebul·lient**
eccentrisity	
	ec·cen·tric·i·ty
eccleziastic	**ec·cle·si·as·tic**
ecco	**echo**
eccocardiology	
	ech·o·car·di·ol·o·gy
eccology	**ecol·o·gy**
ecconomic	**eco·nom·ic**

WRONG	RIGHT
eccosystem	**eco·sys·tem**
eccumenical	
	ec·u·men·i·cal
eccumenism	
	ec·u·men·ism
ecentric	**ec·cen·tric**
echellon	**ech·e·lon**
eching	**etch·ing**
echos	**ech·oes**
ecko	**echo**
eckoic	**echo·ic**
eclare	**éclair**
eclesiastic	**ec·cle·si·as·tic**
ecollogy	**ecol·o·gy**
econamy	**econ·o·my**
ecstacy	**ec·sta·sy**
ect	**etc.**
ecumanism	**ec·u·men·ism**
Ecwador	**Ec·ua·dor**
eczama	**ec·ze·ma**
Edan	**Eden**
edator	**ed·i·tor**
eddable	**ed·i·ble**
eddie	**ed·dy**
eddification	**edi·fi·ca·tion**
eddit	**ed·it**
edducate	**ed·u·cate**
edefy	**ed·i·fy**

59

WRONG	RIGHT	WRONG	RIGHT
edelwise	**edel·weiss**	efigy	**ef·fi·gy**
Edenburg	**Ed·in·burgh**	efluent	**ef·flu·ent** *(flowing)*
edifacation	**edi·fi·ca·tion**		
Edinburo	**Ed·in·burgh**	efort	**ef·fort**
Edipus	**Oed·i·pus**	efrontery	**ef·fron·tery**
editer	**ed·i·tor**	efusive	**ef·fu·sive**
edition	**ad·di·tion** *(adding)*	egaletarian	**egal·i·tar·i·an**
educater	**ed·u·ca·tor**	eger	**ea·ger**
eek	**eke**	eggalitarian	**egal·i·tar·i·an**
eether	**ether** *(in chemistry)*	eggo	**ego**
eface	**ef·face**	eggregious	**egre·gious**
efect	**ef·fect** *(result)*	Egiptian	**Egyp·tian**
efective	**ef·fec·tive** *(having effect)*	egosentric	**ego·cen·tric**
		egrit	**egret**
efectually	**ef·fec·tu·al·ly**	egzaggerate	**ex·ag·ger·ate**
efectuate	**ef·fec·tu·ate**	egzamine	**ex·am·ine** *(test)*
efemminate	**ef·fem·i·nate**	egzema	**ec·ze·ma**
efervescent	**ef·fer·ves·cent**	eightyith	**eight·i·eth**
		eigth	**eighth**
efete	**ef·fete**	eirie	**ee·rie** *(weird)*
effase	**ef·face**	eisel	**ea·sel**
effecacious	**ef·fi·ca·cious**	either	**ether** *(in chemistry)*
effect	**af·fect** *(to influence)*	ejakulate	**ejac·u·late**
effective	**af·fec·tive** *(emotional)*	ejeck	**eject**
		ekanomic	**eco·nom·ic**
effectualy	**ef·fec·tu·al·ly**	eklair	**éclair**
effegy	**ef·fi·gy**	eklectic	**ec·lec·tic**
effemeral	**ephem·er·al**	eklesiastic	**ec·cle·si·as·tic**
effert	**ef·fort**	eklipse	**eclipse**
effervesent	**ef·fer·ves·cent**	eksentric	**ec·cen·tric**
efficiancy	**ef·fi·cien·cy**	ekstasy	**ec·sta·sy**
effluent	**af·flu·ent** *(rich)*	ekumenical	**ec·u·men·i·cal**
effrontary	**ef·fron·tery**		
eficatious	**ef·fi·ca·cious**	elaberate	**elab·o·rate**
eficiency	**ef·fi·cien·cy**	elagence	**el·e·gance**

WRONG	RIGHT	WRONG	RIGHT
element	**el·e·ment**	elimentary	**ele·men·ta·ry** *(basic)*
elamentary	**ele·men·ta·ry** *(basic)*	eliphant	**el·e·phant**
elavate	**el·e·vate**	elipse	**el·lipse**
elboe	**el·bow**	eliptical	**el·lip·ti·cal**
eleck	**elect**	elixer	**elix·ir**
elecktric	**elec·tric**	ellaborate	**elab·o·rate**
electer	**elec·tor**	ellastic	**elas·tic**
electracardiogram	**elec·tro·car·di·o·gram**	ellate	**elate**
electral	**elec·tor·al**	ellder	**eld·er**
electramagnetic	**elec·tro·mag·net·ic**	ellect	**elect**
electrefy	**elec·tri·fy**	ellecteral	**elec·tor·al**
electricly	**elec·tri·cal·ly**	ellection	**elec·tion**
electricute	**elec·tro·cute**	ellectric	**elec·tric**
electrisity	**elec·tric·i·ty**	ellectrolysis	**elec·trol·y·sis**
electristatic	**elec·tro·stat·ic**	ellectron	**elec·tron**
electrokardiogram	**elec·tro·car·di·o·gram**	ellectronic	**elec·tron·ic**
electrollysis	**elec·trol·y·sis**	ellegance	**el·e·gance**
electronnic	**elec·tron·ic**	ellegy	**el·e·gy**
elecution	**el·o·cu·tion**	ellement	**el·e·ment**
elektron	**elec·tron**	ellephant	**el·e·phant**
elementary	**ali·men·ta·ry** *(nourishing)*	ellevate	**el·e·vate**
elementery	**ele·men·ta·ry** *(basic)*	elleven	**elev·en**
elevan	**elev·en**	ellicit	**elic·it** *(evoke)*
elevater	**el·e·va·tor**	ellicit	**il·lic·it** *(unlawful)*
elfs	**elves**	elligible	**el·i·gi·ble**
eligable	**el·i·gi·ble**	elliminate	**elim·i·nate**
eligy	**el·e·gy**	ellipticle	**el·lip·ti·cal**
elimanate	**elim·i·nate**	ellite	**elite** *(best)*
		ellixir	**elix·ir**
		ellocution	**el·o·cu·tion**
		ellongation	**elon·ga·tion**
		elloquent	**el·o·quent**
		ellucidate	**elu·ci·date**
		ellude	**elude** *(escape)*

WRONG	RIGHT	WRONG	RIGHT
ellusion	**elu·sion**	emfasis	**em·pha·sis** (sing.)
	(an escape)	emigrant	**im·mi·grant**
ellusive	**elu·sive**		(one who arrives)
	(hard to grasp)	emigrate	**im·mi·grate**
eloquant	**el·o·quent**		(arrive)
El Salvidor	**El Sal·va·dor**	eminate	**em·a·nate**
elsewere	**else·where**	eminent	**im·mi·nent**
elucedate	**elu·ci·date**		(impending)
elude	**al·lude** (refer to)	emissery	**em·is·sary**
elusive	**al·lu·sive**	emmancipate	
	(referring to)		**eman·ci·pate**
elusive	**il·lu·sive**	emmense	**im·mense**
	(deceptive)	emmigrant	**em·i·grant**
emanent	**em·i·nent**		(one who leaves)
	(prominent)	emmigrate	**em·i·grate**
emansipate	**eman·ci·pate**		(leave)
emashiate	**ema·ci·ate**	emmisary	**em·is·sary**
emaskulate	**emas·cu·late**	emmission	**emis·sion**
embarass	**em·bar·rass**	emmulate	**em·u·late**
embass	**em·boss**	emnity	**en·mi·ty**
embasy	**em·bas·sy**	emolient	**emol·li·ent**
embelish	**em·bel·lish**		(softener)
emberrass	**em·bar·rass**	emollument	**emol·u·ment**
embezle	**em·bez·zle**		(wages)
emblam	**em·blem**	empair	**im·pair**
embom	**em·balm**	empending	**im·pend·ing**
embrase	**em·brace**	emperer	**em·per·or**
embrio	**em·bryo**	emphases	**em·pha·sis**
embroidary	**em·broi·dery**		(sing.)
emend	**amend** (revise)	emphasis	**em·pha·ses** (pl.)
emergancy	**emer·gen·cy**	empireal	**im·pe·ri·al**
emerge	**im·merge** (plunge)		(sovereign)
emerritus	**emer·i·tus**	empithy	**em·pa·thy**
emersion	**im·mer·sion**	employible	**em·ploy·a·ble**
	(plunging)	emporer	**em·per·or**

WRONG	RIGHT	WRONG	RIGHT
emrald	em·er·ald	ennema	en·e·ma
emrey	em·ery	ennigma	enig·ma
enamy	en·e·my	ennumerate	enu·mer·ate
enbankment		enoble	en·no·ble
	em·bank·ment	enormaty	enor·mi·ty
encapsalate		ensamble	en·sem·ble
	en·cap·su·late	ensephalitis	
encefalitis	en·ceph·a·li·tis		en·ceph·a·li·tis
encinderator		ensew	en·sue
	in·cin·er·a·tor	ensine	en·sign
encrimanate		entale	en·tail
	in·crim·i·nate	entanglment	
encumbrence			en·tan·gle·ment
	en·cum·brance	enterprize	en·ter·prise
encuragement		entertaned	en·ter·tained
	en·cour·age·ment	enthusiasticly	
encyclepedia			en·thu·si·as·ti·cal·ly
	en·cy·clo·pe·dia	entirty	en·tire·ty
endevor	en·deav·or	entise	en·tice
endorsment		entomollogy	
	en·dorse·ment		en·to·mol·o·gy
endurence	en·dur·ance		*(insect study)*
endurible	en·dur·a·ble	entomology	
engeneer	en·gi·neer		et·y·mol·o·gy
engenue	in·gé·nue		*(word study)*
engenuity	in·ge·nu·i·ty	entoorage	en·tou·rage
engrosing	en·gross·ing	entrales	en·trails
enhanse	en·hance	entre	en·tree
enima	en·e·ma	entrepeneur	
enjoyible	en·joy·a·ble		en·tre·pre·neur
enlargment		enuff	enough
	en·large·ment	enummerate	enu·mer·ate
enmaty	en·mi·ty	enunciate	an·nun·ci·ate
ennable	en·a·ble		*(announce)*
ennamel	en·am·el	enurgy	en·er·gy

WRONG	RIGHT
envalope	**en·ve·lope** *(n.)*
envelope	**en·vel·op** *(v.)*
enveous	**en·vi·ous**
envirement	
	en·vi·ron·ment
envoke	**in·voke**
	(put into use)
enzime	**en·zyme**
eon	**ion** *(atom)*
epademic	**ep·i·dem·ic**
epadural	**ep·i·du·ral**
epagram	**ep·i·gram**
epalepsy	**ep·i·lep·sy**
epalog	**ep·i·logue**
epataph	**ep·i·taph**
epegraph	**ep·i·graph**
epesode	**ep·i·sode**
ephemmeral	**ephem·er·al**
epic	**ep·och** *(era)*
epicurian	**ep·i·cu·re·an**
epidooral	**ep·i·du·ral**
epifany	**epiph·a·ny**
epillepsy	**ep·i·lep·sy**
Episcapalian	
	Epis·co·pa·li·an
episle	**epis·tle**
epitaf	**ep·i·taph**
epitomy	**epit·o·me**
epoch	**ep·ic** *(story)*
epoxey	**ep·oxy**
eppigram	**ep·i·gram**
equalibrium	
	equi·lib·ri·um
equallity	**equal·i·ty**
equasion	**equa·tion**

WRONG	RIGHT
equater	**equa·tor**
equestrien	**eques·tri·an**
equety	**eq·ui·ty**
equillateral	**equi·lat·er·al**
equillibrium	
	equi·lib·ri·um
equiped	**equipped**
equipmant	**equip·ment**
equitible	**eq·ui·ta·ble**
equivelance	**equiv·a·lence**
equivical	**equiv·o·cal**
eradecate	**erad·i·cate**
erant	**er·rant**
erascible	**iras·ci·ble**
eraser	**era·sure**
	(something erased)
erasure	**eras·er**
	(something that erases)
eratic	**er·rat·ic** *(irregular)*
erge	**urge**
erid	**ar·id**
eriudite	**er·u·dite**
erksome	**irk·some**
erl	**earl**
erly	**ear·ly**
ermin	**er·mine**
ern	**earn** *(deserve)*
ern	**urn** *(vase)*
ernest	**ear·nest**
eroneous	**er·ro·ne·ous**
erotic	**er·rat·ic** *(irregular)*
erratic	**erot·ic** *(sexual)*
errection	**erec·tion**
errend	**er·rand**
errent	**er·rant**

WRONG	RIGHT
errode	**erode**
erronious	**er·ro·ne·ous**
errotic	**erot·ic** *(sexual)*
erruption	**erup·tion**
esaphogus	**esoph·a·gus**
esay	**es·say**
	(try; composition)
escalater	**es·ca·la·tor**
escallate	**es·ca·late**
eschuary	**es·tu·ary**
esence	**es·sence**
esential	**es·sen·tial**
eshelon	**ech·e·lon**
Eskemo	**Es·ki·mo**
esofagus	**esoph·a·gus**
especally	**espe·cial·ly**
espeonage	**es·pi·o·nage**
espouze	**es·pouse**
espreso	**es·pres·so**
essance	**es·sence**
essay	**as·say** *(analyze)*
essentricity	
	ec·cen·tric·i·ty
essoteric	**es·o·ter·ic**
estemation	**esti·ma·tion**
estimible	**es·ti·ma·ble**
estragen	**es·tro·gen**
estrangment	
	es·trange·ment
estuery	**es·tu·ary**
etaquette	**et·i·quette**
et cetara	**et cet·era**
eternaly	**eter·nal·ly**
eternaty	**eter·ni·ty**
ethel	**eth·yl**

WRONG	RIGHT
Etheopia	**Ethi·o·pia**
ether	**ei·ther** *(each)*
etherial	**ethe·re·al**
ethicly	**eth·i·cal·ly**
ethireal	**ethe·re·al**
ethnik	**eth·nic**
etible	**ed·i·ble**
ettiquete	**et·i·quette**
ettymology	**et·y·mol·o·gy**
	(word study)
eturnally	**eter·nal·ly**
etymology	
	en·to·mol·o·gy
	(insect study)
eucher	**eu·chre**
Eucherist	**Eu·cha·rist**
eu de cologne	
	eau de Co·logne
eufemism	**eu·phe·mism**
Eukarist	**Eu·cha·rist**
eukre	**eu·chre**
eullogy	**eu·lo·gy**
euphamism	
	eu·phe·mism
Eurapean	**Eu·ro·pe·an**
euthenasia	**eu·tha·na·sia**
evacative	**evoc·a·tive**
evaccuate	**evac·u·ate**
evacive	**eva·sive**
evadently	**ev·i·dent·ly**
evalluate	**eval·u·ate**
evally	**evil·ly**
evalution	**ev·o·lu·tion**
evangalist	**evan·gel·ist**
evangellical	**evan·gel·i·cal**

WRONG	RIGHT
evaperate	**evap·o·rate**
evassive	**eva·sive**
evedence	**ev·i·dence**
evengelical	**evan·gel·i·cal**
eventially	**even·tu·al·ly**
everywere	**ev·ery·where**
eves	**eaves** *(roof edge)*
evesdrop	**eaves·drop**
evidance	**ev·i·dence**
evidentally	**ev·i·dent·ly**
evily	**evil·ly**
evning	**eve·ning**
evoke	
	in·voke *(put into use)*
evry	**ev·ery**
exackly	**ex·act·ly**
exacution	**ex·e·cu·tion**
exagerrate	**ex·ag·ger·ate**
exagesis	**ex·e·ge·sis**
exalltation	**ex·al·ta·tion**
	(rapture)
exaltation	**ex·ul·ta·tion**
	(rejoicing)
examanation	
	ex·am·i·na·tion
examin	**ex·am·ine** *(test)*
examinor	**ex·am·in·er**
exampel	**ex·am·ple**
examplery	**ex·em·pla·ry**
examplify	**ex·em·pli·fy**
exasparate	**ex·as·per·ate**
exatic	**ex·ot·ic**
exaust	**ex·haust**
exaustion	**ex·haus·tion**
excallence	**ex·cel·lence**

WRONG	RIGHT
excavater	**ex·ca·va·tor**
excede	**ex·ceed** *(surpass)*
exceed	**ac·cede** *(agree)*
exceled	**ex·celled**
excelency	**ex·cel·len·cy**
excelent	**ex·cel·lent**
excell	**ex·cel**
excellancy	**ex·cel·len·cy**
excellant	**ex·cel·lent**
except	**ac·cept** *(receive)*
excepted	**ac·cept·ed**
	(approved)
exceptionly	
	ex·cep·tion·al·ly
excercise	**ex·er·cise** *(use)*
excercism	**ex·or·cism**
excerp	**ex·cerpt**
excess	**ac·cess** *(approach)*
excevate	**ex·ca·vate**
excitible	**ex·cit·a·ble**
excitment	**ex·cite·ment**
excize	**ex·cise**
exclame	**ex·claim**
exclimation	
	ex·cla·ma·tion
exclusave	**ex·clu·sive**
exclussion	**ex·clu·sion**
excomunnicate	
	ex·com·mu·ni·cate
excreet	**ex·crete**
excriment	**ex·cre·ment**
excrushiating	
	ex·cru·ci·at·ing
excurzion	**ex·cur·sion**
excusible	**ex·cus·a·ble**

WRONG	RIGHT	WRONG	RIGHT
execcutive	**ex·ec·u·tive**	expecterant	
exemplafy	**ex·em·pli·fy**		**ex·pec·to·rant**
exemtion	**ex·emp·tion**	expediant	**ex·pe·di·ent**
exentricity	**ec·cen·tric·i·ty**	expell	**ex·pel**
exercise	**ex·or·cise**	expencive	**ex·pen·sive**
	(drive out)	expendature	
exercism	**ex·or·cism**		**ex·pend·i·ture**
exerpt	**ex·cerpt**	expendible	**ex·pend·a·ble**
exersize	**ex·er·cise** *(use)*	experament	
exestential	**ex·is·ten·tial**		**ex·per·i·ment**
exhabition	**ex·hi·bi·tion**	expergate	**ex·pur·gate**
exhail	**ex·hale**	experiance	**ex·pe·ri·ence**
exhertation		expertese	**ex·pert·ise**
	ex·hor·ta·tion	explacate	**ex·pli·cate**
exhillarate	**ex·hil·a·rate**	explane	**ex·plain**
exhorbitant	**ex·or·bi·tant**	explination	
exibit	**ex·hib·it**		**ex·pla·na·tion**
exibition	**ex·hi·bi·tion**	explisit	**ex·plic·it**
exicutionor		explocive	**ex·plo·sive**
	ex·e·cu·tion·er	explotation	
exidus	**ex·o·dus**		**ex·ploi·ta·tion**
exilarate	**ex·hil·a·rate**	exponant	**ex·po·nent**
existance	**ex·ist·ence**	exposer	**ex·po·sure**
exitement	**ex·cite·ment**	expository	**ex·pos·i·to·ry**
exonnerate	**ex·on·er·ate**	expozier	**ex·po·sure**
exorbatent	**ex·or·bi·tant**	expresion	**ex·pres·sion**
exortation	**ex·hor·ta·tion**	expresive	**ex·pres·sive**
expadition	**ex·pe·di·tion**	expreso	**es·pres·so**
expance	**ex·panse**	expressable	**ex·press·i·ble**
expancion	**ex·pan·sion**	expullsion	**ex·pul·sion**
expantion	**ex·pan·sion**	exruciating	
expatriot	**ex·pa·tri·ate**		**ex·cru·ci·at·ing**
expec	**ex·pect**	exsale	**ex·hale**
expecially	**espe·cial·ly**	exseed	**ex·ceed** *(surpass)*
expectent	**ex·pect·ant**	exselled	**ex·celled**

WRONG	RIGHT
exsept	**ex·cept** *(omit)*
exsepted	**ex·cept·ed** *(left out)*
exseptionally	**ex·cep·tion·al·ly**
exsess	**ex·cess** *(surplus)*
exsile	**ex·ile**
exsitement	**ex·cite·ment**
exsize	**ex·cise**
exspanse	**ex·panse**
exspect	**ex·pect**
exspell	**ex·pel**
exspendable	**ex·pend·a·ble**
exspenditure	**ex·pend·i·ture**
exspire	**ex·pire**
exsponge	**ex·punge**
exsport	**ex·port**
exstinguish	**ex·tin·guish**
exsume	**ex·hume**
extant	**ex·tent** *(degree)*
exteerior	**ex·te·ri·or**
extennuating	**ex·ten·u·at·ing**
extent	**ex·tant** *(existing)*
extercate	**ex·tri·cate**
extercurricular	**ex·tra·cur·ric·u·lar**
exterier	**ex·te·ri·or**
exterminater	**ex·ter·mi·na·tor**
extervert	**ex·tro·vert**
extinc	**ex·tinct**

WRONG	RIGHT
extordinary	**ex·traor·di·nary**
extracate	**ex·tri·cate**
extracktion	**ex·trac·tion**
extracuricullar	**ex·tra·cur·ric·u·lar**
extraordinair	**ex·traor·di·naire**
extrapellate	**ex·trap·o·late**
extraterestrial	**ex·tra·ter·res·trial**
extravegant	**ex·trav·a·gant**
extravert	**ex·tro·vert**
extreemly	**ex·treme·ly**
extremast	**ex·trem·ist**
extrematy	**ex·trem·i·ty**
extrordinary	**ex·traor·di·nary**
exuberence	**ex·u·ber·ance**
exulltation	**ex·ul·ta·tion** *(rejoicing)*
exultation	**ex·al·ta·tion** *(rapture)*
exultent	**ex·ult·ant**
exume	**ex·hume**
exxodus	**ex·o·dus**
exzotic	**ex·ot·ic**
exzuberance	**ex·u·ber·ance**
eyelet	**is·let** *(small island)*
eylet	**eye·let** *(small hole)*

F

WRONG	RIGHT
fabrecate	**fab·ri·cate**
fabulus	**fab·u·lous**
facalty	**fac·ul·ty**
faccade	**fa·çade**
faceal	**fa·cial**
facesious	**fa·ce·tious**
facillitate	**facil·i·tate**
facillity	**fa·cil·i·ty**
facinate	**fas·ci·nate**
facist	**fas·cist**
facsimilies	**fac·sim·i·les**
facsion	**fac·tion**
facter	**fac·tor**
factery	**fac·to·ry**
factitious	**fic·ti·tious** *(imaginary)*
factry	**fac·to·ry**
factsimile	**fac·sim·i·le**
factule	**fac·tu·al**
Fahrenhite	**Fahr·en·heit**
faillure	**fail·ure**
fain	**feign** *(pretend)*
faint	**feint** *(pretense)*
fair	**fare** *(fee)*
fairie	**fairy** *(elf)*
fairwell	**fare·well**
fairy	**fer·ry** *(boat)*
faithfull	**faith·ful**
fajeta	**fa·ji·ta**

WRONG	RIGHT
faker	**fa·kir** *(Muslim beggar)*
fakir	**fak·er** *(fraud)*
faksimile	**fac·sim·i·le**
falacy	**fal·la·cy**
falcan	**fal·con**
falible	**fal·li·ble**
falicitous	**felic·i·tous**
faliure	**fail·ure**
fallable	**fal·li·ble**
fallecy	**fal·la·cy**
falloe	**fal·low** *(inactive)*
fallsetto	**fal·set·to**
fallter	**fal·ter**
falonious	**fe·lo·ni·ous**
Faloppian	**Fal·lo·pi·an**
falout	**fall·out**
falow	**fal·low** *(inactive)*
falsefy	**fal·si·fy**
falseto	**fal·set·to**
falsety	**fal·si·ty**
falsly	**false·ly**
falt	**fault**
famely	**fam·i·ly**
fameous	**fa·mous**
familier	**fa·mil·iar**
familierity	**famil·i·ar·i·ty**
familliarize	**famil·iar·ize**
fammine	**fam·ine**

WRONG	RIGHT	WRONG	RIGHT
fancey	**fan·cy**	faston	**fas·ten**
fancifull	**fan·ci·ful**	fatallistic	**fa·tal·is·tic**
fane	**feign** (pretend)	fatallity	**fa·tal·i·ty**
fanfair	**fan·fare**	fataly	**fa·tal·ly**
fannatic	**fa·nat·ic**	fateague	**fa·tigue**
fantastik	**fan·tas·tic**	fatefull	**fate·ful**
fantem	**phan·tom**	fatel	**fa·tal**
fantesy	**fan·ta·sy**	faten	**fat·ten**
farcicle	**far·ci·cal**	fathem	**fath·om**
fare	**fair** (lovely; bazaar)	fatige	**fa·tigue**
farena	**fa·ri·na**	faught	**fought**
Farenheit	**Fahr·en·heit**	faukon	**fal·con**
farensic	**fo·ren·sic**	faun	**fawn**
farewel	**fare·well**		(deer; act servilely)
farfeched	**far-fetched**	faver	**fa·vor**
farmacy	**phar·ma·cy**	faverite	**fa·vor·ite**
farmasuitical	**phar·ma·ceu·ti·cal**	favorible	**fa·vor·a·ble**
Faro	**Phar·aoh**	fawcet	**fau·cet**
	(Egyptian ruler)	fawna	**fau·na**
farse	**farce**	fax paus	**fax pas**
farsical	**far·ci·cal**	faze	**phase** (stage)
fasade	**façade**	feable	**fee·ble**
fascenate	**fas·ci·nate**	feancé	**fi·an·cé** (m.)
fasetious	**fa·ce·tious**	feancé	**fi·an·cée** (f.)
fashien	**fash·ion**	fearfull	**fear·ful**
fashionible	**fash·ion·a·ble**	feasable	**fea·si·ble**
fashist	**fas·cist**	feasant	**pheas·ant**
fasile	**fac·ile**	feasco	**fi·as·co**
fasilitate	**facil·i·tate**	feat	**feet** (pl. of foot)
fasinate	**fas·ci·nate**	featurless	**fea·ture·less**
fassen	**fas·ten**	Febuary	**Feb·ru·ary**
fassenation	**fas·ci·na·tion**	feching	**fetch·ing**
fassion	**fash·ion**	fedaration	**fed·er·a·tion**
fastenner	**fas·ten·er**	fedral	**fed·er·al**
		feeline	**fe·line**

WRONG	RIGHT	WRONG	RIGHT
feend	**fiend**	ferry	**fairy** *(elf)*
feesible	**fea·si·ble**	ferther	**fur·ther**
feet	**feat** *(deed)*	ferthermore	
feetal	**fe·tal**		**fur·ther·more**
feild	**field**	fertillize	**fer·til·ize**
fein	**feign** *(pretend)*	fertive	**fur·tive**
feind	**fiend**	fertle	**fer·tile**
feint	**faint** *(weak)*	fervant	**fer·vent**
feirce	**fierce**	ferved	**fer·vid**
felany	**fel·o·ny**	ferver	**fer·vor**
felisity	**fe·lic·i·ty**	festeval	**fes·ti·val**
fellicitous	**felic·i·tous**	festivaty	**fes·tiv·i·ty**
fellonious	**fe·lo·ni·ous**	festor	**fes·ter**
fellony	**fel·o·ny**	fether	**feath·er**
Fellopian	**Fal·lo·pi·an**	fetis	**fe·tus**
felow	**fel·low**	fettid	**fet·id**
feminity	**fem·i·nin·i·ty**	fettish	**fet·ish**
femminine	**fem·i·nine**	feudal	**fu·tile** *(useless)*
fendish	**fiend·ish**	feudallism	**feu·dal·ism**
feotus	**fe·tus**	feugitive	**fu·gi·tive**
ferce	**fierce**	feul	**fu·el**
feret	**fer·ret**	fewd	**feud**
feric	**fer·ric**	fewdalism	**feu·dal·ism**
ferina	**fa·ri·na**	fiancé	**fi·an·cée** *(f.)*
ferl	**furl**	fiancée	**fi·an·cé** *(m.)*
ferlough	**fur·lough**	fiassco	**fi·as·co**
fermament	**fir·ma·ment**	fibreglass	**fi·ber·glass**
fernace	**fur·nace**	ficas	**fi·cus**
ferniture	**fur·ni·ture**	fickel	**fick·le**
feror	**fu·ror**	ficktion	**fic·tion**
ferous	**fer·rous**	fictitious	**fac·ti·tious**
ferrat	**fer·ret**		*(artificial)*
ferrier	**fur·ri·er**	fictitous	**fic·ti·tious**
ferris	**fer·rous**		*(imaginary)*
ferrocious	**fe·ro·cious**	fiddeler	**fid·dler**

71

WRONG	RIGHT	WRONG	RIGHT
fidellity	**fi·del·i·ty**	finnaly	**fi·nal·ly**
fiftyeth	**fif·ti·eth**		*(in conclusion)*
figarine	**fig·u·rine**	finnancial	**fi·nan·cial**
figerative	**fig·u·ra·tive**	finnesse	**fi·nesse** *(skill)*
figget	**fidg·et**	finnicky	**fin·icky**
figgure	**fig·ure**	finnish	**fin·ish**
figmant	**fig·ment**	fintch	**finch**
figureen	**fig·u·rine**	fir	**fur** *(hair)*
figuretive	**fig·u·ra·tive**	firewerks	**fire·works**
figurhead	**fig·ure·head**	firey	**fi·ery**
fiksation	**fix·a·tion**	firmentation	
filement	**fil·a·ment**		**fer·men·ta·tion**
filet minion		firn	**fern** *(plant)*
	fi·let mi·gnon	first ade	**first aid**
filharmonic		fiscaly	**fis·cal·ly**
	phil·har·mon·ic	fishion	**fis·sion**
fillament	**fil·a·ment**	fishure	**fis·sure**
fillbert	**fil·bert**	fiskle	**fis·cal**
fillial	**fil·i·al**	fistacuffs	**fist·i·cuffs**
fillie	**fil·ly**	fistfull	**fist·ful**
fillter	**fil·ter**	fitfull	**fit·ful**
filthally	**filth·i·ly**	fixcher	**fix·ture**
finalle	**fi·na·le**	fixible	**fix·a·ble**
finallity	**fi·nal·i·ty**	fizle	**fiz·zle**
finallize	**fi·nal·ize**	fizzion	**fis·sion**
finaly	**fi·nal·ly**	flabbie	**flab·by**
	(in conclusion)	flabergast	**flab·ber·gast**
financeer	**fin·an·cier**	flacid	**flac·cid**
financialy	**finan·cial·ly**	fladdery	**flat·tery**
finantial	**fi·nan·cial**	flaged	**flagged**
finely	**fi·nal·ly**	flaggon	**flag·on**
	(in conclusion)	flagrent	**fla·grant**
finerie	**fin·ery**	flair	**flare** *(blaze)*
fingerring	**fin·ger·ing**	flakey	**flaky**
finnale	**fi·na·le**	flaks	**flax**

WRONG	RIGHT
flale	**flail**
flamable	**flam·ma·ble**
flamboyent	**flam·boy·ant**
flamenco	**fla·min·go** *(bird)*
flamingo	**fla·men·co** *(dance)*
flanel	**flan·nel**
flaped	**flapped**
flare	**flair** *(knack)*
flashey	**flashy**
flashlite	**flash·light**
flassid	**flac·cid**
flatery	**flat·tery**
flavering	**fla·vor·ing**
flavorfull	**fla·vor·ful**
flawnt	**flaunt** *(show off)*
flea	**flee** *(run)*
fleace	**fleece**
flee	**flea** *(insect)*
fleecey	**fleecy**
fleese	**fleece**
flegeling	**fledg·ling**
flegmatic	**phleg·mat·ic**
flemm	**phlegm**
flertatious	**flir·ta·tious**
fleshey	**fleshy**
fleur-de-lee	**fleur-de-lis**
flew	**flu** *(influenza)*
flew	**flue** *(pipe)*
flexable	**flex·i·ble**
flimsey	**flim·sy**
flipancy	**flip·pan·cy**
fliped	**flipped**
flippency	**flip·pan·cy**
flirtacious	**flir·ta·tious**

WRONG	RIGHT
flite	**flight** *(air travel)*
flitey	**flighty**
flo	**floe** *(ice)*
flo	**flow** *(glide)*
floatation	**flo·ta·tion**
flod	**flood**
floe	**flow** *(glide)*
floged	**flogged**
floidity	**flu·id·i·ty**
flont	**flaunt**
flook	**fluke**
floped	**flopped**
floppie	**flop·py**
Floreda	**Flor·i·da**
florel	**flo·ral**
florescent	**flu·o·res·cent** *(giving light)*
floresent	**flo·res·cent** *(blooming)*
floride	**flu·o·ride**
florish	**flour·ish**
florral	**flo·ral**
florrid	**flor·id**
florrist	**flo·rist**
flosed	**flossed**
flour	**flow·er** *(part of plant)*
flow	**floe** *(ice)*
flower	**flour** *(grain)*
flownder	**floun·der**
flowt	**flout** *(scoff)*
flu	**flue** *(pipe)*
fluancy	**flu·en·cy**
fluchuate	**fluc·tu·ate**
flue	**flew** *(pt. of fly)*

WRONG	RIGHT
flue	**flu** *(influenza)*
flued	**flu·id**
fluidety	**flu·id·i·ty**
fluoresent	**flo·res·cent** *(blooming)*
fluoresent	**flu·o·res·cent** *(giving light)*
fluorish	**flour·ish**
fluorride	**flu·o·ride**
flur-de-lis	**fleur-de-lis**
flurrie	**flur·ry**
fo	**foe**
foamey	**foamy**
fobia	**pho·bia**
focallize	**fo·cal·ize**
focas	**fo·cus**
foe pas	**faux pas**
foggey	**fo·gy** *(conservative person)*
fogy	**fog·gy** *(misty)*
foibal	**foi·ble**
fokus	**fo·cus**
folage	**fo·li·age**
fole	**foal**
folksey	**folk·sy**
follacle	**fol·li·cle**
follder	**fold·er**
folley	**fol·ly**
folliage	**fo·li·age**
follio	**fo·lio**
folowing	**fol·low·ing**
folter	**fal·ter**
fon	**fawn** *(deer; act servilely)*
fondoo	**fon·due**

WRONG	RIGHT
foney	**pho·ny**
foolhardie	**fool·har·dy**
foose	**fuse**
for	**fore** *(golf cry)*
for	**four** *(number)*
foram	**fo·rum**
forarm	**fore·arm**
forbear	**fore·bear** *(ancestor)*
forbearence	**for·bear·ance**
forbiding	**for·bid·ding** *(dangerous looking)*
forboding	**fore·bod·ing** *(foretelling)*
forcast	**fore·cast**
forcefull	**force·ful**
forclose	**fore·close**
fore	**four** *(number)*
forebear	**for·bear** *(refrain)*
forebearance	**for·bear·ance**
forebearer	**fore·bear** *(ancestor)*
foreboding	**for·bid·ding** *(dangerous looking)*
foreceps	**for·ceps**
forelorn	**for·lorn**
foremula	**for·mu·la**
foresake	**for·sake**
foresite	**fore·sight**
foretitude	**for·ti·tude**
forety	**for·ty**
foreward	**fore·word** *(preface)*

WRONG	RIGHT	WRONG	RIGHT
foreward	**for·ward** *(to the front)*	formullate	**for·mu·late**
forfather	**fore·fa·ther**	fornecation	**for·ni·ca·tion**
forfiet	**for·feit**	forocious	**fe·ro·cious**
forfinger	**fore·fin·ger**	forrage	**for·age**
forfront	**fore·front**	forray	**for·ay**
forgary	**for·gery**	forreign	**for·eign**
forgetfull	**for·get·ful**	forrensic	**fo·ren·sic**
forgeting	**for·get·ting**	forrest	**for·est**
forgo	**fore·go** *(precede)*	forrum	**fo·rum**
forgone	**fore·gone** *(unavoidable)*	forruner	**for·eign·er** *(stranger)*
forgoten	**for·got·ten**	forrunner	**fore·run·ner** *(herald)*
forground	**fore·ground**	forsee	**fore·see**
forhand	**fore·hand**	forseps	**for·ceps**
forhead	**fore·head**	forsight	**fore·sight**
foriegn	**for·eign**	forsithia	**for·syth·ia**
formalldehyde	**form·al·de·hyde**	forstall	**fore·stall**
formallity	**for·mal·i·ty**	fort	**forte** *(skill)*
formallize	**for·mal·ize**	fortatude	**for·ti·tude**
formally	**for·mer·ly** *(in the past)*	forte	**fort** *(fortified place)*
formaly	**for·mal·ly** *(of form)*	forteen	**four·teen**
forman	**fore·man**	fortefy	**for·ti·fy**
formel	**for·mal**	forteith	**for·ti·eth**
formelize	**for·mal·ize**	fortell	**fore·tell**
formely	**for·mer·ly** *(in the past)*	forth	**fourth** *(number)*
formerly	**for·mal·ly** *(of form)*	fortifecation	**for·ti·fi·ca·tion**
formidible	**for·mi·da·ble**	fortouitous	**for·tu·i·tous**
formost	**fore·most**	forward	**fore·word** *(preface)*
formulla	**for·mu·la**	forword	**for·ward** *(to the front)*
		forword	**fore·word** *(preface)*

WRONG	RIGHT
fosfate	**phos·phate**
fosil	**fos·sil**
fossillize	**fos·sil·ize**
fostor	**fos·ter**
fotocopy	**pho·to·copy**
fotoelectric	**pho·to·e·lec·tric**
fotogenic	**pho·to·gen·ic**
fotos	**pho·tos** *(pl.)*
fotosynthesis	**pho·to·syn·the·sis**
foul	**fowl** *(bird)*
foundery	**found·ry**
founten	**foun·tain**
fourfinger	**fore·fin·ger**
fourth	**forth** (forward)
fourty	**for·ty**
fowl	**foul** (filthy)
fowndation	**foun·da·tion**
fowndry	**found·ry**
foyble	**foi·ble**
frachure	**frac·ture**
fractionallize	**frac·tion·al·ize**
fracton	**frac·tion**
fradulent	**fraud·u·lent**
fragill	**frag·ile**
fragrent	**fra·grant**
fraight	**freight**
fraighter	**freight·er**
fraktion	**frac·tion**
fralty	**frail·ty**
framework	**frame·work**
franc	**frank** (honest)
Frances	**Fran·cis** (m.)

WRONG	RIGHT
franchize	**fran·chise**
Francis	**Fran·ces** (f.)
frank	**franc** (coin)
franticly	**fran·ti·cal·ly**
frase	**phrase**
fraternaty	**fra·ter·ni·ty**
fraturnal	**fra·ter·nal**
fraut	**fraught**
frawd	**fraud**
frawdulent	**fraud·u·lent**
frazled	**fraz·zled**
freckel	**freck·le**
freckeled	**freck·led**
fredom	**free·dom**
freedum	**free·dom**
freek	**freak**
freelanse	**free-lance**
freeloder	**free-load·er**
freequency	**fre·quen·cy**
freese	**freeze** (become ice)
freeweeling	**free-wheel·ing**
freind	**friend**
freize	**frieze** (in architecture)
frekle	**freck·le**
frend	**friend**
frenzie	**fren·zy**
frequant	**fre·quent**
frequensy	**fre·quen·cy**
frescoe	**fres·co**
fretfull	**fret·ful**
freting	**fret·ting**
frett	**fret**
friccasee	**fric·as·see**

WRONG	RIGHT
frieght	**freight** (cargo)
frieghter	**freight·er**
frier	**fri·ar**
	(religious person)
frier	**fry·er** (food)
frieze	**freeze** (become ice)
friggate	**frig·ate**
friggid	**frig·id**
frightning	**fright·en·ing**
frigit	**frig·ate**
friing	**fry·ing**
frikassee	**fric·as·see**
friskey	**frisky**
friter	**frit·ter**
frivelous	**friv·o·lous**
frivollity	**fri·vol·i·ty**
Froidian	**Freud·i·an**
frolicksome	**frol·ic·some**
frollic	**frol·ic**
fronteer	**fron·tier**
frosbite	**frost·bite**
frostie	**frosty**
frothey	**frothy**
frouning	**frown·ing**
Fruedian	**Freud·i·an**
frugel	**fru·gal**
fruitfull	**fruit·ful**
fruntier	**fron·tier**
frusstration	**frus·tra·tion**
fryed	**fried**
fuchia	**fuch·sia**
fucilage	**fu·se·lage**
fudal	**feu·dal**
fuge	**fugue**
fuge	**fudge**

WRONG	RIGHT
fugetive	**fu·gi·tive**
fuise	**fuse**
fujative	**fu·gi·tive**
fulback	**full·back**
fulcram	**ful·crum**
fule	**fu·el**
fulfiled	**ful·filled**
fullcrum	**ful·crum**
fullength	**full-length**
fullfil	**ful·fill**
fullfilled	**ful·filled**
fullsome	**ful·some**
fulness	**full·ness**
fumbeling	**fum·bling**
fumegate	**fu·mi·gate**
fumey	**fumy**
functionaly	**func·tion·al·ly**
functionnal	**func·tion·al**
fundamently	
	fun·da·men·tal·ly
fundation	**foun·da·tion**
fundimental	
	fun·da·men·tal
funel	**fun·nel**
funerial	**fu·ne·re·al**
funerral	**fu·ner·al**
fungases	**fun·gus·es**
fungecide	**fun·gi·cide**
funireal	**fu·ne·re·al**
funktion	**func·tion**
funneral	**fun·er·al**
funtion	**func·tion**
fur	**fir** (tree)
fureous	**fu·ri·ous**
furier	**fur·ri·er**

WRONG	RIGHT	WRONG	RIGHT
furlow	**fur·lough**	fushia	**fuch·sia**
furmentation		fusilage	**fu·se·lage**
	fer·men·ta·tion	fussally	**fuss·i·ly**
furn	**fern** (plant)	fusselage	**fu·se·lage**
furnature	**fur·ni·ture**	fussie	**fussy**
furnesh	**fur·nish**	fussion	**fu·sion**
furness	**fur·nace**	futere	**fu·ture**
furow	**fur·row**	futeristic	**futur·is·tic**
furrie	**fur·ry**	futile	**feu·dal**
furrious	**fu·ri·ous**		(of feudalism)
furror	**fu·ror** (frenzy)	futill	**fu·tile** (useless)
furtave	**fur·tive**	futillity	**fu·til·i·ty**
furthurmore		futurristic	**futur·is·tic**
	fur·ther·more	fyllo	**phyl·lo**

G

WRONG	RIGHT
gabanzo	**gar·ban·zo**
gabbardine	**gab·ar·dine**
gabel	**ga·ble** *(roof)*
gadgit	**gadg·et**
gaety	**gai·e·ty**
gaff	**gaffe** *(mistake)*
gaffe	**gaff** *(hook)*
gage	**gauge** *(measure)*
gaget	**gadg·et**
gaging	**gag·ging** *(choking)*
gail	**gale** *(strong wind)*
gailey	**gai·ly**
gait	**gate** *(opening)*
gaje	**gauge** *(measure)*
galant	**gal·lant**
galery	**gal·lery**
galexy	**gal·axy**
galey	**gal·ley**
gallactic	**ga·lac·tic**
gallary	**gal·lery**
gallavant	**gal·li·vant**
gallaxy	**gal·axy**
gallen	**gal·lon**
	(liquid measure)
gallent	**gal·lant**
galleyvant	**gal·li·vant**
gallies	**gal·leys**
gallore	**ga·lore**

WRONG	RIGHT
galloshes	**ga·losh·es**
gallup	**gal·lop**
gallvanize	**gal·va·nize**
gally	**gal·ley**
galon	**gal·lon**
	(liquid measure)
galop	**gal·lop**
galows	**gal·lows**
galvenize	**gal·va·nize**
gama	**gam·ma**
gambet	**gam·bit**
gamble	**gam·bol** *(frolic)*
gambleing	**gam·bling**
gambol	**gam·ble** *(bet)*
gamet	**gam·ut**
gamey	**gamy**
gammut	**gam·ut**
gandola	**gon·do·la**
gandor	**gan·der**
gane	**gain**
gangleing	**gan·gling**
gangreen	**gan·grene**
ganre	**gen·re**
gapeing	**gap·ing**
garanteeing	
	guar·an·tee·ing
garbege	**gar·bage**
gard	**guard**

gardian	**guard·i·an**	gastrick	**gas·tric**
gardin	**gar·den**	gate	**gait** *(walk)*
gardner	**gar·den·er**	gater	**ga·tor**
garet	**gar·ret**	gaudey	**gaudy**
garganchuan		gauk	**gawk**
	gar·gan·tu·an	gaul	**gall**
gargleing	**gar·gling**	gauranteeing	
gargoil	**gar·goyle**		**guar·an·tee·ing**
garilla	**go·ril·la** *(ape)*	gaurd	**guard**
garilla	**guer·ril·la** *(soldier)*	gaurdian	**guard·i·an**
garison	**gar·ri·son**	gaushe	**gauche**
garlend	**gar·land**	gavle	**gav·el**
garlick	**gar·lic**	gawnt	**gaunt**
garmint	**gar·ment**	gawntlet	**gauntlet**
garnesh	**gar·nish**	gawze	**gauze**
garrage	**ga·rage**	gayety	**gai·e·ty**
garralous	**gar·ru·lous**	gayla	**ga·la**
garrason	**gar·ri·son**	gayze	**gaze**
garrbled	**gar·bled**	gazele	**ga·zelle**
garrish	**gar·ish**	gazete	**ga·zette**
garrit	**gar·ret**	gazibo	**ga·ze·bo**
garrlic	**gar·lic**	geagraphical	
garson	**gar·çon**		**ge·o·graph·i·cal**
garulous	**gar·ru·lous**	gealogy	**ge·ol·o·gy**
gasahol	**gas·o·hol**	geametric	**ge·o·met·ric**
gasaline	**gas·o·line**	gease	**geese**
gasha	**gei·sha**	geens	**genes**
gasious	**gas·e·ous**		*(hereditary units)*
gaskit	**gas·ket**	geer	**gear**
gaslite	**gas·light**	gel	**jell** *(become jelly)*
gassamer	**gos·sa·mer**	gell	**gel**
gasseous	**gas·e·ous**		*(jelly-like substance)*
gasslight	**gas·light**	gellatin	**gel·a·tin**
gassoline	**gas·o·line**	gellding	**geld·ing**
gastly	**ghast·ly**	gelly	**jel·ly**

WRONG	RIGHT
Gemmini	**Gem·i·ni**
genasis	**gen·e·sis**
geneology	**ge·ne·al·o·gy**
generalaty	**gen·er·al·i·ty**
generaly	**gen·er·al·ly**
generater	**gen·er·a·tor**
generick	**ge·ner·ic**
generousity	**gen·er·os·i·ty**
generus	**gen·er·ous**
genes	**jeans** *(trousers)*
genetal	**gen·i·tal**
geneticly	**ge·net·i·cal·ly**
geneus	**ge·nius** *(talent)*
genger	**gin·ger**
geniel	**ge·nial**
genius	**ge·nus** *(class)*
genneration	**gen·er·a·tion**
genneric	**ge·ner·ic**
genoside	**gen·o·cide**
genrally	**gen·er·al·ly**
genrous	**gen·er·ous**
genteal	**gen·teel** *(refined)*
genteel	**gen·tile** *(not Jewish)*
gentile	**gen·tle** *(not rough)*
gentile	**gen·teel** *(refined)*
gentle	**gen·tile** *(not Jewish)*
gentley	**gen·tly**
genuen	**gen·u·ine**
genufleck	**gen·u·flect**
genus	**ge·nius** *(talent)*
geografical	**ge·o·graph·i·cal**
geomettric	**ge·o·met·ric**

WRONG	RIGHT
geraffe	**gi·raffe**
gerage	**ga·rage**
geraneum	**ge·ra·ni·um**
gerble	**ger·bil**
gereatrics	**ger·i·at·rics**
gerkin	**gher·kin**
germacide	**ger·mi·cide**
germain	**ger·mane**
germanate	**ger·mi·nate**
geschure	**ges·ture** *(movement)*
geshtalt	**ge·stalt**
gess	**guess** *(surmise)*
gest	**guest** *(person)*
gest	**jest**
gestickulate	**ges·tic·u·late**
gestolt	**ge·stalt**
geting	**get·ting**
getogether	**get·to·geth·er**
getto	**ghet·to**
geurilla	**guer·ril·la** *(soldier)*
geuss	**guess** *(surmise)*
gezebo	**ga·ze·bo**
gezelle	**ga·zelle**
gheto	**ghet·to**
ghool	**ghoul**
gibe	**jibe** *(agree)*
giberish	**gib·ber·ish**
giblit	**gib·let**
gidance	**guid·ance**
giddyness	**gid·di·ness**
gient	**gi·ant**
giesha	**gei·sha**
gigalo	**gig·o·lo**
gigantick	**gi·gan·tic**

81

WRONG	RIGHT	WRONG	RIGHT
gigbite	**gi·ga·byte**	glaukoma	**glau·co·ma**
gigling	**gig·gling**	gleem	**gleam**
gileless	**guile·less**	gleen	**glean**
gillotine	**guil·lo·tine**	glibb	**glib**
gilt	**guilt** *(blame)*	glideing	**glid·ing**
gimick	**gim·mick**	glimer	**glim·mer**
gimlit	**gim·let**	glimse	**glimpse**
gimnasium	**gym·na·si·um**	glissen	**glis·ten**
ginea pig	**guin·ea pig**	glitery	**glit·tery**
ginecology	**gyn·e·col·o·gy**	globel	**glob·al**
gingam	**ging·ham**	gloomey	**gloomy**
ginnie	**jin·ni**	glorafy	**glo·ri·fy**
gipsum	**gyp·sum**	glorius	**glo·ri·ous**
girafe	**gi·raffe**	glossery	**glos·sa·ry**
giration	**gy·ra·tion**	glossey	**glossy**
girm	**germ**	glote	**gloat**
giro	**gy·ro** *(lamb sandwich)*	gloucoma	**glau·co·ma**
giroscope	**gy·ro·scope**	gluecose	**glu·cose**
gise	**guise** *(aspect)*	glueing	**glu·ing**
giser	**gey·ser**	glumy	**gloomy**
giss	**gist**	gluttenous	**glut·ton·ous**
gitar	**gui·tar**	glyserine	**glyc·er·in**
giudance	**guid·ance**	gnarlled	**gnarled**
giveing	**giv·ing**	gnawwing	**gnaw·ing**
gizzerd	**giz·zard**	gnoam	**gnome**
glaceir	**gla·cier**	gnoo	**gnu**
glaciel	**gla·cial**	gobbeling	**gob·bling**
gladeator	**glad·i·a·tor**	goblen	**gob·lin**
gladeolas	**glad·i·o·lus**	gobling	**gob·bling**
glamorus	**glam·or·ous**	goblit	**gob·let**
glanceing	**glanc·ing**	goche	**gauche**
glanduler	**glan·du·lar**	gock	**gawk**
glareing	**glar·ing**	goddy	**gaudy**
glashal	**gla·cial**	gode	**goad**
glasier	**gla·cier**	godess	**god·dess**

WRONG	RIGHT
gofer	**go·pher** *(animal)*
gofor	**go·fer** *(errand runner)*
gogles	**gog·gles**
goldan	**gold·en**
golf	**gulf** *(bay; gap)*
goll	**gall**
gollbladder	**gall·blad·der**
gollden	**gold·en**
gondala	**gon·do·la**
gondoleer	**gon·do·lier**
gonorrea	**gon·or·rhea**
gont	**gaunt**
gontlet	**gaunt·let**
goofey	**goofy**
goolash	**gou·lash**
gophor	**go·pher** *(animal)*
gorami	**gou·ra·mi**
gord	**gourd**
gorey	**gory**
gorgous	**gor·geous**
gorila	**go·ril·la** *(ape)*
gorilla	**guer·ril·la** *(soldier)*
gorjeous	**gor·geous**
gormet	**gour·met**
gorrila	**go·ril·la** *(ape)*
gosamer	**gos·sa·mer**
gosip	**gos·sip**
gosspel	**gos·pel**
gossup	**gos·sip**
gost	**ghost**
goucho	**gau·cho**
goul	**ghoul**
gourmey	**gour·met**
goverment	**gov·ern·ment**

WRONG	RIGHT
governer	**gov·er·nor**
govurn	**gov·ern**
gowge	**gouge**
gowt	**gout**
goyter	**goi·ter**
goz	**gauze**
grabing	**grab·bing**
gracius	**gra·cious**
grackel	**grack·le**
gradiant	**gra·di·ent**
gradiation	**gra·da·tion**
gradualy	**grad·u·al·ly**
graduit	**grad·u·ate**
graff	**graft**
graff	**graph**
grafic	**graph·ic**
grafite	**graph·ite**
grafitti	**graf·fi·ti**
gragarious	**gre·gar·i·ous**
grainary	**gran·a·ry**
gram	**gra·ham** *(flour)*
gramaticly	**gram·mat·i·cal·ly**
grammer	**gram·mar**
granade	**gre·nade**
grandaughter	**grand·daugh·ter**
grandeose	**gran·di·ose**
grandure	**gran·deur** *(grandness)*
granery	**gran·a·ry**
granet	**gran·ite** *(stone)*
granite	**grant·ed** *(pt. of grant)*
grannola	**gran·o·la**

WRONG	RIGHT	WRONG	RIGHT
grannular	**gran·u·lar**	greatfull	**grate·ful**
granstand	**grand·stand**	greedally	**greed·i·ly**
granted	**gran·ite** *(stone)*	greenary	**green·ery**
granuler	**gran·u·lar**	greenkeeper	
grapfruit	**grape·fruit**		**greens·keep·er**
graphick	**graph·ic**	Greenwhich	**Green·wich**
grapling	**grap·pling**	Greese	**Greece**
grappel	**grap·ple**	greesy	**greasy**
grapvine	**grape·vine**	gregarrious	**gre·gar·i·ous**
grase	**grace**	greif	**grief**
grassey	**grassy**	greivance	**griev·ance**
grasshoper	**grass·hop·per**	greiving	**griev·ing**
grate	**great** *(large)*	greivous	**griev·ous**
gratefull	**grate·ful**	gremlen	**grem·lin**
gratefy	**grat·i·fy**	grenery	**green·ery**
grateing	**grat·ing**	grennade	**gre·nade**
gratetude	**grat·i·tude**	grennadine	**gren·a·dine**
gratious	**gra·cious**	Grennich	**Green·wich**
grattitude	**grat·i·tude**	griddiron	**grid·i·ron**
gratuetous	**gra·tu·i·tous**	gridle	**grid·dle**
gravelly	**grave·ly** *(soberly)*	grieveing	**griev·ing**
gravely	**grav·el·ly**	grievence	**griev·ance**
	(full of gravel)	grievius	**griev·ous**
gravetate	**grav·i·tate**	griffiti	**graf·fi·ti**
gravety	**grav·i·ty**	griling	**grill·ing**
gravey	**gra·vy**	grimey	**grimy**
gravill	**grav·el**	grimmace	**gri·mace**
gravstone	**grave·stone**	grimmly	**grim·ly**
gravvity	**grav·i·ty**	grined	**grind**
gravyard	**grave·yard**	grinestone	**grind·stone**
grazeing	**graz·ing**	grining	**grin·ning**
Greace	**Greece**	griping	**grip·ping** *(holding)*
greasey	**greasy**	gripping	**grip·ing**
great	**greet** *(meet)*		*(complaining)*
great	**grate** *(scrape)*	grissle	**gris·tle**

WRONG	RIGHT	WRONG	RIGHT
grizzely	**griz·zly** *(bear)*	grumbleing	**grum·bling**
grizzly	**gris·ly** *(horrible)*	grungey	**grun·gy**
groan	**grown** *(mature)*	grusome	**grue·some**
grogy	**grog·gy**	gruvel	**grov·el**
groing	**grow·ing**	gruwel	**gru·el**
grone	**groan** *(moan)*	guacomole	**gua·ca·mo·le**
grone	**grown** *(mature)*	guage	**gauge** *(measure)*
grool	**gru·el**	guaranteing	
grooling	**gru·el·ing**		**guar·an·tee·ing**
groosome	**grue·some**	guardean	**guard·i·an**
gropeing	**grop·ing**	guerila	**guer·ril·la** *(soldier)*
grose	**gross**	guerilla	**go·ril·la** *(ape)*
grosery	**gro·cery**	gues	**guest** *(person)*
grotesk	**gro·tesque**	gufaw	**guf·faw**
groth	**growth**	guideing	**guid·ing**
groto	**grot·to**	guidence	**guid·ance**
grouchey	**grouchy**	guilless	**guile·less**
groupy	**group·ie**	guilotine	**guil·lo·tine**
grouseing	**grous·ing**	guilt	**gilt** *(coated)*
grovell	**grov·el**	guinnea pig	**guin·ea pig**
growchy	**grouchy**	guittar	**gui·tar**
growel	**growl**	gulet	**gul·let**
groweth	**growth**	gulf	**golf** *(game)*
grown	**groan** *(moan)*	gullable	**gul·li·ble**
growsing	**grous·ing**	gulley	**gul·ly**
growt	**grout**	gullit	**gul·let**
growwing	**grow·ing**	gultch	**gulch**
groyn	**groin**	gumtion	**gump·tion**
grubing	**grub·bing**	gumy	**gum·my**
gruby	**grub·by**	guning	**gun·ning**
grudgeingly	**grudg·ing·ly**	guocamole	**gua·ca·mo·le**
gruesum	**grue·some**	gurdle	**gir·dle**
gruge	**grudge**	gurgleing	**gur·gling**
grugingly	**grudg·ing·ly**	gurny	**gur·ney**
gruling	**gru·el·ing**	gurth	**girth**

WRONG	RIGHT	WRONG	RIGHT
guset	**gus·set**	guys	**guise** (*aspect*)
gussto	**gus·to**	guyser	**gey·ser**
guter	**gut·ter**	gygabyte	**gi·ga·byte**
gutteral	**gut·tur·al**	gymnaseum	
guvernatorial			**gym·na·si·um**
	guber·na·to·ri·al	gynacology	**gyn·e·col·o·gy**
guvernment	**gov·ern·ment**	gypsom	**gyp·sum**
guvnor	**gov·er·nor**	gyrascope	**gy·ro·scope**

H

WRONG	RIGHT
habbitation	**hab·i·ta·tion**
habbitual	**ha·bit·u·al**
habet	**hab·it**
habetation	**hab·i·ta·tion**
habitible	**hab·it·a·ble**
hachery	**hatch·ery**
hachet	**hatch·et**
haching	**hatch·ing**
hachway	**hatch·way**
hacknied	**hack·neyed**
hadock	**had·dock**
haf	**half** (n.)
haggerd	**hag·gard**
hagle	**hag·gle**
haikoo	**hai·ku**
hail	**hale** (healthy; force)
hainous	**hei·nous**
hair	**heir** (inheritor)
hair	**hare** (rabbit)
hairbrained	**hare·brained**
hairey	**hairy** (hair-covered)
hairlip	**hare·lip**
hairloom	**heir·loom**
hairpeace	**hair·piece**
hairy	**har·ry** (harass)
haiven	**ha·ven**
haize	**haze**
haizel	**ha·zel**

WRONG	RIGHT
hakneyed	**hack·neyed**
halapeno	**ja·la·pe·ño**
hale	**hail** (ice; call)
halebut	**hal·i·but**
halelujah	**hal·le·lu·jah**
half	**halve** (v.)
hall	**haul** (pull)
hallibut	**hal·i·but**
hallo	**ha·lo** (ring of light)
hallowed	**hol·lowed** (made empty inside)
hallucenation	**hal·lu·ci·na·tion**
hallucenogenic	**hal·lu·ci·no·gen·ic**
halmark	**hall·mark**
halow	**hal·low** (venerate)
halow	**ha·lo** (ring of light)
halowed	**hal·lowed** (venerated)
Haloween	**Hal·low·een**
halsyon	**hal·cy·on**
halucinnation	**hal·lu·ci·na·tion**
halucinogenic	**hal·lu·ci·no·gen·ic**
halve	**half** (n.)
hamberger	**ham·burg·er**

WRONG	RIGHT
hamering	**ham·mer·ing**
hammuck	**ham·mock**
hanbook	**hand·book**
handcuf	**hand·cuff**
handecapped	**hand·i·capped**
handecraft	**hand·i·craft**
handelbar	**han·dle·bar**
handeling	**han·dling**
handfull	**hand·ful**
handicaped	**hand·i·capped**
handiman	**hand·y·man**
handkercheif	**hand·ker·chief**
handlely	**hand·i·ly**
handriting	**hand·writ·ing**
handsome	**han·som** *(carriage)*
handsomly	**hand·some·ly**
handsum	**hand·some** *(good-looking)*
handwriten	**hand·writ·ten**
handycraft	**hand·i·craft**
handywork	**hand·i·work**
hangar	**hang·er** *(garment holder)*
hangcuff	**hand·cuff**
hanger	**hang·ar** *(aircraft shed)*
hankerchief	**hand·ker·chief**
hansome	**han·som** *(carriage)*

WRONG	RIGHT
hansome	**hand·some** *(good-looking)*
hapened	**hap·pened**
haphazerd	**hap·haz·ard**
haram	**ha·rem**
harang	**ha·rangue**
harbenger	**har·bin·ger**
harber	**har·bor**
hardwear	**hard·ware**
hardy	**hearty** *(wholehearted)*
hardyness	**har·di·ness** *(boldness)*
hare	**hair** *(fur)*
haresy	**her·e·sy**
harey	**har·ry** *(harass)*
harlekin	**har·le·quin**
harlet	**har·lot**
harliquin	**har·le·quin**
harmanic	**har·mon·ic**
harmfull	**harm·ful**
harmoneca	**har·mon·i·ca**
harmoneous	**har·mo·ni·ous**
harmoney	**har·mo·ny**
harmonicly	**har·mon·i·cal·ly**
harmonnic	**har·mon·ic**
harnes	**har·ness**
harowing	**har·row·ing**
harpsicord	**harp·si·chord**
harrangue	**ha·rangue**
harrassment	**har·ass·ment**
harrem	**ha·rem**
harry	**hairy** *(hair-covered)*

WRONG	RIGHT
hart	**heart** *(organ)*
hartache	**heart·ache**
harth	**hearth**
harty	**hearty** *(wholehearted)*
harvister	**har·vest·er**
hasheesh	**hash·ish**
hassen	**has·ten**
hassuck	**has·sock**
hast	**haste**
hastey	**hasty**
hatable	**hate·a·ble**
hatchary	**hatch·ery**
hatchit	**hatch·et**
hatefull	**hate·ful**
hater	**hat·ter** *(hat-maker)*
hatrid	**ha·tred**
hatter	**hat·er** *(one who hates)*
hauk	**hawk**
hauthorn	**haw·thorn**
hauture	**hau·teur**
hauty	**haugh·ty**
havan	**ha·ven**
Havanna	**Ha·vana**
havec	**hav·oc**
haveing	**hav·ing**
havock	**hav·oc**
Hawai	**Ha·waii**
Hawaien	**Ha·wai·ian**
hawl	**haul** *(pull)*
hawnch	**haunch** *(hindquarter)*
hawnted	**haunt·ed**
hawteur	**hau·teur**

WRONG	RIGHT
hawthorne	**haw·thorn**
hawty	**haugh·ty**
haxsaw	**hack·saw**
hay	**hey** *(interj.)*
hazally	**ha·zi·ly**
hazerd	**haz·ard**
hazerdous	**haz·ard·ous**
hazey	**ha·zy**
hazle	**ha·zel**
hazzard	**haz·ard**
head	**heed** *(attend to)*
headake	**head·ache**
headfone	**head·phone**
headquorters	**head·quar·ters**
headress	**head·dress**
heal	**heel** *(part of foot)*
healler	**heal·er**
healthfull	**health·ful**
hear	**here** *(on this place)*
hearafter	**here·af·ter**
hearby	**here·by**
heard	**herd** *(group)*
heart	**hart** *(deer)*
heartake	**heart·ache**
heartally	**heart·i·ly**
heartbeet	**heart·beat**
heartbern	**heart·burn**
heartbraking	**heart·break·ing**
heartiness	**har·di·ness** *(boldness)*
heartrendering	**heart·rend·ing**
hearty	**har·dy** *(bold)*

89

WRONG	RIGHT	WRONG	RIGHT
heathan	**hea·then**	heiroglyphics	**hi·er·o·glyph·ics**
heathe	**heath**	he'l	**he'll** (he will)
heavilly	**heav·i·ly**	helecopter	**hel·i·cop·ter**
heavin	**heav·en**	Helenistic	**Hel·len·is·tic**
heavinly	**heav·en·ly**	heleum	**he·li·um**
heaviset	**heavy·set**	hell	**he'll** (he will)
Hebrue	**He·brew**	hellash	**hell·ish**
heckel	**heck·le**	hellicopter	**hel·i·cop·ter**
heckeler	**heck·ler**	hellium	**he·li·um**
hecks	**hex**	hellix	**he·lix**
hectac	**hec·tic**	helmit	**hel·met**
hedache	**head·ache**	helpfull	**help·ful**
hedanist	**he·do·nist**	helth	**health**
heddress	**head·dress**	helthful	**health·ful**
hede	**heed** (attend to)	helthy	**healthy**
hedgeing	**hedg·ing**	hemaglobin	**he·mo·glo·bin**
hedgrow	**hedge·row**	hemarroid	**hem·or·rhoid**
hedonnist	**he·do·nist**	hemed	**hemmed**
hedquarters	**head·quar·ters**	hemlok	**hem·lock**
heel	**heal** (cure)	hemmisphere	**hem·i·sphere**
heelium	**he·li·um**	hemmorage	**hem·or·rhage**
heelix	**he·lix**	hemmroid	**hem·or·rhoid**
heep	**heap**	hemogloben	**he·mo·glo·bin**
heeth	**heath**	hemorrage	**hem·or·rhage**
heeve	**heave**	hemorroid	**hem·or·rhoid**
heffer	**heif·er**	hencforth	**hence·forth**
heffty	**hefty**	henpek	**hen·peck**
hege	**hedge**	hense	**hence**
hegehog	**hedge·hog**	hensforth	**hence·forth**
hegerow	**hedge·row**	hentchman	**hench·man**
heightan	**height·en**		
heinious	**hei·nous**		
heirarchy	**hi·er·ar·chy**		
heires	**heir·ess**		

WRONG	RIGHT
herafter	**here·af·ter**
heram	**ha·rem**
herasy	**her·e·sy**
herbacide	**her·bi·cide**
herbel	**herb·al**
herby	**here·by**
herculian	**her·cu·le·an**
herd	**heard** (pt. of hear)
here	**hear** (listen)
hereditery	**he·red·i·tary**
heresay	**hear·say**
heretige	**her·it·age**
hering	**her·ring**
heritic	**her·e·tic**
herkulean	**her·cu·le·an**
herloom	**heir·loom**
hermatage	**her·mit·age**
hermet	**her·mit**
hermitege	**her·mit·age**
hernea	**her·nia**
heroe	**he·ro** (sing.)
heroin	**her·o·ine** (f.; hero)
heroine	**her·o·in** (narcotic)
herold	**her·ald**
heros	**he·roes** (pl.)
herpez	**her·pes**
herrald	**her·ald**
herrediary	**he·red·i·tary**
herresy	**her·e·sy**
herretic	**her·e·tic**
herritage	**her·it·age**
herroic	**he·ro·ic**
herroin	**her·o·in** (narcotic)
herroine	**her·o·ine** (f.; hero)

WRONG	RIGHT
herron	**her·on**
herrowing	**har·row·ing**
her's	**hers**
herse	**hearse**
herth	**hearth**
hesetancy	**hes·i·tan·cy**
hesetate	**hes·i·tate**
hesitasion	**hes·i·ta·tion**
hesitency	**hes·i·tan·cy**
heterogeneous	**het·er·og·e·nous** (of different origin)
heterrosexual	**het·er·o·sex·u·al**
hethen	**hea·then**
hether	**heath·er**
hetrogenius	**het·er·o·ge·ne·ous** (of different origin)
hevally	**heav·i·ly**
heven	**heav·en**
hevy	**heavy**
hevyweight	**heavy·weight**
hew	**hue** (color)
hey	**hay** (dried grass)
heywire	**hay·wire**
hi alai	**jai alai**
hiararchy	**hi·er·ar·chy**
hiasinth	**hy·a·cinth**
hiatas	**hi·a·tus**
hibrid	**hy·brid**
hiburnate	**hi·ber·nate**
hichair	**high·chair**
hichhike	**hitch·hike**
hickery	**hick·o·ry**

91

WRONG	RIGHT	WRONG	RIGHT
hickup	**hic·cup**	hinesight	**hind·sight**
hiddeous	**hid·e·ous**	hingeing	**hing·ing**
hidrant	**hy·drant**	hiperbola	**hy·per·bo·la**
hidraulic	**hy·drau·lic**		*(curve)*
hidrochloric		hiperbole	**hy·per·bo·le**
	hy·dro·chlo·ric		*(exaggeration)*
hidroelectric		hipertension	
	hy·dro·e·lec·tric		**hy·per·ten·sion**
hidrogen	**hy·dro·gen**		*(high blood pressure)*
hieena	**hy·e·na**	hiperventilation	
hiefer	**heif·er**		**hy·per·ven·ti·la·tion**
hieght	**height**	hiphen	**hy·phen**
hienous	**hei·nous**	hipnosis	**hyp·no·sis** *(sing.)*
hier	**heir** *(inheritor)*	hipochondriac	
hierchy	**hi·er·ar·chy**		**hy·po·chon·dri·ac**
hieress	**heir·ess**	hipocrisy	**hy·poc·ri·sy**
hierloom	**heir·loom**	hipodermic	**hy·po·der·mic**
hierogliphics		hipopotamus	
	hi·er·o·glyph·ics		**hip·po·pot·a·mus**
hietus	**hi·a·tus**	hipotension	
higiene	**hy·giene**		**hy·po·ten·sion**
hijact	**hi·jack**		*(low blood pressure)*
hikory	**hick·o·ry**	hipothesis	**hy·poth·e·sis**
hiku	**hai·ku**		*(sing.)*
hilaraty	**hi·lar·i·ty**	hipothetical	
hilarrious	**hi·lar·i·ous**		**hy·po·thet·i·cal**
hilbilly	**hill·bil·ly**	hipparcritical	
hilight	**high·light**		**hyp·o·crit·i·cal**
hillarious	**hi·lar·i·ous**		*(deceitful)*
hillarity	**hi·lar·i·ty**	Hippocritic	**Hip·po·crat·ic**
hillbillie	**hill·bil·ly**		*(of Hippocrates)*
hiltop	**hill·top**	hirarchy	**hi·er·ar·chy**
Himilayas	**Hi·ma·la·yas**	hi-rise	**high-rise**
himn	**hymn** *(song)*	hiroglyphics	
hinderance	**hin·drance**		**hi·er·o·glyph·ics**

WRONG	RIGHT
Hispannic	**His·pan·ic**
hisself	**him·self**
histemine	**his·ta·mine**
histerectomy	**hys·ter·ec·to·my**
histeria	**hys·te·ria**
histerical	**hys·ter·i·cal**
histery	**his·to·ry**
historecal	**his·tor·i·cal**
historrian	**his·to·ri·an**
histreonic	**his·tri·on·ic**
hitchike	**hitch·hike**
hiway	**high·way**
hoan	**hone**
hoar	**whore**
hoard	**horde** *(crowd)*
hoarie	**hoary**
hobbeling	**hob·bling**
hobbie	**hob·by**
hobgoblen	**hob·gob·lin**
hobknob	**hob·nob**
hocky	**hock·ey**
hoged	**hogged**
hogepoge	**hodge·podge**
holacaust	**hol·o·caust**
Holand	**Hol·land**
hole	**whole** *(entire)*
holeday	**hol·i·day**
holesale	**whole·sale**
holey	**ho·ly** *(sacred)*
holey	**whol·ly** *(totally)*
hollandase	**hol·lan·daise**
Hollend	**Hol·land**
hollendaise	**hol·lan·daise**
holliday	**hol·i·day**

WRONG	RIGHT
hollie	**hol·ly** *(plant)*
hollistic	**ho·lis·tic**
hollocaust	**hol·o·caust**
hollograph	**hol·o·graph**
hollow	**hal·low** *(venerate)*
hollowed	**hal·lowed** *(venerated)*
Holloween	**Hal·low·een**
hollster	**hol·ster**
holly	**ho·ly** *(sacred)*
holocost	**hol·o·caust**
holy	**hol·ly** *(plant)*
holy	**holey** *(with holes)*
holy	**whol·ly** *(totally)*
Holywood	**Hol·ly·wood**
homacidal	**hom·i·ci·dal**
homage	**hom·mage** *(tribute)*
homaly	**hom·i·ly**
homanym	**hom·o·nym**
hombray	**hom·bre**
homested	**home·stead**
homeword	**home·ward**
homisidal	**hom·i·ci·dal**
homley	**home·ly**
hommage	**hom·age** *(reverence)*
hommicidal	**hom·i·ci·dal**
hommily	**hom·i·ly**
hommogenize	**ho·mog·e·nize**
hommonym	**hom·o·nym**
homofobia	**ho·mo·pho·bia**

WRONG	RIGHT	WRONG	RIGHT
homogenious	**ho·mo·ge·ne·ous**	horezontal	**hor·i·zon·tal**
homoginize	**ho·mog·e·nize**	horible	**hor·ri·ble**
homosexule	**ho·mo·sex·u·al**	horify	**hor·ri·fy**
Honalulu	**Hon·o·lu·lu**	horison	**ho·ri·zon**
honering	**hon·or·ing**	horizontel	**hor·i·zon·tal**
honeysukle	**hon·ey·suck·le**	hornit	**hor·net**
honnesty	**hon·es·ty**	horor	**hor·ror**
honney	**hon·ey**	horrable	**hor·ri·ble**
honnorable	**hon·or·a·ble**	horrably	**hor·ri·bly**
Honoloolu	**Hon·o·lu·lu**	horred	**hor·rid**
honorible	**hon·or·a·ble**	horrefy	**hor·ri·fy**
honted	**haunt·ed**	horrer	**hor·ror**
hony	**hon·ey**	horrescope	**hor·o·scope**
honycomb	**hon·ey·comb**	horrizen	**ho·ri·zon**
honymoon	**hon·ey·moon**	horrizontal	**hor·i·zon·tal**
honysuckle	**hon·ey·suck·le**	hors derve	**hors d'oeu·vre**
hoodlem	**hood·lum**	horse	**hoarse** *(harsh)*
hoola	**hu·la**	horshoe	**horse·shoe**
hopefull	**hope·ful**	hortaculture	**hor·ti·cul·ture**
hopfully	**hope·ful·ly**	hosery	**ho·siery**
hoping	**hop·ping**	hospess	**hos·pice**
	(bouncing)	hospetable	**hos·pi·ta·ble**
hopping	**hop·ing**	hospetal	**hos·pi·tal**
	(wanting)	hospetality	**hos·pi·tal·i·ty**
hopscotch	**hop·scotch**	hospiece	**hos·pice**
horascope	**hor·o·scope**	hospitallity	**hos·pi·tal·i·ty**
horde	**hoard** *(reserve)*	hospitallization	**hos·pi·tal·i·za·tion**
hor dourve	**hors d'oeu·vre**	hospitible	**hos·pi·ta·ble**
hore	**hoar** *(frost)*	hostege	**hos·tage**
hore	**whore**	hostel	**hos·tile**
horemone	**hor·mone**		*(unfriendly)*
horendous	**hor·ren·dous**	hostes	**host·ess**
		hostile	**hos·tel** *(inn)*

WRONG	RIGHT	WRONG	RIGHT
hostillity	**hos·til·i·ty**	humilliation	**humil·i·a·tion**
hottel	**ho·tel**	humillity	**hu·mil·i·ty**
houling	**howl·ing**	humingbird	**hum·ming·bird**
houmous	**hum·mus**	hummanity	**hu·man·i·ty**
houskeeper	**house·keep·er**	hummidifier	**humid·i·fi·er**
houswife	**house·wife**	hummiliation	**humil·i·a·tion**
hovvel	**hov·el**	hummility	**hu·mil·i·ty**
hovver	**hov·er**	humorous	**hu·mer·us** *(bone)*
howlling	**howl·ing**	humous	**hu·mus**
hownd	**hound**	hunch	**haunch** *(hindquarter)*
hoxe	**hoax**	hunderd	**hun·dred**
hoziery	**ho·siery**	hundreth	**hun·dredth**
huch	**hutch**	hungerly	**hun·gri·ly**
huddeling	**hud·dling**	hungery	**hun·gry**
hue	**hew** *(chop)*	Hungery	**Hun·ga·ry**
huged	**hugged**	hungrilly	**hun·gri·ly**
hukster	**huck·ster**	hunny	**hon·ey**
hulla	**hu·la**	huntch	**hunch**
human	**hu·mane** *(kind)*	hurbol	**herb·al**
humane	**hu·man** *(person)*	hurdel	**hur·dle** *(barrier)*
humaniterian	**human·i·tar·i·an**	hurdeling	**hur·dling**
humannity	**hu·man·i·ty**	hurdle	**hur·tle** *(rush)*
humbelest	**hum·blest**	huricane	**hur·ri·cane**
humbley	**hum·bly**	hurnia	**her·nia**
humed	**hu·mid**	hurpes	**her·pes**
humen	**hu·man** *(person)*	hurrecane	**hur·ri·cane**
humenism	**hu·man·ism**	hurrey	**hur·ry**
humer	**hu·mor**	hurring	**hur·ry·ing**
humerous	**hu·mer·us** *(bone)*	hurse	**hearse**
humerous	**hu·mor·ous** *(funny)*	hurtel	**hur·tle** *(rush)*
humidefier	**humid·i·fi·er**		
humidety	**hu·mid·i·ty**		

WRONG	RIGHT	WRONG	RIGHT
hurtfull	**hurt·ful**	hygene	**hy·giene**
hurtle	**hur·dle** *(barrier)*	hym	**hymn** *(song)*
husbandery	**hus·band·ry**	hymnel	**hym·nal**
husbend	**hus·band**	hypacondriac	
huskie	**husky**		**hy·po·chon·dri·ac**
hussie	**hus·sy**	hypadermic	
hussle	**hus·tle**		**hy·po·der·mic**
huvel	**hov·el**	hypatension	
huver	**hov·er**		**hy·po·ten·sion**
hyacenth	**hy·a·cinth**		*(low blood pressure)*
hybred	**hy·brid**	hypathetical	
hydergen	**hy·dro·gen**		**hy·po·thet·i·cal**
hydracarbon		hyperallergenic	
	hy·dro·car·bon		**hy·po·al·ler·gen·ic**
hydrachloric			*(not allergenic)*
	hy·dro·chlo·ric	hyperbola	**hy·per·bo·le**
hydraelectric			*(exaggeration)*
	hy·dro·e·lec·tric	hyperbole	**hy·per·bo·la**
hydrafoil	**hy·dro·foil**		*(curve)*
hydragen	**hy·dro·gen**	hypercritical	
hydraphobia			**hyp·o·crit·i·cal**
	hy·dro·pho·bia		*(deceitful)*
hydraullic	**hy·drau·lic**	hyperdermic	
hydrent	**hy·drant**		**hy·po·der·mic**
hydrocarben		hypertension	
	hy·dro·car·bon		**hy·po·ten·sion**
hydrocloric			*(low blood pressure)*
	hy·dro·chlo·ric	hypertention	
hydrofobia			**hy·per·ten·sion**
	hy·dro·pho·bia		*(high blood pressure)*
hydrolic	**hy·drau·lic**	hyperventillation	
hyecinth	**hy·a·cinth**		**hy·per·ven·ti·la·tion**
hyeena	**hy·e·na**	hyphan	**hy·phen**
hyfen	**hy·phen**	hyphennate	**hy·phen·ate**
hygeinic	**hy·gi·en·ic**	hypnatism	**hyp·no·tism**

WRONG	RIGHT
hypnoses............**hyp·no·sis** *(sing.)*	hypothesis .....**hy·poth·e·ses** *(pl.)*
hypnosis .....**hyp·no·ses** *(pl.)*	hypothetacal......................**hy·po·thet·i·cal**
hypnottic............**hyp·not·ic**	hypothurmia......................**hy·po·ther·mia**
hypocrasy ....**hy·poc·ri·sy**	hypottenuse......................**hy·pot·e·nuse**
Hypocratic ....**Hip·po·crat·ic** *(of Hippocrates)*	hyppacrisy........**hy·poc·ri·sy**
hypocrit............**hyp·o·crite**	hyppochondriac ....**hy·po·chon·dri·ac**
hypocritical......................**hy·per·crit·i·cal** *(too critical)*	hyppothalamus...................**hy·po·thal·a·mus**
hypotension......................**hy·per·ten·sion** *(high blood pressure)*	hyppothesis ....**hy·poth·e·sis** *(sing.)*
hypothalmus ....**hy·po·thal·a·mus**	hysterrectomy....................**hys·ter·ec·to·my**
hypotheses .....**hy·poth·e·sis** *(sing.)*	hysterria ....**hys·te·ria**
	hysterrical.........**hys·ter·i·cal**

I

WRONG	RIGHT
iadine	**io·dine**
ian	**ion** *(atom)*
ibuprofin	**ibu·pro·fen**
iceburg	**ice·berg**
iceing	**ic·ing**
icey	**icy**
icickle	**ici·cle**
icilly	**ici·ly**
iconnoclast	**icon·o·clast**
icycle	**ici·cle**
iddiocy	**id·i·o·cy**
idealisticly
	ide·al·is·ti·cal·ly
ideallism	**ide·al·ism**
idealogical	**ide·o·log·i·cal**
idealy	**ide·al·ly**
idee	**idea**
ideel	**ide·al**
ideelism	**ide·al·ism**
ideelistically
	ide·al·is·ti·cal·ly
ideelly	**ide·al·ly**
idel	**idyll** *(short poem)*
idel	**idol** *(object of worship)*
idel	**idle** *(inactive)*
identafy	**iden·ti·fy**
identefication
	iden·ti·fi·ca·tion

WRONG	RIGHT
identety	**iden·ti·ty**
identicly	**iden·ti·cal·ly**
ideologecal	**ide·o·log·i·cal**
ideom	**id·i·om**
ideomatic	**id·i·o·mat·ic**
ideosyncrasy
	id·i·o·syn·cra·sy
ideot	**id·i·ot**
iderdown	**ei·der·down**
idia	**idea**
idiacy	**id·i·o·cy**
idiam	**id·i·om**
idiat	**id·i·ot**
idillic	**idyl·lic**
idiosincrasy
	id·i·o·syn·cra·sy
idle	**idol** *(object of worship)*
idle	**idyll** *(short poem)*
idol	**idle** *(inactive)*
idollatrous	**idol·a·trous**
idollatry	**idol·a·try**
idollize	**idol·ize**
idological	**ide·o·log·i·cal**
idolotrous	**idol·a·trous**
idolotry	**idol·a·try**
idyll	**idol**
	(object of worship)

98

WRONG	RIGHT	WRONG	RIGHT
idyll	**idle** *(inactive)*	Illinoi	**Il·li·nois**
idyllick	**idyl·lic**	illisit	**il·lic·it** *(unlawful)*
iglue	**ig·loo**	illitteracy	**il·lit·er·a·cy**
ignaramus	**ig·no·ra·mus**	illogecal	**il·log·i·cal**
ignerance	**ig·no·rance**	illucidate	**elu·ci·date**
igneus	**ig·ne·ous**	illude	**elude** *(escape)*
ignight	**ig·nite**	illumenation	
igniminious			**il·lu·mi·na·tion**
	ig·no·min·i·ous	illusion	**al·lu·sion**
ignious	**ig·ne·ous**		*(reference)*
ignomineous		illusion	**elu·sion**
	ig·no·min·i·ous		*(an escape)*
ignoreing	**ig·nor·ing**	illusive	**elu·sive**
ignorence	**ig·no·rance**		*(hard to grasp)*
igregious	**egre·gious**	illustrater	**il·lus·tra·tor**
iguanna	**igua·na**	illustrius	**il·lus·tri·ous**
igwana	**igua·na**	ilogical	**il·log·i·cal**
ikonoclast	**icon·o·clast**	ilumination	
iland	**is·land**		**il·lu·mi·na·tion**
Ilead	**Il·i·ad**	ilusion	**il·lu·sion**
ilegal	**il·le·gal**		*(false idea)*
ilegible	**il·leg·i·ble**	ilustration	**il·lus·tra·tion**
ilegitimate	**il·le·git·i·mate**	ilustrator	**il·lus·tra·tor**
ilet	**is·let** *(small island)*	ilustrious	**il·lus·tri·ous**
ilicit	**il·lic·it** *(unlawful)*	imaciate	**ema·ci·ate**
Ilinois	**Il·li·nois**	imaculate	**im·mac·u·late**
iliteracy	**il·lit·er·a·cy**	imaganation	
iliterate	**il·lit·er·ate**		**imag·i·na·tion**
Illanois	**Il·li·nois**	imagenary	**imag·i·nary**
illate	**elate**	imaginible	**imag·i·na·ble**
illegable	**il·leg·i·ble**	imanent	**im·ma·nent**
illegle	**il·le·gal**		*(inherent)*
Illiad	**Il·i·ad**	imasculate	**emas·cu·late**
illicit	**elic·it** *(evoke)*	imatate	**im·i·tate**
illigitimate	**il·le·git·i·mate**	imaterial	**im·ma·te·ri·al**

99

WRONG	RIGHT	WRONG	RIGHT
imature	**im·ma·ture**	immagination	**imag·i·na·tion**
imbalm	**em·balm**	immanent	**im·mi·nent**
imbargo	**em·bar·go**		*(impending)*
imbark	**em·bark**	immatereal	**im·ma·te·ri·al**
imbarras	**em·bar·rass**	immedeacy	**im·me·di·a·cy**
imbellish	**em·bel·lish**	immediatly	**im·me·di·ate·ly**
imbesile	**im·be·cile**		
imbew	**im·bue**	immerge	**emerge**
imbezzle	**em·bez·zle**		*(come out)*
imbodiment	**em·bod·i·ment**	immersable	**im·mers·i·ble**
imboss	**em·boss**	immersion	**emer·sion**
imbrace	**em·brace**		*(emerging)*
imbroider	**em·broi·der**	immigrant	**em·i·grant**
imediacy	**im·me·di·a·cy**		*(one who leaves)*
imediately	**im·me·di·ate·ly**	immigrate	**em·i·grate**
imemorial	**im·me·mo·ri·al**		*(leave)*
imense	**im·mense**	immigrent	**im·mi·grant**
imensity	**im·men·si·ty**		*(one who arrives)*
imeritus	**emer·i·tus**	imminent	**em·i·nent**
imersible	**im·mers·i·ble**		*(prominent)*
imige	**im·age**	imminent	**im·ma·nent**
imigrant	**im·mi·grant**		*(inherent)*
	(one who arrives)	immitate	**im·i·tate**
imigrate	**im·mi·grate**	immoble	**im·mo·bile**
	(arrive)	immolument	**emol·u·ment**
iminent	**im·mi·nent**		*(wages)*
	(impending)	immorallity	**im·mo·ral·i·ty**
imission	**emis·sion**	immortallize	**im·mor·tal·ize**
immacculate	**im·mac·u·late**	immortel	**im·mor·tal**
immage	**im·age**	immovible	**im·mov·a·ble**
immaginable	**imag·i·na·ble**	immunety	**im·mu·ni·ty**
immaginary	**imag·i·nary**		

WRONG	RIGHT	WRONG	RIGHT
immutible	**im·mu·ta·ble**	imperseptible	**im·per·cep·ti·ble**
imobile	**im·mo·bile**	impersonnate	**im·per·son·ate**
imoderate	**im·mod·er·ate**	impersonnel	**im·per·son·al**
imodest	**im·mod·est**	impertinance	**im·per·ti·nence**
imolate	**im·mo·late**	impervius	**im·per·vi·ous**
imoral	**im·mor·al**	impetence	**im·po·tence**
imorality	**im·mo·ral·i·ty**	impettuous	**im·pet·u·ous**
imortal	**im·mor·tal**	impettus	**im·pe·tus**
imotional	**emo·tion·al**	impireal	**im·pe·ri·al**
impack	**im·pact**		*(sovereign)*
impare	**im·pair**	impirical	**em·pir·i·cal**
imparment	**im·pair·ment**	implacible	**im·plac·a·ble**
impasioned	**im·pas·sioned**	implecation	**im·pli·ca·tion**
impasition	**im·po·si·tion**	impliment	**im·ple·ment**
impass	**im·passe**	implisit	**im·plic·it**
impassable	**im·pas·si·ble**	imployee	**em·ploy·ee**
	(cannot feel pain)	implyed	**im·plied**
impassible	**im·pass·a·ble**	impollite	**im·po·lite**
	(cannot be passed)	importence	**im·por·tance**
impateince	**im·pa·tience**	imposeing	**im·pos·ing**
impeccible	**im·pec·ca·ble**	imposibility	**im·pos·si·bil·i·ty**
impedement	**im·ped·i·ment**	imposter	**im·pos·tor**
impeech	**im·peach**		*(deceiver)*
impeed	**im·pede**	impostor	**im·pos·ture**
impeling	**im·pel·ling**		*(deception)*
impell	**im·pel**	impotant	**im·po·tent**
impenatrable	**im·pen·e·tra·ble**	impovrish	**im·pov·er·ish**
impenge	**im·pinge**	impracticle	**im·prac·ti·cal**
imperceptable	**im·per·cep·ti·ble**	impregnible	**im·preg·na·ble**
imperetive	**im·per·a·tive**	impresion	**im·pres·sion**
impermiable	**im·per·me·a·ble**		

WRONG	RIGHT	WRONG	RIGHT
imprisise	**im·pre·cise**	inbalance	**im·bal·ance**
improbible	**im·prob·a·ble**	inbibe	**im·bibe**
impromtu	**im·promp·tu**	incalcuble	
impropriaty			**in·cal·cu·la·ble**
	im·pro·pri·e·ty	incandessent	
improvasation			**in·can·des·cent**
	im·prov·i·sa·tion	incapasitate	
improvment			**in·ca·pac·i·tate**
	im·prove·ment	incarserate	**in·car·cer·ate**
impudance	**im·pu·dence**	incedence	**in·ci·dence**
impullsive	**im·pul·sive**	incence	**in·cense**
impunaty	**im·pu·ni·ty**	incendery	**in·cen·di·ary**
impune	**im·pugn**	incephalitis	
impuraty	**im·pu·ri·ty**		**en·ceph·a·li·tis**
impurmeable		incersion	**in·cur·sion**
	im·per·me·able	incessent	**in·ces·sant**
impurvious	**im·per·vi·ous**	incestus	**in·ces·tu·ous**
imulsion	**emul·sion**	incidently	**in·ci·den·tal·ly**
imunity	**im·mu·ni·ty**	incinerater	**in·cin·er·a·tor**
imutable	**im·mu·ta·ble**	incipiant	**in·cip·i·ent**
inable	**en·a·ble**	inciser	**in·ci·sor**
inaccessable		inclemment	**in·clem·ent**
	in·ac·ces·si·ble	inclinnation	**in·cli·na·tion**
inacurate	**in·ac·cu·rate**	inclusave	**in·clu·sive**
inadvertantly		incode	**en·code**
	in·ad·vert·ent·ly	incogneto	**in·cog·ni·to**
inagural	**in·au·gu·ral**	incoherance	
inallienable	**in·al·ien·a·ble**		**in·co·her·ence**
inamel	**en·am·el**	incombency	
inanamate	**in·an·i·mate**		**in·cum·ben·cy**
inapropriate		incomeing	**in·com·ing**
	in·ap·pro·pri·ate	incompareable	
inapt	**in·ept** (clumsy)		**in·com·pa·ra·ble**
inate	**in·nate**	incompatable	
inaugral	**in·au·gu·ral**		**in·com·pat·i·ble**

WRONG	RIGHT	WRONG	RIGHT
incompatent ....in·com·pe·tent	incredulus .....in·cred·u·lous
incomperhensible................in·com·pre·hen·si·ble	increese ....in·crease
incompettent ....in·com·pe·tent	incrimminate ....in·crim·i·nate
incomprable.....................in·com·pa·ra·ble	incroach ....en·croach
incomprehensable ....in·com·pre·hen·si·ble	incubater ....in·cu·ba·tor
incomunicado....................in·com·mu·ni·cado	incumbincy......................in·cum·ben·cy
inconceivible ....in·con·ceiv·a·ble	incureable ....in·cur·a·ble
incongrous...in·con·gru·ous	incurr ....in·cur
incongruant ....in·con·gru·ent	incurzion............in·cur·sion
inconsievable ....in·con·ceiv·a·ble	incyclopedia ....en·cy·clo·pe·dia
inconspickuous..................in·con·spic·u·ous	indacate ....in·di·cate
incontrovertable ....in·con·tro·vert·i·ble	indanger ....en·dan·ger
inconveneince ....in·con·ven·ience	indead.................in·deed
incoppacitate ....in·ca·pac·i·tate	indecks ....in·dex
incorigible ....in·cor·ri·gi·ble	indefinitly.....in·def·i·nite·ly
incorperate....in·cor·po·rate	indegence..........in·di·gence
incorruptable ....in·cor·rupt·i·ble	*(poverty)*
incrament.........in·cre·ment	indellible............in·del·i·ble
increaseingly ....in·creas·ing·ly	indemmify.......in·dem·ni·fy
incredable ....in·cred·i·ble	indemnaty.........in·dem·ni·ty
	indenchured ...in·den·tured
	independant ....in·de·pend·ent
	indescribeable ....in·de·scrib·a·ble
	indesent ....in·de·cent
	indespensable ....in·dis·pen·sa·ble
	indestructable ....in·de·struct·i·ble
	indetted.............in·debt·ed
	indevidual.......in·di·vid·u·al

103

WRONG	RIGHT	WRONG	RIGHT

WRONG	RIGHT
indicater	**in·di·ca·tor**
Indien	**In·di·an**
indiffrence	**in·dif·fer·ence**
indigence	**in·di·gents**
	(poor persons)
indigense	**in·di·gence**
	(poverty)
indiginous	**in·dig·e·nous**
indignaty	**in·dig·ni·ty**
indignent	**in·dig·nant**
indipendent	
	in·de·pend·ent
indireck	**in·di·rect**
indiscrimanate	
	in·dis·crim·i·nate
indispensible	
	in·dis·pen·sa·ble
indisscretion	
	in·dis·cre·tion
inditment	**in·dict·ment**
	(formal charge)
individal	**in·di·vid·u·al**
individuallity	
	in·di·vid·u·al·i·ty
indoctranate	
	in·doc·tri·nate
indollent	**in·do·lent**
indommitable	
	in·dom·i·ta·ble
indorsment	
	en·dorse·ment
indubbitably	
	in·du·bi·ta·bly
inducktion	**in·duc·tion**
inducment	**in·duce·ment**

WRONG	RIGHT
indulgance	**in·dul·gence**
indurance	**en·dur·ance**
indusement	**in·duce·ment**
industralize	
	in·dus·tri·al·ize
industreal	**in·dus·tri·al**
industrey	**in·dus·try**
industriallize	
	in·dus·tri·al·ize
inebreated	**in·e·bri·at·ed**
inedable	**in·ed·i·ble**
ineficient	**in·ef·fi·cient**
inelligible	**in·el·i·gi·ble**
inemical	**in·im·i·cal**
inepp	**in·ept** *(clumsy)*
inept	**in·apt** *(not apt)*
inequity	**in·iq·ui·ty**
	(wickedness)
inevatible	**in·ev·i·ta·ble**
infallable	**in·fal·li·ble**
infaltrate	**in·fil·trate**
infamercial	**in·fo·mer·cial**
infamus	**in·fa·mous**
infantsy	**in·fan·cy**
infattuation	**in·fat·u·a·tion**
infecktion	**in·fec·tion**
infectuous	**in·fec·tious**
infedelity	**in·fi·del·i·ty**
infency	**in·fan·cy**
infenite	**in·fi·nite**
infenitesimal	
	in·fin·i·tes·i·mal
infinitive	**in·fin·i·tive**
infentry	**in·fan·try**
inferance	**in·fer·ence**

WRONG	RIGHT	WRONG	RIGHT
inferier	in·fe·ri·or	ingit	in·got
infermation		ingraciate	in·gra·ti·ate
	in·for·ma·tion	ingraned	in·grained
inferr	in·fer	ingrave	en·grave
infidellity	in·fi·del·i·ty	ingrediant	in·gre·di·ent
infilltrate	in·fil·trate	ingrossing	en·gross·ing
infinetesimal		inhabbitable	
	in·fin·i·tes·i·mal		in·hab·it·a·ble
infinetive	in·fin·i·tive	inhabitent	in·hab·it·ant
infinety	in·fin·i·ty	inharent	in·her·ent
infinnite	in·fi·nite	inheret	in·her·it
infirior	in·fe·ri·or	inheritence	in·her·it·ance
infirmry	in·fir·ma·ry	inhibbition	in·hi·bi·tion
inflamable	in·flam·ma·ble	inhibiter	in·hib·i·tor
inflamation		inhirent	in·her·ent
	in·flam·ma·tion	inhospittable	
inflateing	in·flat·ing		in·hos·pi·ta·ble
inflatible	in·flat·a·ble	inibition	in·hi·bi·tion
inflationery	in·fla·tion·ary	ining	in·ning
inflexable	in·flex·i·ble	iniquity	in·eq·ui·ty
inflick	in·flict		*(unfairness)*
influance	in·flu·ence	inititive	in·i·ti·a·tive
influencial	in·flu·en·tial	injeck	in·ject
influinza	in·flu·en·za	injenue	in·gé·nue
informallity	in·for·mal·i·ty	injenuity	in·ge·nu·i·ty
informent	in·form·ant	injenuous	in·gen·u·ous
infrequint	in·fre·quent	injery	in·ju·ry
infringeing	in·fring·ing	injest	in·gest
infurnal	in·fer·nal	injoin	en·join
infurno	in·fer·no	injunktion	in·junc·tion
infuryate	in·fu·ri·ate	injurius	in·ju·ri·ous
ingagement		inkandescent	
	en·gage·ment		in·can·des·cent
ingenius	in·gen·ious	inkey	inky
ingenuety	in·ge·nu·i·ty	inkubation	in·cu·ba·tion

WRONG	RIGHT	WRONG	RIGHT
inlayed	in·laid	innerview	in·ter·view
innacence	in·no·cence	innimical	in·im·i·cal
innane	in·ane	innitial	in·i·tial
innanimate	in·an·i·mate	innitiate	in·i·ti·ate
innapt	in·apt *(not apt)*	innitiative	in·i·ti·a·tive
innavation	in·no·va·tion	innoccuous	in·noc·u·ous
innebriated	in·e·bri·at·ed	innoculation	
inneresting	in·ter·est·ing		in·oc·u·la·tion
innerject	in·ter·ject	innordinate	in·or·di·nate
innerlude	in·ter·lude	innosense	in·no·cence
innermediary		innundate	in·un·date
	in·ter·me·di·ary	innure	in·ure
innermediate		inoble	ig·no·ble
	in·ter·me·di·ate	inocculation	
innermission			in·oc·u·la·tion
	in·ter·mis·sion	inocence	in·no·cence
innermittent		inocent	in·no·cent
	in·ter·mit·tent	inocuous	in·noc·u·ous
innernational		inordenate	in·or·di·nate
	in·ter·na·tion·al	inormous	enor·mous
innerogative		inovation	in·no·va·tion
	in·ter·rog·a·tive	inpacted	im·pact·ed
innerpersonal		inpale	im·pale
	in·ter·per·son·al	inpartial	im·par·tial
innerracial	in·ter·ra·cial	inpeach	im·peach
innersect	in·ter·sect	inpending	im·pend·ing
innersection		inpersonal	im·per·son·al
	in·ter·sec·tion	inpersonate	
innersperse	in·ter·sperse		im·per·son·ate
innertia	in·er·tia	inpractical	im·prac·ti·cal
innerupt	in·ter·rupt	inprecise	im·pre·cise
innerval	in·ter·val	inprint	im·print
innervene	in·ter·vene	inpromptu	im·promp·tu
innervention		inpropriety	
	in·ter·ven·tion		im·pro·pri·e·ty

WRONG	RIGHT
inquery	**in·quiry**
inquireing	**in·quir·ing**
inquisative	**in·quis·i·tive**
inrage	**en·rage**
insalation	**in·su·la·tion**
insamnia	**in·som·nia**
insanety	**in·san·i·ty**
inseck	**in·sect**
insecticede	**in·sec·ti·cide**
insemanation	**in·sem·i·na·tion**
insendiary	**in·cen·di·ary**
insense	**in·cense**
insentive	**in·cen·tive**
inseperable	**in·sep·a·ra·ble**
insergence	**in·sur·gence**
inserrection	**in·sur·rec·tion**
insessant	**in·ces·sant**
insestuous	**in·ces·tu·ous**
insicure	**in·se·cure**
insidence	**in·ci·dence**
insideous	**in·sid·i·ous**
insight	**in·cite** *(rouse)*
insignea	**in·sig·nia**
insinerator	**in·cin·er·a·tor**
insinnuate	**in·sin·u·ate**
insiped	**in·sip·id**
insipient	**in·cip·i·ent**
insision	**in·ci·sion**
insisive	**in·ci·sive**
insisor	**in·ci·sor**
insistance	**in·sist·ence**
insite	**in·sight** *(understanding)*

WRONG	RIGHT
insite	**in·cite** *(rouse)*
insollent	**in·so·lent**
insomnea	**in·som·nia**
inspeck	**in·spect**
inspecter	**in·spec·tor**
insperation	**in·spi·ra·tion**
instagate	**in·sti·gate**
instalation	**in·stal·la·tion**
instance	**in·stants** *(moments)*
instantaneus	**in·stan·ta·ne·ous**
instants	**in·stance** *(occasion)*
instatution	**in·sti·tu·tion**
insted	**in·stead**
insterment	**in·stru·ment**
instince	**in·stance** *(occasion)*
instinctave	**in·stinc·tive**
instink	**in·stinct**
instrament	**in·stru·ment**
instruck	**in·struct**
instructer	**in·struc·tor**
insue	**en·sue**
insuffrable	**in·suf·fer·a·ble**
insulater	**in·su·la·tor**
insulen	**in·su·lin**
insuler	**in·su·lar**
insullation	**in·su·la·tion**
insurection	**in·sur·rec·tion**
insurence	**in·sur·ance**
insurjence	**in·sur·gence**
insurt	**in·sert**
intail	**en·tail**

WRONG	RIGHT	WRONG	RIGHT
intamet	**in·ti·mate**	intermision	**in·ter·mis·sion**
intanation	**in·to·na·tion**	intermitent	**in·ter·mit·tent**
intangable	**in·tan·gi·ble**	intermural	**in·tra·mu·ral**
inteference	**in·ter·fer·ence**	internationel	**in·ter·na·tion·al**
integrel	**in·te·gral**	internel	**in·ter·nal**
integrety	**in·teg·ri·ty**	interogate	**in·ter·ro·gate**
intelectual	**in·tel·lec·tu·al**	interogative	**in·ter·rog·a·tive**
inteligence	**in·tel·li·gence**	interpersonnal	**in·ter·per·son·al**
inteligible	**in·tel·li·gi·ble**	interpetation	**in·ter·pre·ta·tion**
intence	**in·tense**	interpollate	**in·ter·po·late**
intensefy	**in·ten·si·fy**		*(insert; estimate)*
intensety	**in·ten·si·ty**	interseck	**in·ter·sect**
intentionly	**in·ten·tion·al·ly**	intersecktion	**in·ter·sec·tion**
interacial	**in·ter·ra·cial**	intersede	**in·ter·cede**
interceed	**in·ter·cede**	intersept	**in·ter·cept**
interchangable	**in·ter·change·a·ble**	intersession	**in·ter·ces·sion**
interdisiplinary	**in·ter·dis·ci·pli·nary**		*(an interceding)*
interductory	**in·tro·duc·to·ry**	interspurse	**in·ter·sperse**
interem	**in·ter·im**	interupt	**in·ter·rupt**
interferance	**in·ter·fer·ence**	interveiw	**in·ter·view**
interger	**in·te·ger**	intervel	**in·ter·val**
intergral	**in·te·gral**	intervenous	**in·tra·ve·nous**
intergrate	**in·te·grate**	intervension	**in·ter·ven·tion**
intergration	**in·te·gra·tion**	intervine	**in·ter·vene**
interier	**in·te·ri·or**	intestenal	**in·tes·tin·al**
interjeck	**in·ter·ject**	intice	**en·tice**
interlood	**in·ter·lude**		
intermedeary	**in·ter·me·di·ary**		

WRONG	RIGHT	WRONG	RIGHT
intiger	**in·te·ger**	intuative	**in·tu·i·tive**
intigrate	**in·te·grate**	intuision	**in·tu·i·tion**
intimadate	**in·tim·i·date**	inturn	**in·tern**
intimmacy	**in·ti·ma·cy**	inuendo	**in·nu·en·do**
intimmate	**in·ti·mate**	inumerable	**in·nu·mer·a·ble**
intirety	**en·tire·ty**		
intirior	**in·te·ri·or**	inunciate	**enun·ci·ate**
intolerence	**in·tol·er·ance**		*(pronounce)*
intollerable	**in·tol·er·a·ble**	inurtia	**in·er·tia**
intoxacate	**in·tox·i·cate**	invacation	**in·vo·ca·tion**
intracacy	**in·tri·ca·cy**	invadeing	**in·vad·ing**
intraduce	**in·tro·duce**	invagle	**in·vei·gle**
intraductory	**in·tro·duc·to·ry**	invallid	**in·va·lid**
		invalluable	**in·val·u·a·ble**
intramurral	**in·tra·mu·ral**	invantory	**in·ven·to·ry**
intransagent	**in·tran·si·gent**	invaribly	**in·var·i·a·bly**
		invatation	**in·vi·ta·tion**
intransative	**in·tran·si·tive**	invay	**in·veigh**
intravenus	**in·tra·ve·nous**	invazion	**in·va·sion**
intraverted	**in·tro·vert·ed**	invecktive	**in·vec·tive**
intreeg	**in·trigue**	inventer	**in·ven·tor**
intreging	**in·trigu·ing**	investagate	**in·ves·ti·gate**
intrensic	**in·trin·sic**	investature	**in·ves·ti·ture**
intreppid	**in·trep·id**	invetarate	**in·vet·er·ate**
intresting	**in·ter·est·ing**	inviegh	**in·veigh**
intricasy	**in·tri·ca·cy**	inviegle	**in·vei·gle**
intrige	**in·trigue**	invigerate	**in·vig·or·ate**
intrigueing	**in·trigu·ing**	invinsible	**in·vin·ci·ble**
intrinsick	**in·trin·sic**	invisable	**in·vis·i·ble**
introductry	**in·tro·duc·to·ry**	involuntery	**in·vol·un·tary**
		invurse	**in·verse**
introduse	**in·tro·duce**	inyure	**in·ure**
introvurted	**in·tro·vert·ed**	ion	**eon** *(time period)*
intrust	**en·trust**	iphemeral	**ephem·er·al**
intruzion	**in·tru·sion**	iradiate	**ir·ra·di·ate**

WRONG	RIGHT	WRONG	RIGHT
irassible	**iras·ci·ble**	irratation	**ir·ri·ta·tion**
irational	**ir·ra·tion·al**	irreduceable	**ir·re·duc·i·ble**
irection	**erec·tion**	irrefutible	**ir·ref·u·ta·ble**
ireducible	**ir·re·duc·i·ble**	irreguler	**ir·reg·u·lar**
irefutable	**ir·ref·u·ta·ble**	irrelavent	**ir·rel·e·vant**
iregular	**ir·reg·u·lar**	irrepairable	**ir·rep·a·ra·ble**
irellevant	**ir·rel·e·vant**	irreproachible	
iren	**iron**		**ir·re·proach·a·ble**
ireny	**iro·ny**	irresistable	**ir·re·sist·i·ble**
ireplaceable		irresponsable	
	ir·re·place·a·ble		**ir·re·spon·si·ble**
irepparable	**ir·rep·a·ra·ble**	irretreivable	
irepressible			**ir·re·triev·a·ble**
	ir·re·press·i·ble	irreverance	**ir·rev·er·ence**
ireproachable		irreversable	**ir·re·vers·i·ble**
	ir·re·proach·a·ble	irrevokable	**ir·rev·o·ca·ble**
ires	**iris**	irridescent	**ir·i·des·cent**
iresistible	**ir·re·sist·i·ble**	irritent	**ir·ri·tant**
iresponsible		irritible	**ir·ri·ta·ble**
	ir·re·spon·si·ble	irronical	**iron·i·cal**
iretrievable		isalate	**iso·late**
	ir·re·triev·a·ble	isametrics	**iso·met·rics**
ireverence	**ir·rev·er·ence**	isatope	**iso·tope**
ireversible	**ir·re·vers·i·ble**	ishue	**is·sue**
irevocable	**ir·rev·o·ca·ble**	isle	**aisle** *(passage)*
iridessent	**ir·i·des·cent**	Islem	**Is·lam**
irie	**aer·ie** *(nest)*	islet	**eye·let** *(small hole)*
irigate	**ir·ri·gate**	ismus	**isth·mus**
iritable	**ir·ri·ta·ble**	isometricks	**iso·met·rics**
iritation	**ir·ri·ta·tion**	Isreal	**Is·ra·el**
irksum	**irk·some**	isshue	**is·sue**
irode	**erode**	issolate	**iso·late**
ironicle	**iron·i·cal**	issometrics	**iso·met·rics**
irradicate	**erad·i·cate**	isue	**is·sue**
irragate	**ir·ri·gate**	Itallian	**Ital·ian**

J

WRONG	RIGHT
jackel	**jack·al**
jackit	**jack·et**
jacknife	**jack·knife**
jaged	**jag·ged**
jagwire	**jag·uar**
Jahovah	**Je·ho·vah**
jaid	**jade**
jai lai	**jai alai**
jailbrake	**jail·break**
jailler	**jail·er**
jalapino	**ja·la·peño**
jalousy	**jal·ou·sie** (shade)
jalousy	**jeal·ousy**
jam	**jamb** (side post)
Jamaca	**Ja·mai·ca**
jamb	**jam** (jelly)
jamberee	**jam·bo·ree**
jamed	**jammed**
jangeled	**jan·gled**
janiter	**jan·i·tor**
Jannuary	**Jan·u·ary**
janquil	**jon·quil**
Jappanese	**Jap·a·nese**
jared	**jarred**
jargen	**jar·gon**
jasmen	**jas·mine**
jaundes	**jaun·dice**
jauntey	**jaun·ty**

WRONG	RIGHT
javellin	**jav·e·lin**
jawl	**jowl**
jawnt	**jaunt**
jax	**jacks**
jazmine	**jas·mine**
jeallous	**jeal·ous**
jealoussy	**jeal·ousy**
jealousy	**jal·ou·sie** (shade)
jeans	**genes**
	(hereditary units)
jeapardy	**jeop·ardy**
jear	**jeer**
jeens	**jeans** (trousers)
Jehoveh	**Je·ho·vah**
jejoon	**je·june**
jelatin	**gel·a·tin**
jell	**gel**
	(jelly-like substance)
jelley	**jel·ly**
jellyed	**jel·lied**
jelous	**jeal·ous**
jem	**gem**
jender	**gen·der**
jenealogy	**ge·ne·al·o·gy**
jenetically	**ge·net·i·cal·ly**
jenial	**ge·nial**
jenie	**jin·ni**
jenital	**gen·i·tal**

WRONG	RIGHT	WRONG	RIGHT
jenius	**ge·nius** *(talent)*	jiger	**jig·ger**
jenre	**gen·re**	jiggsaw	**jig·saw**
jentry	**gen·try**	jigled	**jig·gled**
jepardy	**jeop·ardy**	jijune	**je·june**
jeranium	**ge·ra·ni·um**	jimied	**jim·mied**
jerbil	**ger·bil**	jin	**gin**
jeriatrics	**ger·i·at·rics**	jingley	**jin·gly**
jerkey	**jerky**	jinks	**jinx**
jernalism	**jour·nal·ism**	jinny	**jin·ni**
jersies	**jer·seys**	jipsum	**gyp·sum**
Jeruselam	**Je·ru·sa·lem**	jiro	**gy·ro**
Jessuit	**Jes·u·it**		*(lamb sandwich)*
jestation	**ges·ta·tion**	jist	**gist**
jester	**ges·ture**	jive	**gibe** *(taunt)*
	(movement)	jocand	**joc·und**
jesticulate	**ges·tic·u·late**	jockular	**joc·u·lar**
jestor	**jest·er** *(clown)*	jocky	**jock·ey**
jetisson	**jet·ti·son**	joger	**jog·ger**
jeuse	**juice**	johnquil	**jon·quil**
Jewash	**Jew·ish**	joinning	**join·ing**
Jewery	**Jew·ry**	jokeing	**jok·ing**
jewjitsu	**ju·jit·su**	jokund	**joc·und**
jewl	**jew·el**	jondice	**jaun·dice**
jewler	**jew·el·er**	jonquill	**jon·quil**
jewlery	**jew·el·ry**	jont	**jaunt**
jewlip	**ju·lep**	jontey	**jaun·ty**
jewvenile	**ju·ven·ile**	joobilation	**ju·bi·la·tion**
ji ali	**jai alai**	Jordon	**Jor·dan**
jiant	**gi·ant**	jornalism	**jour·nal·ism**
jibbrish	**gib·ber·ish**	jossle	**jos·tle**
jibe	**gibe** *(taunt)*	joted	**jot·ted**
jibe	**jive** *(nonsense)*	joul	**jowl**
jiblet	**gib·let**	journallism	**jour·nal·ism**
jifey	**jif·fy**	journel	**jour·nal**
jigalo	**gig·o·lo**	journied	**jour·neyed**

113

WRONG	RIGHT
journy	**jour·ney**
jovvial	**jo·vi·al**
joyfullness	**joy·ful·ness**
jubalee	**ju·bi·lee**
jubelation	**ju·bi·la·tion**
jubillant	**ju·bi·lant**
jubillation	**ju·bi·la·tion**
jubillee	**ju·bi·lee**
juce	**juice**
juddicious	**ju·di·cious**
Judeism	**Ju·da·ism**
judgemint	**judg·ment**
judiciery	**ju·di·ci·ary**
judicous	**ju·di·cious**
judishal	**ju·di·cial**
juggeler	**jug·u·lar**
	(of the throat)
juggeler	**jug·gler**
	(performer)
juggeling	**jug·gling**
juggement	**judg·ment**
juggler	**jug·u·lar**
	(of the throat)
jugitsu	**ju·jit·su**
jugling	**jug·gling**
jugular	**jug·gler**
	(performer)
juguler	**jug·u·lar**
	(of the throat)
juicey	**juicy**
juidicial	**ju·di·cial**
juidiciary	**ju·di·ci·ary**
juidicious	**ju·di·cious**
juiniper	**ju·ni·per**
juise	**juice**

WRONG	RIGHT
jule	**jew·el**
julien	**ju·li·enne**
julip	**ju·lep**
jullienne	**ju·li·enne**
juncsure	**junc·ture**
jungel	**jun·gle**
junier	**jun·ior**
junipar	**ju·ni·per**
junkit	**jun·ket**
junktion	**junc·tion**
junkture	**junc·ture**
juornal	**jour·nal**
Jupeter	**Ju·pi·ter**
jurasdiction	**ju·ris·dic·tion**
jurasprudence	**ju·ris·pru·dence**
jurer	**ju·ror**
jurey	**ju·ry**
jurisdiksion	**ju·ris·dic·tion**
jurisprudance	**ju·ris·pru·dence**
jurk	**jerk**
jurnal	**jour·nal**
jurney	**jour·ney**
jurrisdiction	**ju·ris·dic·tion**
jurrisprudence	**ju·ris·pru·dence**
jurry	**ju·ry**
jurseys	**jer·seys**
justace	**jus·tice**
justafiable	**jus·ti·fi·a·ble**
justafication	**jus·ti·fi·ca·tion**

WRONG	RIGHT	WRONG	RIGHT
justafy	**jus·ti·fy**	justise	**jus·tice**
justapose	**jux·ta·pose**	juvanile	**ju·ven·ile**
justfieble	**jus·ti·fi·a·ble**	juxtipose	**jux·ta·pose**
justifacation		jymnasium	**gym·na·si·um**
	jus·ti·fi·ca·tion	jyration	**gy·ra·tion**

K

WRONG	RIGHT	WRONG	RIGHT
kadre	**ca·dre**	kendle	**kin·dle**
Kajun	**Ca·jun**	kendling	**kin·dling**
kakhi	**kha·ki**	kendred	**kin·dred**
kalleidoscope		kenetic	**ki·net·ic**
	ka·lei·do·scope	kennal	**ken·nel**
kalrabi	**kohl·ra·bi**	kenship	**kin·ship**
kamcorder	**cam·cord·er**	Kentukey	**Ken·tucky**
kamono	**ki·mo·no**	keosk	**ki·osk**
kangeroo	**kan·ga·roo**	kerasene	**ker·o·sene**
kanine	**ca·nine**	kercheif	**ker·chief**
kaos	**cha·os**	kernel	**colo·nel** *(officer)*
karafe	**ca·rafe**	kettel	**ket·tle**
Karea	**Ko·rea**	kewe	**ki·wi**
karet	**car·at**	key	**quay** *(wharf)*
	(gem weight)	keybord	**key·board**
karrat	**kar·at** *(1/24)*	keyestone	**key·stone**
karrate	**ka·ra·te**	kiak	**kay·ak**
kawala	**ko·a·la**	kibbutz	**kib·itz** *(meddle)*
Kawanis	**Ki·wa·nis**	kibutz	**kib·butz**
keal	**keel**		*(settlement)*
kean	**keen**	kiche	**quiche**
kebob	**ke·bab**	kichen	**kitch·en**
kechup	**ketch·up**	kidnies	**kid·neys**
kee lime pie	**key lime pie**	kielbassa	**kiel·ba·sa**
keewee	**ki·wi**	kilabite	**kil·o·byte**
kelo	**ki·lo**	kilagram	**kil·o·gram**
kemp	**kempt**	kilameter	**ki·lo·me·ter**
ken	**kin** *(relatives)*	kilawatt	**kil·o·watt**

WRONG	RIGHT
kilbasa	**kiel·ba·sa**
killogram	**kil·o·gram**
killometer	**ki·lo·me·ter**
killowatt	**kil·o·watt**
kimona	**ki·mo·no**
kin	**ken** (*understanding*)
kindel	**kin·dle**
kindeling	**kin·dling**
kinderd	**kin·dred**
kindergarden	**kin·der·gar·ten**
kinely	**kind·ly**
kingdum	**king·dom**
kingley	**king·ly**
kingpen	**king·pin**
kinkey	**kinky**
kinly	**kind·ly**
kinnetic	**ki·net·ic**
kiser roll	**kai·ser roll**
kitch	**kitsch**
kitchan	**kitch·en**
kitchenwear	**kitch·en·ware**
kiten	**kit·ten**
kleptomaneac	**klep·to·ma·ni·ac**
kluts	**klutz**
knackworst	**knack·wurst**
knak	**knack**
knapsak	**knap·sack**
knave	**nave** (*part of a church*)
knaveish	**knav·ish**
knead	**need** (*require*)
kneal	**kneel**

WRONG	RIGHT
kneed	**knead** (*work dough*)
knicknack	**knick·knack**
knicks	**nix** (*disapprove of*)
knifeing	**knif·ing**
knifes	**knives** (*pl.*)
knikers	**knick·ers** (*short pants*)
knite	**knight** (*rank*)
kniting	**knit·ting**
knitwit	**nit·wit**
knive	**knife** (*sing.*)
knoby	**knob·by**
knoted	**knot·ted**
knowledgable	**knowl·edge·a·ble**
knowlege	**knowl·edge**
knuckel	**knuck·le**
koalla	**ko·a·la**
koasher	**ko·sher**
kolidoscope	**ka·lei·do·scope**
kolrabi	**kohl·ra·bi**
koochen	**ku·chen**
Koria	**Ko·rea**
Korran	**Ko·ran**
Kremlen	**Krem·lin**
kuken	**ku·chen**
kumkwat	**kum·quat**
kurchief	**ker·chief**
kurnel	**ker·nel** (*grain*)
kuzoo	**ka·zoo**
kwafure	**coif·fure** (*hair style*)

WRONG	RIGHT	WRONG	RIGHT
kwagmire	**quag·mire**	kwintet	**quin·tet**
kwagulate	**co·ag·u·late**	kwixotic	**quix·ot·ic**
kwala	**ko·a·la**	Kwonset	**Quon·set**
Kwanze	**Kwan·zaa**	kworum	**quo·rum**
kwell	**quell**	kyudos	**ku·dos**

L

WRONG	RIGHT
labarinth	**lab·y·rinth**
labborious	**la·bo·ri·ous**
laber	**la·bor**
laberatory	**lab·o·ra·to·ry**
laberor	**la·bor·er**
labirynth	**lab·y·rinth**
lable	**la·bel**
laborrious	**la·bo·ri·ous**
labotomy	**lo·bot·o·my**
labratory	**lab·o·ra·to·ry**
labrinth	**lab·y·rinth**
lacerration	**lac·er·a·tion**
lached	**latched**
lachkey	**latch·key**
lacker	**lac·quer**
lackidaisical	**lack·a·dai·si·cal**
lackies	**lack·eys**
lacks	**lax** *(loose)*
lacksative	**lax·a·tive**
lacktic	**lac·tic**
lacluster	**lack·lus·ter**
lacquor	**lac·quer**
lacross	**la·crosse**
lacsivious	**las·civ·i·ous**
ladden	**lad·en**
ladder	**lat·ter** *(more recent)*
lade	**laid** *(pt. of lay)*

WRONG	RIGHT
ladel	**la·dle**
ladeling	**la·dling**
lader	**lad·der** *(framework of steps)*
ladys	**la·dies** *(pl.)*
laety	**la·i·ty**
laffable	**laugh·a·ble**
lafter	**laugh·ter**
lager	**lag·ger** *(one who lags)*
lagger	**la·ger** *(beer)*
laggoon	**la·goon**
laghable	**laugh·a·ble**
lagitemate	**legit·i·mate**
lai	**lei** *(wreath)*
laim	**lame** *(crippled)*
lain	**lane** *(road)*
laing	**lay·ing**
lair	**lay·er** *(stratum)*
laissay faire	**lais·sez faire**
laithe	**lathe** *(cutting machine)*
lakadaisical	**lack·a·dai·si·cal**
lakluster	**lack·lus·ter**
lam	**lamb** *(sheep)*
lama	**lla·ma** *(animal)*
lamay	**la·mé** *(fabric)*

119

WRONG	RIGHT	WRONG	RIGHT
lamb	**lam** *(flight)*	larrynx	**lar·ynx**
Lambrewsco	**Lam·brus·co**	larseny	**lar·ce·ny**
lamenated	**lam·i·nat·ed**	larve	**lar·va**
lamma	**la·ma** *(monk)*	lasania	**la·sa·gna**
lamme	**la·mé** *(fabric)*	lasor	**la·ser**
lamment	**la·ment**	lassagna	**la·sa·gna**
lamminated	**lam·i·nat·ed**	lasseration	**lac·er·a·tion**
lamppoon	**lam·poon**	lassivious	**las·civ·i·ous**
lampray	**lam·prey**	lassoo	**las·so**
landow	**lan·dau**	Las Vagas	**Las Ve·gas**
landscaipe	**land·scape**	latant	**la·tent**
lane	**lain** *(pp. of lie)*	late	**lat·te**
lanelin	**lan·o·lin**		*(coffee with milk)*
langauge	**lan·guage**	latecks	**la·tex**
langerrie	**lin·ge·rie**	Laten	**Lat·in**
langourous	**lan·guor·ous**	Lateno	**La·ti·no**
langwid	**lan·guid**	later	**lat·ter** *(more recent)*
langwish	**lan·guish**	laterrel	**lat·er·al**
lankey	**lanky**	latetude	**lat·i·tude**
lanlady	**land·la·dy**	lath	**lathe**
lanlord	**land·lord**		*(cutting machine)*
lannolin	**lan·o·lin**	lathargic	**le·thar·gic**
lanscape	**land·scape**	lathe	**lath** *(wood strip)*
lanturn	**lan·tern**	latice	**lat·tice**
laped	**lapped**	latreen	**la·trine**
lappel	**la·pel**	latter	**lad·der**
laquer	**lac·quer**		*(framework of steps)*
larciny	**lar·ce·ny**	latter	**lat·er** *(subsequently)*
lare	**lair** *(den)*	latteral	**lat·er·al**
lareit	**lar·i·at**	lattess	**lat·tice**
larengitis	**lar·yn·gi·tis**	lattex	**la·tex**
largly	**large·ly**	lattitude	**lat·i·tude**
larinx	**lar·ynx**	laudible	**laud·a·ble**
larriat	**lar·i·at**	laughible	**laugh·a·ble**
larryngitis	**lar·yn·gi·tis**	laugter	**laugh·ter**

WRONG	RIGHT	WRONG	RIGHT
laundermat	**laun·dro·mat**	leakedge	**leak·age**
laundery	**laun·dry**	leakey	**leaky**
laurreate	**lau·re·ate**	lean	**lien** *(legal claim)*
laurrel	**lau·rel**	lear	**leer**
lauyer	**law·yer**	leatard	**le·o·tard**
lavendar	**lav·en·der**	leavenning	**leav·en·ing**
lavertory	**lav·a·to·ry**	leaway	**lee·way**
lavesh	**lav·ish**	Lebinon	**Leb·a·non**
lavinder	**lav·en·der**	Lebra	**Li·bra**
lavitory	**lav·a·to·ry**	lechra	**lech·er·ous**
lavva	**la·va**	lectrolysis	**elec·trol·y·sis**
lavvish	**lav·ish**	lecturn	**lec·tern**
lawd	**laud** *(praise)*	lecturor	**lec·tur·er**
lawfull	**law·ful**	led	**lead**
lawsoot	**law·suit**		*(chemical; to guide)*
lawwer	**law·yer**	ledgend	**leg·end**
lax	**lacks** *(needs)*	ledgeslature	**leg·is·la·ture**
lax	**lox** *(salmon)*		*(lawmaking body)*
laxitive	**lax·a·tive**	ledgible	**leg·i·ble**
lay	**lei** *(wreath)*	ledgor	**ledg·er**
layed	**laid** *(pt. of lay)*	leech	**leach** *(filter)*
layity	**la·i·ty**	leef	**leaf** *(plant organ)*
lazally	**la·zi·ly**	leeflet	**leaf·let**
lazay faire	**lais·sez faire**	leegal	**le·gal**
lazer	**la·ser**	leegion	**le·gion**
lazey	**la·zy**	leek	**leak** *(escape)*
leach	**leech** *(worm)*	leen	**lean** *(bend; thin)*
leacherous	**lech·er·ous**	leep	**leap**
lead	**led** *(pt. of lead)*	leeves	**leaves**
leader	**li·ter** *(metric unit)*	leeward	**lee·ward**
leafey	**leafy**	leftenant	**lieu·ten·ant**
leaflit	**leaf·let**	legable	**leg·i·ble**
leage	**league**	legallity	**le·gal·i·ty**
leaison	**li·ai·son**	legallization	
leak	**leek** *(vegetable)*		**legal·i·za·tion**

WRONG	RIGHT	WRONG	RIGHT
legand	**leg·end**	lerch	**lurch**
legasy	**leg·a·cy**	lerning	**learn·ing**
legel	**le·gal**	lerynx	**lar·ynx**
legeslation	**leg·is·la·tion**	lese	**lease**
leggacy	**leg·a·cy**	lessen	**les·son** (instruction)
leggendary	**leg·end·ary**	lesser	**les·sor** (landlord)
legger	**ledg·er**	lesson	**less·en** (decrease)
leggislation	**leg·is·la·tion**	lessor	**less·er** (smaller)
leggume	**leg·ume**	lest	**least**
legian	**le·gion**	lesure	**lei·sure**
legilazation	**legal·i·za·tion**	leter	**li·ter** (metric unit)
legindary	**leg·end·ary**	lethel	**le·thal**
leging	**leg·ging**	lether	**leath·er**
legionaire	**legion·naire**	leting	**let·ting**
legislater	**leg·is·la·tor** (lawmaker)	letrine	**la·trine**
		lettice	**let·tuce**
legislator	**leg·is·la·ture** (lawmaking body)	leud	**lewd**
legitamate	**legit·i·mate**	leutenant	**lieu·ten·ant**
legoom	**leg·ume**	levarege	**lev·er·age**
lein	**lien** (legal claim)	leve	**leave**
leisier	**lei·sure**	levee	**levy** (tax)
leisurly	**lei·sure·ly**	leven	**elev·en**
leiu	**lieu**	levening	**leav·en·ing**
leman	**lem·on** (fruit)	levetation	**lev·i·ta·tion**
lemonaid	**lem·on·ade**	levie	**lev·ee** (embankment)
leniant	**le·ni·ent**	levie	**levy** (tax)
lentel	**len·til** (pea)	levrage	**lev·er·age**
lenthen	**lenght·en**	levy	**lev·ee** (embankment)
lenthy	**lengthy**	ley	**lei** (wreath)
lentil	**lin·tel** (beam)	liabillity	**li·a·bil·i·ty**
leoperd	**leop·ard**	liable	**li·bel** (defame)
leperosy	**lep·ro·sy**	liannize	**li·on·ize**
leprachaun	**lep·re·chaun**	liar	**lyre** (harp)
leprasy	**lep·ro·sy**	liason	**li·ai·son**
		liballous	**li·bel·ous**

122

WRONG	RIGHT	WRONG	RIGHT
libarian	**li·brar·i·an**	lightin	**light·en**
libary	**li·brary**	lightning	**light·en·ing**
libbelous	**li·bel·ous**		*(making less heavy)*
libberalize	**lib·er·al·ize**	likelyhood	**like·li·hood**
libberally	**lib·er·al·ly**	likley	**like·ly**
libberation	**lib·er·a·tion**	liklihood	**like·li·hood**
libberty	**lib·er·ty**	likness	**like·ness**
libedo	**li·bi·do**	lile	**lisle**
libel	**li·a·ble** *(likely)*	lillac	**li·lac**
liberalize	**lib·er·al·ize**	lilly	**lily**
liberetto	**li·bret·to**	lim	**limb** *(branch)*
liberration	**lib·er·a·tion**	limb	**limn** *(draw)*
Libia	**Lib·ya**	limboe	**lim·bo**
libility	**li·a·bil·i·ty**	Lime	**Lyme** *(disease)*
lible	**li·bel** *(defame)*	limetation	**lim·i·ta·tion**
lible	**li·a·ble** *(likely)*	limitting	**lim·it·ing**
libralize	**lib·er·al·ize**	limmerick	**lim·er·ick**
librally	**lib·er·al·ly**	limmitation	**lim·i·ta·tion**
librarean	**li·brar·i·an**	limmiting	**lim·it·ing**
librery	**li·brary**	limosine	**lim·ou·sine**
libreto	**li·bret·to**	limph	**lymph**
licarice	**lic·o·rice**	limrick	**lim·er·ick**
licence	**li·cense**	limstone	**lime·stone**
licencious	**licen·tious**	linament	**lin·i·ment** *(salve)*
licker	**liq·uor**	linan	**lin·en**
	(alcoholic drink)	linch	**lynch**
licorish	**lic·o·rice**	lindseed	**lin·seed**
lie	**lye** *(alkaline substance)*	lineament	**lin·i·ment**
lien	**lean** *(bend; thin)*		*(salve)*
liesure	**lei·sure**	linege	**lin·age**
liesurely	**lei·sure·ly**		*(number of lines)*
lieutenent	**lieu·ten·ant**	lineing	**lin·ing**
liggament	**lig·a·ment**	lingeray	**lin·ge·rie**
lightening	**light·ning**	lingueenie	**lin·gui·ne**
	(flash of light)	lingwistics	**lin·guis·tics**

123

WRONG	RIGHT	WRONG	RIGHT
linier	**lin·e·ar**	lisense	**li·cense**
liniment	**lin·e·a·ment** *(outline)*	lisentious	**licen·tious**
linjerie	**lin·ge·rie**	listenning	**lis·ten·ing**
linkege	**link·age**	litagation	**lit·i·ga·tion**
links	**lynx** *(animal)*	litarel	**lit·er·al** *(actual)*
linnament	**lin·i·ment** *(salve)*	litargy	**lit·ur·gy**
linneage	**lin·e·age** *(ancestry)*	liteny	**lit·a·ny**
		liter	**lit·ter** *(rubbish; young)*
linneament	**lin·e·a·ment** *(outline)*	literachure	**lit·er·a·ture**
linnear	**lin·e·ar**	literal	**lit·to·ral** *(on the shore)*
linnen	**lin·en**		
linnoleum	**li·no·le·um**	literaly	**lit·er·al·ly**
linsede	**lin·seed**	literecy	**lit·er·a·cy**
lintel	**len·til** *(pea)*	literrary	**lit·er·ary**
lintil	**lin·tel** *(beam)*	lith	**lithe**
linx	**links** *(golf course)*	litheum	**lith·i·um**
linx	**lynx** *(animal)*	litmas	**lit·mus**
Lio	**Leo**	litning	**light·ning** *(flash of light)*
lionnize	**li·on·ize**		
lipposuction	**lip·o·suc·tion**	litning	**light·en·ing** *(make less heavy)*
lip-sink	**lip-sync**		
liqeur	**li·queur** *(flavored liquor)*	litoral	**lit·to·ral** *(on the shore)*
		litrature	**lit·er·a·ture**
liquadate	**liq·ui·date**	littany	**lit·a·ny**
liquafy	**liq·ue·fy**	littelest	**lit·tlest**
liquer	**liq·uor** *(alcoholic drink)*	litter	**li·ter** *(metric unit)*
		litteral	**lit·er·al** *(actual)*
liquor	**li·queur** *(flavored liquor)*	litteral	**lit·to·ral** *(on the shore)*
		litterary	**lit·er·ary**
lire	**li·ar** *(one who tells lies)*	litterature	**lit·er·a·ture**
lire	**lyre** *(harp)*	littergy	**lit·ur·gy**
lirecal	**lyr·i·cal**	littigation	**lit·i·ga·tion**
		liutenant	**lieu·ten·ant**

WRONG	RIGHT	WRONG	RIGHT
livary	**liv·ery**	logarhythm	**log·a·rithm**
liveable	**liv·a·ble**	loge	**lodge** *(house)*
livelyhood	**live·li·hood**	loger	**log·ger** *(lumberjack)*
liverworst	**liv·er·wurst**	logger	**la·ger** *(beer)*
livley	**live·ly**	loggistics	**lo·gis·tics**
livlihood	**live·li·hood**	logicly	**log·i·cal·ly**
livry	**liv·ery**	logorithm	**log·a·rithm**
livver	**liv·er**	loiterring	**loi·ter·ing**
livvid	**liv·id**	lolypop	**lol·li·pop**
lizerd	**liz·ard**	lome	**loam**
llama	**la·ma** *(monk)*	lone	**loan** *(something lent)*
load	**lode** *(ore)*	lonelyness	**lone·li·ness**
loan	**lone** *(solitary)*	longetude	**lon·gi·tude**
loar	**lore**	longevety	**lon·gev·i·ty**
loath	**loathe** *(detest)*	lonliness	**lone·li·ness**
loathe	**loath** *(unwilling)*	looau	**lu·au**
loathesome	**loath·some**	loobricant	**lu·bri·cant**
lobbie	**lob·by**	loocid	**lu·cid**
lobbotomy	**lo·bot·o·my**	loominary	**lu·mi·nary**
lobstar	**lob·ster**	loored	**lu·rid** *(startling)*
local	**lo·cale** *(place)*	loose	**lose** *(mislay)*
locale	**lo·cal** *(of a district)*	loosing	**los·ing** *(mislaying)*
locallity	**lo·cal·i·ty**	loot	**lute**
locallize	**lo·cal·ize**		*(musical instrument)*
localy	**lo·cal·ly**	loped	**lopped** *(cut)*
locamotive	**lo·co·mo·tive**	loreate	**lau·re·ate**
loccation	**lo·ca·tion**	lorel	**lau·rel**
loces	**lo·cus** *(place)*	lose	**loose** *(free)*
lockit	**lock·et**	loseing	**los·ing** *(mislaying)*
locks	**lox** *(salmon)*	lose-leaf	**loose-leaf**
locus	**lo·cust** *(grasshopper)*	losenge	**loz·enge**
lode	**load** *(burden)*	lossed	**lost**
lodge	**loge** *(theater box)*	Los Vegas	**Las Ve·gas**
lodgeing	**lodg·ing**	lotery	**lot·tery**
lofer	**loaf·er**	lotien	**lo·tion**

125

WRONG	RIGHT
lotis	**lo·tus**
lottary	**lot·tery**
lou	**lieu**
loud	**laud** (praise)
loungeing	**loung·ing**
lousey	**lousy**
Lousiana	**Lou·i·si·ana**
lovliness	**love·li·ness**
lovly	**love·ly**
lowse	**louse**
loyelty	**loy·al·ty**
loyer	**law·yer**
lubrecant	**lu·bri·cant**
lubricater	**lubri·ca·tor**
luced	**lu·cid**
Lucefer	**Lu·ci·fer**
luckey	**lucky**
lucretive	**lu·cra·tive**
lucsious	**lus·cious**
lude	**lewd**
ludecrous	**lu·di·crous**
luggege	**lug·gage**
Luisiana	**Lou·i·si·ana**
lukemia	**leu·ke·mia**
lukerative	**lu·cra·tive**
lukwarm	**luke·warm**
lulaby	**lull·a·by**
lumanescent
....	**lumi·nes·cent**

WRONG	RIGHT
lumbar	**lum·ber** (timber)
lumbego	**lum·ba·go**
lumber	**lum·bar** (of the loins)
lumenous	**lu·mi·nous**
luminesent
....	**lumi·nes·cent**
lumminary	**lu·mi·nary**
lunchen	**lunch·eon**
lunessy	**lu·na·cy**
lung	**lunge** (thrust)
lunge	**lung** (breathing organ)
lunnacy	**lu·na·cy**
luow	**lu·au**
lured	**lu·rid** (startling)
lushious	**lus·cious**
lusid	**lu·cid**
lustey	**lusty**
lustfull	**lust·ful**
lute	**loot** (plunder)
Lutharen	**Lu·ther·an**
luxerious	**lux·u·ri·ous**
luxery	**lux·u·ry**
luxurient	**lux·u·ri·ant**
lyrecs	**lyr·ics**
lyrrical	**lyr·i·cal**

M

WRONG   RIGHT

WRONG	RIGHT
mabbe	may·be
macabb	ma·ca·bre
macarroni	mac·a·ro·ni
macarroon	mac·a·roon
maccaroni	mac·a·ro·ni
maccaroon	mac·a·roon
macedamia	mac·a·dam·ia
macerel	mack·er·el
mach	match (equal)
machanation	mach·i·na·tion
machanic	me·chan·ic
machene	ma·chine
machesmo	ma·chis·mo
machette	ma·che·te
Machievellian	Mach·i·a·vel·li·an
machinary	ma·chin·ery
machinest	ma·chin·ist
mackaral	mack·er·el
mackaroni	mac·a·ro·ni
mackaroon	mac·a·roon
mackentosh	mack·in·tosh (coat)
mackerrel	mack·er·el
Mackiavellian	Mach·i·a·vel·li·an

WRONG	RIGHT
mackination	mach·i·na·tion
mackintosh	Mc·In·tosh (apple)
mackrame	mac·ra·mé
macobre	ma·ca·bre
macramay	mac·ra·mé
madam	mad·ame (title)
madame	mad·am (lady)
madamoiselle	made·moi·selle
maddam	mad·am (lady)
madder	mat·ter (substance)
made	maid (servant)
madem	mad·am (lady)
mademoizelle	mademoiselle
maden	maid·en
mader	mad·der (angrier)
Madera	Ma·deira
madicinal	me·dic·i·nal
madley	mad·ly
madmaselle	made·moi·selle
madona	ma·don·na
magasine	mag·a·zine
magestic	ma·jes·tic

127

WRONG	RIGHT	WRONG	RIGHT
magesty	**maj·es·ty**	magnetick	**mag·net·ic**
maggazine	**mag·a·zine**	magnettism	**mag·net·ism**
maggic	**mag·ic**	magnezium	**mag·ne·si·um**
maggit	**mag·got**		*(element)*
maggma	**mag·ma**	magnifficence	
maggnolia	**mag·no·lia**		**mag·nif·i·cence**
maggpie	**mag·pie**	magnificant	
magick	**mag·ic**		**mag·nif·i·cent**
magickal	**mag·i·cal**	magnifisense	
maginta	**ma·gen·ta**		**mag·nif·i·cence**
magisian	**ma·gi·cian**	magnifyer	**mag·ni·fi·er**
magistarial	**mag·is·te·ri·al**	magninimity	
magistrait	**mag·is·trate**		**mag·na·nim·i·ty**
magizine	**mag·a·zine**	magnolya	**mag·no·lia**
magna cum loude		magor	**ma·jor**
	mag·na cum lau·de	magorette	**ma·jor·ette**
magnafication		magot	**mag·got**
	mag·ni·fi·ca·tion	magpye	**mag·pie**
magnanimaty		mahagany	**ma·hog·a·ny**
	mag·na·nim·i·ty	mahem	**may·hem**
magnanimus		mahogony	**ma·hog·a·ny**
	mag·nan·i·mous	maid	**made** *(prepared)*
magnate		maidin	**maid·en**
	mag·net	mail	**male** *(masculine)*
	(iron attracter)	main	**mane** *(hair)*
magnatise	**mag·net·ize**	mainge	**mange**
magnatude	**mag·ni·tude**	mainger	**man·ger**
magnesia		mainia	**ma·nia**
	mag·ne·si·um	mainnaise	**may·on·naise**
	(element)	maintane	**main·tain**
magnesium	**mag·ne·sia**	maintenence	
	(laxative)		**main·te·nance**
magnet		mair	**mare** *(female horse)*
	mag·nate	maitre dee	**mai·tre d'**
	(important person)	maize	**maze** *(labyrinth)*

WRONG	RIGHT	WRONG	RIGHT
majarity	ma·jor·i·ty	malevalence	
majenta	ma·gen·ta		malev·o·lence
majer	ma·jor	malevolant	malev·o·lent
majerette	ma·jor·ette	malfeesance	
majestick	ma·jes·tic		mal·fea·sance
majesticly	ma·jes·ti·cal·ly	malicius	ma·li·cious
majic	mag·ic	malignansy	ma·lig·nan·cy
majisterial	mag·is·te·ri·al	malignent	ma·lig·nant
majistrate	mag·is·trate	maline	ma·lign
majisty	maj·es·ty	malise	mal·ice
majong	mah·jongg	mall	maul *(injure)*
majoraty	ma·jor·i·ty	mallable	mal·le·a·ble
majoret	ma·jor·ette	malladjusted	
makadamia	mac·a·dam·ia		mal·ad·just·ed
makaw	ma·caw	malladroit	mal·a·droit
makeing	mak·ing	mallady	mal·a·dy
makismo	ma·chis·mo	mallapropism	
makup	make·up		mal·a·prop·ism
malace	mal·ice	mallaria	ma·lar·ia
maladdy	mal·a·dy	mallarkey	ma·lar·key
maladroyt	mal·a·droit	mallcontent	mal·con·tent
malaize	ma·laise	mallerd	mal·lard
malaprapism		mallevolence	
	mal·a·prop·ism		malev·o·lence
malard	mal·lard	mallevolent	malev·o·lent
malasses	mo·las·ses	mallfeasance	
malatto	mu·lat·to		mal·fea·sance
malayse	ma·laise	mallformation	
malcantent	mal·con·tent		mal·for·ma·tion
male	mail *(letters)*	mallfunction	
maleable	mal·le·a·ble		mal·func·tion
malee	me·lee	mallice	mal·ice
maleria	ma·lar·ia	mallicious	ma·li·cious
malest	mo·lest	mallify	mol·li·fy
malet	mal·let	mallignant	ma·lig·nant

WRONG	RIGHT
mallinger	**ma·lin·ger**
mallit	**mal·let**
mallnourished	**mal·nour·ished**
mallnutrition	**mal·nu·tri·tion**
mallodorous	**mal·o·dor·ous**
mallpractice	**mal·prac·tice**
mallted	**malt·ed**
malnurished	**mal·nour·ished**
maloderous	**mal·o·dor·ous**
mamal	**mam·mal**
mamary	**mam·ma·ry**
mame	**maim**
mammagraphy	**mam·mog·ra·phy**
mammel	**mam·mal**
mammery	**mam·ma·ry**
mammeth	**mam·moth**
mammry	**mam·ma·ry**
mamogram	**mam·mo·gram**
mamography	**mam·mog·ra·phy**
mamoth	**mam·moth**
mana	**man·na**
manacal	**man·a·cle**
manacotti	**man·i·cot·ti**
manacure	**man·i·cure**
manafest	**man·i·fest**
manafesto	**man·i·fes·to**
manafold	**man·i·fold**
managable	**man·age·a·ble**

WRONG	RIGHT
manageing	**man·ag·ing**
managemint	**man·age·ment**
managerie	**me·nag·er·ie**
managment	**man·age·ment**
managor	**man·ag·er**
manarch	**mon·arch**
manarchy	**mon·ar·chy**
mancion	**man·sion**
mandable	**man·di·ble**
mandalin	**man·do·lin**
mander	**maun·der**
manderin	**man·da·rin**
mandetory	**man·da·to·ry**
mandolen	**man·do·lin**
mane	**main** *(important)*
manea	**ma·nia**
maneac	**ma·ni·ac**
manefest	**man·i·fest**
manege	**man·age** *(control)*
maneger	**man·ag·er**
manequin	**man·ne·quin**
maner	**man·ner** *(method)*
manerism	**man·ner·ism**
manestery	**mon·as·tery**
manetain	**main·tain**
mangel	**man·gle**
mangey	**man·gy**
mangleing	**man·gling**
mangrel	**mon·grel**
Manhatten	**Man·hat·tan**
maniack	**ma·ni·ac**
maniacle	**ma·ni·a·cal**

130

WRONG	RIGHT
manicle	**man·a·cle**
manicurest	**man·i·cur·ist**
manifess	**man·i·fest**
manifessto	**man·i·fes·to**
manilla	**ma·nila**
manipalate	**manip·u·late**
maniplative	**manip·u·la·tive**
manippulate	**manip·u·late**
manipulater	**manip·u·la·tor**
manitor	**mon·i·tor**
manje	**mange**
manjer	**man·ger**
mankine	**man·kind**
manley	**man·ly**
mannacle	**man·a·cle**
mannage	**man·age** *(control)*
mannaise	**may·on·naise**
manndate	**man·date**
mannekin	**man·ne·quin**
manner	**man·or** *(estate)*
manneuver	**ma·neu·ver**
mannicure	**man·i·cure**
mannifest	**man·i·fest**
mannifesto	**man·i·fes·to**
mannifold	**man·i·fold**
mannila	**ma·nila**
mannipulate	**manip·u·late**
mannor	**man·ner** *(method)*
mannsion	**man·sion**
mannual	**man·u·al**

WRONG	RIGHT
mannufacture	**man·u·fac·ture**
mannure	**ma·nure**
manocle	**mon·o·cle**
manogamy	**mo·nog·a·my**
manologue	**mon·o·logue**
manopolize	**mo·nop·o·lize**
manopoly	**mo·nop·o·ly**
manotonous	**mo·not·o·nous**
manslotter	**man·slaugh·ter**
mansoon	**mon·soon**
manster	**mon·ster**
manstrosity	**mon·stros·i·ty**
mantal	**man·tel** *(shelf)*
mantel	**man·tle** *(cloak)*
mantice	**man·tis**
mantle	**man·tel** *(shelf)*
manuel	**man·u·al**
manuer	**ma·nure**
manuever	**ma·neu·ver**
manufacter	**man·u·fac·ture**
manuskript	**man·u·script**
manuver	**ma·neu·ver**
manyascript	**man·u·script**
mapel	**ma·ple**
maping	**map·ping**
marader	**ma·raud·er**
maragold	**mar·i·gold**
maranade	**mar·i·nade**
maranara	**ma·ri·na·ra**
maranate	**mar·i·nate** *(v.)*

WRONG	RIGHT	WRONG	RIGHT
maraner	**mar·i·ner**	mariuana	**ma·ri·jua·na**
marascheno	**mar·a·schi·no**	marjeram	**mar·jo·ram**
maratal	**mar·i·tal**		*(plant)*
	(of marriage)	marjin	**mar·gin**
maratime	**mar·i·time**	marjinalia	**mar·gi·na·lia**
marbel	**mar·ble**	marjorine	**mar·ga·rine**
marbleing	**mar·bling**		*(spread)*
mare	**may·or** *(official)*	markee	**mar·quee**
mareachi	**ma·ri·a·chi**	marketible	**mar·ket·a·ble**
marejuana	**ma·ri·jua·na**	marketting	**mar·ket·ing**
marena	**ma·ri·na**	markidly	**mark·ed·ly**
marenate	**mar·i·nate** *(v.)*	markit	**mar·ket**
marene	**ma·rine**	Marksism	**Marxism**
mareonette	**mar·i·o·nette**	marlen	**mar·lin** *(fish)*
margen	**mar·gin**	marmelade	**mar·ma·lade**
margenalia	**mar·gi·na·lia**	marow	**mar·row**
margerine	**mar·ga·rine**	marquey	**mar·quee**
	(spread)	marr	**mar**
marginale	**mar·gin·al**	marraca	**ma·ra·ca**
marginallia	**mar·gi·na·lia**	marrage	**mar·riage**
marginel	**mar·gin·al**	marraschino	
margrin	**mar·ga·rine**		**mar·a·schi·no**
	(spread)	marrathon	**mar·a·thon**
mariage	**mar·riage**	marrble	**mar·ble**
marianette	**mar·i·o·nette**	marriachi	**ma·ri·a·chi**
maridian	**me·rid·i·an**	marriagable	
maried	**mar·ried**		**mar·riage·a·ble**
maring	**mar·ring**	marriege	**mar·riage**
maringue	**me·ringue**	marrigold	**mar·i·gold**
	(pie topping)	marrijuana	**ma·ri·jua·na**
marinnara	**ma·ri·na·ra**	marrimba	**ma·rim·ba**
marionet	**mar·i·o·nette**	marrinade	**mar·i·nade**
marital	**mar·tial** *(military)*	marrinara	**ma·ri·na·ra**
maritle	**mar·i·tal**	marrinate	**mar·i·nate** *(v.)*
	(of marriage)	marrionette	**mar·i·o·nette**

WRONG	RIGHT
marrital	**mar·i·tal** *(of marriage)*
marry	**mer·ry** *(happy)*
marryed	**mar·ried**
marshal	**mar·tial** *(military)*
marshall	**mar·shal** *(law officer)*
Marshen	**Mar·tian** *(of Mars)*
marshmellow	**marsh·mal·low**
Marsian	**Mar·tian** *(of Mars)*
marsipan	**mar·zi·pan**
marsupeal	**mar·su·pi·al**
marten	**mar·tin** *(bird)*
martenet	**mar·ti·net**
martengale	**mar·tin·gale**
marteni	**mar·ti·ni**
marter	**mar·tyr**
martial	**mar·i·tal** *(of marriage)*
martial	**mar·shal** *(law officer)*
martin	**mar·ten** *(mammal)*
Martin	**Mar·tian** *(of Mars)*
martinette	**mar·ti·net**
martordom	**mar·tyr·dom**
marune	**ma·roon**
marvalous	**mar·vel·ous**
marvell	**mar·vel**
marvelus	**mar·vel·ous**
marygold	**mar·i·gold**
marzapan	**mar·zi·pan**

WRONG	RIGHT
masa	**me·sa**
masachism	**mas·o·chism**
Masachusetts	**Mas·sa·chu·setts**
masacre	**mas·sa·cre**
masage	**mas·sage** *(a rubbing)*
masc	**mask** *(cover)*
mascera	**mas·ca·ra**
mascet	**mas·cot**
masculen	**mas·cu·line**
mase	**mace**
masen	**ma·son**
masenry	**ma·son·ry**
maseur	**mas·seur** *(m.)*
maseuse	**mas·seuse** *(f.)*
mashete	**ma·che·te**
mashination	**mach·i·na·tion**
mashine	**ma·chine**
masive	**mas·sive**
mask	**masque** *(masked ball)*
maskara	**mas·ca·ra**
maskerade	**mas·quer·ade**
maskot	**mas·cot**
maskuline	**mas·cu·line**
masokism	**mas·o·chism**
masoleum	**mau·so·le·um**
masonrey	**ma·son·ry**
masque	**mask** *(cover)*
masquito	**mos·qui·to**
masquorade	**mas·quer·ade**
massacer	**mas·sa·cre**

WRONG	RIGHT
Massachusets	**Mas·sa·chu·setts**
massage	**mes·sage** *(communication)*
massaje	**mas·sage** *(a rubbing)*
massakre	**mas·sa·cre**
masscara	**mas·ca·ra**
massectomy	**mas·tec·to·my**
masser	**mas·seur** *(m.)*
massiah	**mes·si·ah**
massochism	**mas·o·chism**
masson	**ma·son**
Massonic	**Ma·son·ic**
massquerade	**mas·quer·ade**
massticate	**mas·ti·cate**
masstiff	**mas·tiff**
masstodon	**mas·to·don**
massuer	**mas·seur** *(m.)*
massuse	**mas·seuse** *(f.)*
mastacate	**mas·ti·cate**
mastadon	**mas·to·don**
mastead	**mast·head**
masterbate	**mas·tur·bate**
masterey	**mas·tery**
masterfull	**mas·ter·ful**
masterley	**mas·ter·ly**
mastermine	**mas·ter·mind**
masterry	**mas·tery**
mastro	**ma·es·tro**
mat	**matte** *(dull finish)*
matabolism	**me·tab·o·lism**

WRONG	RIGHT
matallic	**me·tal·lic**
matcher	**ma·ture** *(full-grown)*
matchuration	**mat·u·ra·tion**
mateing	**mat·ing** *(joining)*
matenee	**mat·i·nee**
mater de	**mai·tre d'**
material	**ma·te·ri·el** *(supplies)*
materiallism	**ma·te·ri·al·ism**
materiallize	**ma·te·ri·al·ize**
materiel	**ma·te·ri·al** *(cloth)*
maternaty	**ma·ter·ni·ty**
maternel	**ma·ter·nal**
math	**moth**
mathamatical	**math·e·mat·i·cal**
mathematicks	**math·e·mat·ics**
mathematitian	**math·e·ma·ti·cian**
mathmatical	**math·e·mat·i·cal**
mathmatician	**math·e·ma·ti·cian**
mathmatics	**math·e·matics**
maticulous	**metic·u·lous**
matinay	**mat·i·nee**
mating	**mat·ting** *(interweaving)*

WRONG	RIGHT	WRONG	RIGHT
matirial	**ma·te·ri·al** *(cloth)*	maudlen	**maud·lin**
matiriel	**ma·te·ri·el**	maukish	**mawk·ish**
	(supplies)	maul	**mall**
matoor	**ma·ture**		*(shopping center)*
	(full-grown)	mausolium	**mau·so·le·um**
matramonial		mave	**mauve** *(purple)*
	mat·ri·mo·ni·al	mavrick	**mav·er·ick**
matrearch	**ma·tri·arch**	maxamal	**max·i·mal**
matre d'	**mai·tre d'**	maxamize	**max·i·mize**
matren	**ma·tron**	maxamum	**max·i·mum**
matress	**mat·tress**	maxem	**max·im**
matriark	**ma·tri·arch**	mayem	**may·hem**
matricks	**ma·trix**	mayer	**may·or** *(official)*
matrickulate	**matric·u·late**	mayme	**maim**
matriculateing		mayonaise	**may·on·naise**
	matric·u·lat·ing	mayorality	**may·or·al·ty**
matrimonal		maze	**maize** *(corn)*
	mat·ri·mo·ni·al	mcintosh	**mack·in·tosh**
matriside	**mat·ri·cide**		*(coat)*
mattador	**mat·a·dor**	meak	**meek**
matte	**mat**	mean	**mien** *(manner)*
	(floor covering)	meanial	**me·ni·al**
matter	**mad·der** *(angrier)*	meaningfull	**mean·ing·ful**
mattinee	**mat·i·nee**	meanning	**mean·ing**
matting	**mat·ing** *(joining)*	measels	**mea·sles**
mattled	**mot·tled**	measley	**mea·sly**
mattriculate	**matric·u·late**	measureable	
mattrimonial			**meas·ur·a·ble**
	mat·ri·mo·ni·al	measureing	**meas·ur·ing**
mattrimony	**mat·ri·mo·ny**	measurment	
mattriss	**mat·tress**		**meas·ure·ment**
matturation	**mat·u·ra·tion**	meat	**meet** *(encounter)*
maturaty	**ma·tu·ri·ty**	meat	**mete** *(distribute)*
maturnal	**ma·ter·nal**	meatey	**meaty**
maturnity	**ma·ter·ni·ty**	meazles	**mea·sles**

WRONG	RIGHT
meazure	**meas·ure**
mebbe	**may·be**
mecaw	**ma·caw**
mechanicle	**me·chan·i·cal**
mechannic	**me·chan·ic**
mechenism	**mech·a·nism**
meckanic	**me·chan·ic**
meckanism	**mech·a·nism**
medacal	**med·i·cal**
medacation	**med·i·ca·tion**
medal	**med·dle** *(interfere)*
medal	**met·al** *(iron, etc.)*
medalion	**me·dal·lion**
medatation	**med·i·ta·tion**
Medaterranean	
	Med·i·ter·ra·ne·an
meddallion	**me·dal·lion**
meddication	
	med·i·ca·tion
Meddilterranean	
	Med·i·ter·ra·ne·an
meddle	**med·al** *(award)*
meddle	**met·tle** *(courage)*
meddlesum	
	med·dle·some
medea	**me·dia**
medean	**me·di·an**
medecine	**med·i·cine**
Medeira	**Ma·dei·ra**
medel	**med·al** *(award)*
medelist	**med·al·ist**
medeocre	**me·di·o·cre**
medeocrity	**me·di·oc·ri·ty**
medeum	**me·di·um**
medeval	**me·di·e·val**

WRONG	RIGHT
mediateing	**me·di·at·ing**
mediater	**me·di·a·tor**
medicel	**med·i·cal**
medick	**med·ic**
medievil	**me·di·e·val**
mediocer	**me·di·o·cre**
mediocraty	**me·di·oc·ri·ty**
mediokre	**me·di·o·cre**
medion	**me·di·an**
medisinal	**me·dic·i·nal**
medisine	**med·i·cine**
Mediteranean	
	Med·i·ter·ra·ne·an
medle	**med·dle** *(interfere)*
medlesome	**med·dle·some**
medly	**med·ley**
medow	**mead·ow**
meeger	**mea·ger**
meel	**meal**
meen	**mean** *(middle)*
meer	**mere**
meesles	**mea·sles**
meesly	**mea·sly**
meet	**meat** *(food)*
meet	**mete** *(distribute)*
meeting	**met·ing** *(distributing)*
meetting	**meet·ing** *(encountering)*
megabite	**meg·a·byte**
megallopolis	
	meg·a·lop·o·lis
meggaphone	
	meg·a·phone
meggaton	**meg·a·ton**

WRONG	RIGHT	WRONG	RIGHT
meladic	**me·lod·ic**	memor	**mem·oir**
meladrama	**mel·o·dra·ma**	memorabillia	
melady	**mel·o·dy**		**mem·o·ra·bil·ia**
melaise	**ma·laise**	memorandom	
melan	**mel·on**		**mem·o·ran·dum**
melancolly	**mel·an·choly**	memoreal	**me·mo·ri·al**
melaria	**ma·lar·ia**	memrable	**mem·o·ra·ble**
melay	**me·lee**	memry	**mem·o·ry**
meld	**melt** *(dissolve)*	memwar	**mem·oir**
melenoma	**mel·a·no·ma**	menajerie	**me·nag·er·ie**
melinger	**ma·lin·ger**	menapause	**men·o·pause**
melinkoly	**mel·an·choly**	menase	**men·ace**
melled	**meld**	menastrate	**men·stru·ate**
	(cards; blend)	mendacant	**men·di·cant**
mellodic	**me·lod·ic**	meneal	**me·ni·al**
mellodious	**me·lo·di·ous**	menice	**men·ace**
mellodrama	**mel·o·dra·ma**	mennopause	
mellody	**mel·o·dy**		**men·o·pause**
mellon	**mel·on**	menshun	**men·tion**
mellt	**melt** *(dissolve)*	menstrate	**men·stru·ate**
melodick	**me·lod·ic**	menstrul	**men·stru·al**
melodius	**me·lo·di·ous**	ment	**meant** *(pt. of mean)*
melow	**mel·low**	ment	**mint**
melt	**meld** *(cards; blend)*	mentallity	**men·tal·i·ty**
memarandum		mentaly	**men·tal·ly**
	mem·o·ran·dum	mentel	**men·tal**
membor	**mem·ber**	menthal	**men·thol**
membrain	**mem·brane**	mently	**men·tal·ly**
memerabilia		menue	**menu**
	mem·o·ra·bil·ia	merange	**me·ringue**
memerize	**mem·o·rize**		*(pie topping)*
memery	**mem·o·ry**	meraschino	**mar·a·schi·no**
memior	**mem·oir**	merathon	**mar·a·thon**
memmorial	**me·mo·ri·al**	merauder	**ma·raud·er**
memmorize	**mem·o·rize**	mercanary	**mer·ce·nary**

WRONG	RIGHT	WRONG	RIGHT
merchendise ....**mer·chan·dise**		mesage ....**mes·sage** *(communication)*	
merchent............**mer·chant**		mesenger ....**mes·sen·ger**	
mercurey..............**mer·cu·ry**		mesiah.................**mes·si·ah**	
mercyful ....**mer·ci·ful**		message ....**mas·sage** *(a rubbing)*	
mercyless............**mer·ci·less**		messinger ....**mes·sen·ger**	
merder ....**mur·der**		mesure.................**meas·ure**	
mere .....**mare** *(female horse)*		metabalism ...**me·tab·o·lism**	
meret ....**mer·it**		metafor ....**met·a·phor**	
meretorious....................... ....**mer·i·to·ri·ous**		metal.......**med·al** *(award)*	
meridean ....**me·rid·i·an**		metal........**met·tle** *(courage)*	
merinade ....**mar·i·nade**		metalic ....**me·tal·lic**	
merine ....**ma·rine**		metalurgy ....**met·al·lur·gy**	
meritorius ....**mer·i·to·ri·ous**		metamorfosis ....**met·a·mor·pho·sis** *(sing.)*	
merje ....**merge**			
merkantile ....**mer·can·tile**		metamorphick ....**met·a·mor·phic**	
merky.....................**murky**		metamorphosis ....**met·a·mor·pho·ses** *(pl.)*	
merly ....**mere·ly**			
mermade ....**mer·maid**		mete ....**meet** *(encounter)*	
mermur ....**mur·mur**		mete ....**meat** *(food)*	
merridian..........**me·rid·i·an**		metear ....**me·te·or**	
merrimint ....**mer·ri·ment**		metearology ....**mete·or·ol·o·gy**	
merrit ....**mer·it**			
merritorious ....**mer·i·to·ri·ous**		meteing ....**met·ing** *(distributing)*	
merrow ....**mar·row**		metellurgy ......**met·al·lur·gy**	
merry ....**mar·ry** *(wed)*		meterology ....**mete·or·ol·o·gy**	
merryment ......**mer·ri·ment**			
mersenary ....**mer·ce·nary**		methadical......**method·i·cal**	
mersiful...............**mer·ci·ful**		methadology....................... ....**meth·od·ol·o·gy**	
mersiless..............**mer·ci·less**			
mersy ....**mer·cy**			
merth ....**mirth**			

138

methed ....**meth·od**
meticulous.....**metic·u·lous**
meting ....**meeting**
　　　　　(encountering)
metle.........**met·tle** *(courage)*
metomorphosis...................
.........**met·a·mor·pho·sis**
　　　　　　　　(sing.)
metranome ....**met·ro·nome**
metrapolitan ....
............**met·ro·pol·i·tan**
metrick ....**met·ric**
metricle ....**met·ri·cal**
metropollitan ....
............**met·ro·pol·i·tan**
mettabolism ....
...............**me·tab·o·lism**
mettal.......**met·al** *(iron, etc.)*
mettamorphic ....
...............**met·a·mor·phic**
mettamorphosis ....
........**met·a·mor·pho·sis**
　　　　　　　　(sing.)
mettaphor.........**met·a·phor**
metticulous .....**metic·u·lous**
mettronome ....
...............**met·ro·nome**
mettropolitan ....
............**met·ro·pol·i·tan**
Mexaco................**Mex·i·co**
mezanine ....**mez·za·nine**
mezmerize ....**mes·mer·ize**
Micheal ....**Mi·chael**
micraphone ....
.................**mi·cro·phone**

micrascope .....**mi·cro·scope**
micrawave ....**mi·cro·wave**
microfeche ....**mi·cro·fiche**
microfone......**mi·cro·phone**
microscopec ....
...............**mi·cro·scop·ic**
micsellanious ....
............**mis·cel·la·ne·ous**
miday....................**mid·day**
middair ....**mid·air**
middel ....**mid·dle**
middleing............**mid·dling**
midgit ....**midg·et**
midieval ....**me·di·e·val**
midle.....................**mid·dle**
midling...............**mid·dling**
midruff..................**mid·riff**
mien ....**mean** *(middle)*
miget ....**midg·et**
might ....**mite**
　　　(insect; small amount)
migrane ....**mi·graine**
migrateing ....**mi·grat·ing**
migrent ....**mi·grant**
mika ....**mi·ca**
mikrofiche ....**mi·cro·fiche**
mikrofilm ....**mi·cro·film**
milatary ....**mil·i·tary**
mildley...................**mild·ly**
mildue..................**mil·dew**
mileiu ....**mi·lieu**
milenium.......**mil·len·ni·um**
milicia ....**mi·li·tia**
miligram............**mil·li·gram**
milimeter.........**mil·li·me·ter**

WRONG	RIGHT
milinery	**mil·li·nery**
	(hat shop)
milion	**mil·lion**
milionaire	**mil·lion·aire**
militent	**mil·i·tant**
militery	**mil·i·tary**
miliue	**mi·lieu**
milktoast	**milque·toast**
	(timid person)
milkyness	**milk·i·ness**
millagram	**mil·li·gram**
millameter	**mil·li·me·ter**
milldew	**mil·dew**
milleage	**mile·age**
millenary	**mil·li·nery**
	(hat shop)
millenium	**mil·len·ni·um**
millieu	**mi·lieu**
millinery	**mil·le·nary**
	(a thousand)
millionare	**mil·lion·aire**
millit	**mil·let**
millitant	**mil·i·tant**
millitary	**mil·i·tary**
millitia	**mi·li·tia**
milliun	**mil·lion**
Millwaukee	**Mil·wau·kee**
mimeagraph	
	mim·e·o·graph
mimick	**mim·ic**
mimickry	**mim·ic·ry**
mimmeograph	
	mim·e·o·graph
mimmic	**mim·ic**
minamal	**min·i·mal**

WRONG	RIGHT
minamum	**min·i·mum**
minarity	**mi·nor·i·ty**
minaster	**min·is·ter**
minasterial	**min·is·te·ri·al**
minastrone	**mine·strone**
minature	**min·i·a·ture**
minceing	**minc·ing**
mind	**mine** *(pron.)*
mine	**mind** *(intellect)*
miner	**mi·nor**
	(underage person)
minerel	**min·er·al**
Minesota	**Min·ne·so·ta**
miniscule	**mi·nus·cule**
ministery	**min·is·try**
ministrone	**mine·strone**
minits	**min·utes**
miniture	**min·i·a·ture**
Minnasota	**Min·ne·so·ta**
minneral	**min·er·al**
minnestrone	**mine·strone**
minniature	**min·i·a·ture**
minnicam	**min·i·cam**
minnimal	**min·i·mal**
minnimum	**min·i·mum**
minnister	**min·is·ter**
minnisterial	**min·is·te·ri·al**
minor	**min·er**
	(mine worker)
minoraty	**mi·nor·i·ty**
minow	**min·now**
minsing	**minc·ing**
mint	**meant** *(pt. of mean)*
mintion	**men·tion**
mintsmeat	**mince·meat**

WRONG	RIGHT	WRONG	RIGHT
minuette	**min·u·et**	misscarriage	**...mis·car·riage**
minural	**min·er·al**	misscellaneous	
minuts	**min·utes**		**...mis·cel·la·ne·ous**
miracel	**mir·a·cle**	misschief	**...mis·chief**
mirackulous	**mirac·u·lous**	misschievous	
miraje	**mi·rage**		**...mis·chie·vous**
miriad	**myr·i·ad**	missconstrue	
miricle	**mir·a·cle**		**...mis·con·strue**
mirrage	**mi·rage**	missdemeanor	
mirrer	**mir·ror**		**...mis·de·mean·or**
mirrh	**myrrh**	missellaneous	
mirtle	**myr·tle**		**...mis·cel·la·ne·ous**
miscarrege	**mis·car·riage**	missfit	**...mis·fit**
miscelaneous		missfortune	**...mis·for·tune**
	...mis·cel·la·ne·ous	missile	**mis·sal** *(book)*
mischeif	**mis·chief**	missionery	**mis·sion·ary**
mischevious		Missisippi	**Mis·sis·sippi**
	...mis·chie·vous	missle	**mis·sile** *(projectile)*
misconstrew		misslead	**mis·lead**
	...mis·con·strue	missletoe	**mis·tle·toe**
misdemeaner		missogynist	**mis·og·y·nist**
	...mis·de·mean·or	missplace	**mis·place**
mishapen	**mis·shap·en**	misspronounce	
misile	**mis·sile**		**...mis·pro·nounce**
mision	**mis·sion**	missrepresent	
misionary	**mis·sion·ary**		**...mis·rep·re·sent**
Misissippi	**Mis·sis·sippi**	misstake	**mis·take**
Misouri	**Mis·souri**	misstress	**mis·tress**
mispell	**mis·spell**	misstrial	**mis·tri·al**
mispernounce		Missuri	**Mis·souri**
	...mis·pro·nounce	mist	**midst** *(middle)*
misrable	**mis·er·a·ble**	misterious	**mys·te·ri·ous**
misrey	**mis·ery**	mistey	**misty**
missal	**mis·sile** *(projectile)*	mistical	**mys·ti·cal**
missap	**mis·hap**	misticism	**mys·ti·cism**

141

WRONG	RIGHT	WRONG	RIGHT
mistify	**mys·ti·fy**	modifecation	**mod·i·fi·ca·tion**
mistique	**mys·ti·que**	modjule	**mod·ule**
mistriss	**mis·tress**	modlin	**maud·lin**
mistro	**ma·es·tro**	modren	**mod·ern**
mitagate	**mit·i·gate**	moduler	**mod·u·lar**
mite	**might** (aux.v.; power)	mogel	**mo·gul**
miten	**mit·ten**	moing	**mow·ing**
mithical	**myth·i·cal**	moissen	**mois·ten**
mithological	**myth·o·log·i·cal**	moister	**mois·ture** (wetness)
mithology	**my·thol·o·gy**	molacule	**mol·e·cule**
mitst	**midst** (middle)	molases	**mo·las·ses**
mittigate	**mit·i·gate**	moldey	**moldy**
mittin	**mit·ten**	moleculer	**mo·lec·u·lar**
mixchure	**mix·ture**	moler	**mo·lar**
mizer	**mi·ser**	molesstation	**moles·ta·tion**
mizerable	**mis·er·a·ble**	molify	**mol·li·fy**
mizery	**mis·ery**	mollecular	**mo·lec·u·lar**
mnemonick	**mne·mon·ic**	mollecule	**mol·e·cule**
moan	**mown** (pp. of mow)	mollesk	**mol·lusk**
moat	**mote** (particle)	mollest	**mo·lest**
mobillize	**mo·bi·lize**	mollestation	**moles·ta·tion**
moble	**mo·bile**	mollten	**mol·ten**
mockasin	**moc·ca·sin**	molusk	**mol·lusk**
mockry	**mock·ery**	momentem	**mo·men·tum**
modal	**mod·el** (a copy)	momenterily	**momen·tar·i·ly**
modallity	**mo·dal·i·ty**	momentery	**mo·men·tary**
modaration	**mod·er·a·tion**	momento	**me·men·to**
moddern	**mod·ern**	momentus	**mo·men·tous**
moddest	**mod·est**	momint	**mo·ment**
moddo	**mot·to**	monacle	**mon·o·cle**
modecum	**mod·i·cum**	monagamy	**mo·nog·a·my**
modefier	**mod·i·fi·er**	monagram	**mon·o·gram**
model	**mod·al** (of a mode)		
moderater	**mod·er·a·tor**		

WRONG	RIGHT	WRONG	RIGHT
monagraph	mon·o·graph	monostery	mon·as·tery
monalith	mon·o·lith	monotany	mo·not·o·ny
monalogue	mon·o·logue	monotnous	
monapolize	mo·nop·o·lize		mo·not·o·nous
monapoly	mo·nop·o·ly	Monseigneur	Mon·si·gnor
monarcical	mo·nar·chi·cal		*(Catholic title)*
monarcy	mon·ar·chy	Monsignor	Mon·sei·gneur
monark	mon·arch		*(French title)*
monasstic	mo·nas·tic	monstrosaty	
monastary	mon·as·tery		mon·stros·i·ty
monatone	mon·o·tone	monstrus	mon·strous
monder	maun·der	monsune	mon·soon
mone	moan *(groan)*	montaj	mon·tage
mone	mown *(pp. of mow)*	monthley	month·ly
mongrul	mon·grel	monumentel	
monimental			mon·u·men·tal
	mon·u·men·tal	mony	money
monitary	mon·e·tary	mooce	moose
moniter	mon·i·tor	moodey	moody
monky	mon·key	mool	mule
monnarchical		moor	more *(additional)*
	mo·nar·chi·cal	moosse	mousse *(food)*
monnetary	mon·e·tary	moping	mop·ping
monney	mon·ey		*(washing)*
monnitor	mon·i·tor	mopping	mop·ing
monnogram	mon·o·gram		*(sulking)*
monnolith	mon·o·lith	moral	mo·rale *(spirit)*
monnotny	mo·not·o·ny	moralaty	mo·ral·i·ty
monnumental		morale	mor·al *(ethical)*
	mon·u·men·tal	morall	mo·rale *(spirit)*
mononukleosis		morallistic	mor·al·is·tic
	mon·o·nu·cle·o·sis	morallity	mo·ral·i·ty
monoply	mo·nop·o·ly	moran	mo·ron
monopollize		moratoreum	
	mo·nop·o·lize		mor·a·to·ri·um

WRONG	RIGHT
morays	**mo·res**
morbed	**mor·bid**
morbidety	**mor·bid·i·ty**
morchuary	**mor·tu·ary**
more	**moor** (secure a ship)
morel	**mor·al** (ethical)
morelistick	**mor·al·is·tic**
morfine	**mor·phine**
morgage	**mort·gage**
morge	**morgue**
moring	**moor·ing**
moritorium	**mor·a·to·ri·um**
Morman	**Mor·mon**
morning	**mourn·ing** (grieving)
morover	**more·over**
morphene	**mor·phine**
morral	**mor·al** (ethical)
morrale	**mo·rale** (spirit)
morrass	**mo·rass**
morratorium	**mor·a·to·ri·um**
morron	**mo·ron**
morrose	**mo·rose**
morsle	**mor·sel**
mortafy	**mor·ti·fy**
mortallity	**mor·tal·i·ty**
mortarbord	**mor·tar·board**
mortel	**mor·tal**
morter	**mor·tar**
mortgege	**mort·gage**
mortitian	**mor·ti·cian**
mortle	**mor·tal**

WRONG	RIGHT
mortuery	**mor·tu·ary**
mosaick	**mo·sa·ic**
mosion	**mo·tion**
mosk	**mosque**
moskito	**mos·qui·to**
mossoleum	**mau·so·le·um**
motavate	**mo·ti·vate**
mote	**moat** (ditch)
moteef	**mo·tif**
motell	**mo·tel**
moter	**mo·tor**
motercade	**mo·tor·cade**
motiff	**mo·tif**
motled	**mot·tled**
motly	**mot·ley**
moto	**mot·to**
motorcaid	**mo·tor·cade**
motorcross	**mo·to·cross**
motorcykle	**mo·tor·cy·cle**
motorest	**mo·tor·ist**
motsarella	**moz·za·rel·la**
mottel	**mo·tel** (inn)
mottivate	**mo·ti·vate**
mottley	**mot·ley**
mouce	**mouse** (rodent)
mounteneer	**moun·tain·eer**
mountin	**moun·tain**
mountnous	**moun·tain·ous**
mournfull	**mourn·ful**
mourning	**morn·ing** (part of day)
mouse	**mousse** (food)
mouthfull	**mouth·ful**

WRONG	RIGHT
move	**mauve** *(purple)*
moveing	**mov·ing**
movemint	**move·ment**
movey	**mov·ie**
movible	**mov·a·ble**
movment	**move·ment**
mown	**moan** *(groan)*
mownd	**mound**
mownt	**mount**
mowse	**mouse** *(rodent)*
mowthful	**mouth·ful**
mowwing	**mow·ing**
moysture	**mois·ture** *(wetness)*
mozaic	**mo·sa·ic**
mozarella	**moz·za·rella**
muchually	**mu·tu·al·ly**
mucous	**mu·cus** *(n.)*
mucsle	**mus·cle** *(brawn)*
mucus	**mu·cous** *(adj.)*
muddey	**mud·dy**
mudey	**moody**
mudled	**mud·dled**
muffen	**muf·fin**
mufler	**muf·fler**
muger	**mug·ger**
muggey	**mug·gy**
mukraker	**muck·rak·er**
mulato	**mu·lat·to**
mulet	**mul·let**
mullberry	**mul·ber·ry**
mullish	**mul·ish**
mullit	**mul·let**
multafarious	**mul·ti·far·i·ous**

WRONG	RIGHT
multaple	**mul·ti·ple**
multaplication	**mul·ti·pli·ca·tion**
multaplicity	**mul·ti·plic·i·ty**
multatude	**mul·ti·tude**
multatudinous	**mul·ti·tu·di·nous**
multch	**mulch**
multecultural	**mul·ti·cul·tur·al**
multeplexer	**mul·ti·plex·er**
multifairious	**mul·ti·far·i·ous**
multipal	**mul·ti·ple**
multiplacation	**mul·ti·pli·ca·tion**
multiplisity	**mul·ti·plic·i·ty**
multitudanous	**mul·ti·tu·di·nous**
mumbleing	**mum·bling**
mummyfy	**mum·mi·fy**
mundain	**mun·dane**
Munday	**Mon·day**
munger	**mon·ger**
municipallity	**mu·nic·i·pal·i·ty**
municiple	**mu·nic·i·pal**
munifisent	**munif·i·cent**
munisipality	**mu·nic·i·pal·i·ty**
munk	**monk**
munkey	**mon·key**
munnitions	**mu·ni·tions**
munth	**month**

murcantile	**mer·can·tile**	musstache	**mus·tache**
murcurial	**mer·cu·ri·al**	musterd	**mus·tard**
murcury	**mer·cu·ry**	mutanous	**mu·ti·nous**
murcy	**mer·cy**	mute	**moot** *(debatable)*
murderus	**mur·der·ous**	muteable	**mu·ta·ble**
murel	**mu·ral**	mutent	**mu·tant**
murge	**merge**	muteny	**mu·ti·ny**
murkey	**murky**	muther	**moth·er**
murmer	**mur·mur**	mutible	**mu·ta·ble**
murral	**mu·ral**	mutillate	**mu·ti·late**
murtle	**myr·tle**	mutinus	**mu·ti·nous**
muscet	**mus·ket**	mutten	**mut·ton**
muscle	**mus·sel** *(shellfish)*	muttilate	**mu·ti·late**
muscrat	**musk·rat**	mutualy	**mu·tu·al·ly**
musculer	**mus·cu·lar**	muzeum	**mu·se·um**
museing	**mus·ing**	muzic	**mu·sic**
mushmelon	**musk·mel·on**	muzical	**mu·si·cal**
mushrum	**mush·room**		*(of music)*
musicall	**mu·si·cale**	muzle	**muz·zle**
	(social affair)	muzlin	**mus·lin**
musick	**mu·sic**	myread	**myr·i·ad**
musicle	**mu·si·cal**	myrh	**myrrh**
	(of music)	myrtel	**myr·tle**
musitian	**mu·si·cian**	mysoginist	**mis·og·y·nist**
musium	**mu·se·um**	mystefy	**mys·ti·fy**
muskatel	**mus·ca·tel**	mysteke	**mys·tique**
muskey	**musky**	mysterius	**mys·te·ri·ous**
muskit	**mus·ket**	mystickal	**mys·ti·cal**
muskmellon	**musk·mel·on**	mystirious	**mys·te·ri·ous**
muslen	**mus·lin**	mystisism	**mys·ti·cism**
mussey	**mussy**	mystry	**mys·tery**
mussle	**mus·sel** *(shellfish)*	mythalogical	
mussle	**mus·cle** *(brawn)*		**myth·o·log·i·cal**
mussmelon	**musk·mel·on**	mythalogy	**my·thol·o·gy**
mussrat	**musk·rat**	mythicel	**myth·i·cal**

N

WRONG	RIGHT
Nabraska	Ne·bras·ka
nachure	na·ture
nack	knack
nader	na·dir
naeve	na·ive
naevete	na·ive·té
naghty	naugh·ty
nagotiate	ne·go·ti·ate
naigh	neigh *(whinny)*
naivte	na·ive·té
namly	name·ly
namsake	name·sake
nannie	nan·ny
naped	napped
napken	nap·kin
napsack	knap·sack
naration	nar·ra·tion
narative	nar·ra·tive
narator	nar·ra·tor
narcisism	nar·cis·sism
naritive	nar·ra·tive
narkotic	nar·cot·ic
narled	gnarled
narow	nar·row
narrater	nar·ra·tor
narretive	nar·ra·tive
narsicism	nar·cis·sism
Nasau	Nas·sau

WRONG	RIGHT
nasel	na·sal
nashing	gnash·ing
Nassaw	Nas·sau
nastey	nas·ty
nat	gnat
natave	na·tive
natel	na·tal
naterallize	nat·u·ral·ize
naterally	nat·u·ral·ly
natetorium	nata·to·ri·um
natianally	nation·al·ly
natily	nat·ti·ly
nationallistic	
	nation·al·is·tic
nationallity	nation·al·i·ty
nationallize	nation·al·ize
nationaly	nation·al·ly
nativety	na·tiv·i·ty
nattally	nat·ti·ly
nattivity	na·tiv·i·ty
natur	na·ture
naturallize	nat·u·ral·ize
naturely	nat·u·ral·ly
naturralist	nat·u·ral·ist
nausiate	nau·se·ate
nausious	nau·seous
nauticle	nau·ti·cal
nauty	naugh·ty

WRONG	RIGHT	WRONG	RIGHT
Navada	**Ne·vada**	neckless	**neck·lace**
navagation	**nav·i·ga·tion**	necktarine	**nec·tar·ine**
navagible	**nav·i·ga·ble**	necsesary	**nec·es·sary**
naval	**na·vel** (*umbilicus*)	necter	**nec·tar**
nave	**knave** (*rogue*)	necterine	**nec·tar·ine**
navegator	**nav·i·ga·tor**	nee	**knee**
Naveho	**Nav·a·ho**	nee	**né** (*m.; born*)
navel	**na·val** (*of a navy*)	need	**knead** (*work dough*)
navery	**knav·ery**	neel	**kneel**
navice	**nov·ice**	nefew	**neph·ew**
navigater	**nav·i·ga·tor**	neggation	**ne·ga·tion**
navish	**knav·ish**	neggative	**neg·a·tive**
navvigation	**nav·i·ga·tion**	neggotiate	**ne·go·ti·ate**
nawing	**gnaw·ing**	neghbor	**neigh·bor**
nawtical	**nau·ti·cal**	negitive	**neg·a·tive**
nay	**neigh** (*whinny*)	neglagible	**neg·li·gi·ble**
nay	**nee** (*f.; born*)	negleck	**neg·lect**
nazel	**na·sal**	neglectfull	**neg·lect·ful**
Nazereth	**Naz·a·reth**	neglegee	**neg·li·gee**
Nazie	**Na·zi**	negligable	**neg·li·gi·ble**
nead	**knead** (*work dough*)	negligance	**neg·li·gence**
neaded	**need·ed** (*required*)	neglige	**neg·li·gee**
nealism	**ni·hil·ism**	neice	**niece**
nean	**ne·on**	neighber	**neigh·bor**
Neanderthol		neither	**neth·er** (*lower*)
	Nean·der·thal	neklace	**neck·lace**
neaphyte	**ne·o·phyte**	nektar	**nec·tar**
Neapollitan	**Nea·pol·i·tan**	nell	**knell**
neatenning	**neat·en·ing**	nemeses	**nem·e·sis** (*sing.*)
nebulla	**neb·u·la**	nemesis	**nem·e·ses** (*pl.*)
nebullous	**neb·u·lous**	nemonic	**mne·mon·ic**
necesary	**nec·es·sary**	neophite	**ne·o·phyte**
necesity	**ne·ces·si·ty**	Neopolitan	**Nea·pol·i·tan**
necessarally	**nec·es·sar·i·ly**	nepatism	**nep·o·tism**
neckercheif	**neck·er·chief**	neralgia	**neu·ral·gia**

WRONG	RIGHT
neroses	**neu·ro·ses** *(pl.)*
nerration	**nar·ra·tion**
nerture	**nur·ture**
nervana	**nir·va·na**
nervey	**nervy**
nervus	**nerv·ous**
nesesary	**nec·es·sary**
nesesity	**ne·ces·si·ty**
nessle	**nes·tle**
neted	**net·ted**
nether	**nei·ther** *(not either)*
Netherlords	**Neth·er·lands**
netled	**net·tled**
network	**net·work**
neuance	**nu·ance**
neumatic	**pneu·mat·ic**
neumonia	**pneu·mo·nia**
neurallgia	**neu·ral·gia**
neurollogy	**neu·rol·o·gy**
neuroses	**neu·ro·sis** *(sing.)*
neurosis	**neu·ro·ses** *(pl.)*
neurottic	**neu·rot·ic**
neute	**newt**
neuteron	**neu·tron**
neutrallity	**neu·tral·i·ty**
neutrallize	**neu·tral·ize**
neutril	**neu·tral**
neverthaless	**nev·er·the·less**
New Jersy	**New Jer·sey**
newliwed	**new·ly·wed**
New Orleens	**New Or·le·ans**
newral	**neu·ral**

WRONG	RIGHT
newveau riche	**nou·veau riche**
New Zeeland	**New Zea·land**
nexous	**nex·us**
ney	**nay** *(no)*
ney	**nee** *(f.; born)*
ney	**neigh** *(whinny)*
Niagera	**Ni·ag·a·ra**
nialism	**ni·hil·ism**
nibbeling	**nib·bling**
nicatine	**nic·o·tine**
niceaty	**ni·ce·ty**
Niceragua	**Nic·a·ra·gua**
nich	**niche**
nickers	**knick·ers** *(short pants)*
nickknack	**knick·knack**
nickotine	**nic·o·tine**
nicks	**nix** *(disapprove of)*
nie	**nigh**
nieghbor	**neigh·bor**
niese	**niece**
niether	**nei·ther** *(not either)*
nieve	**na·ive**
nife	**knife**
nigation	**ne·ga·tion**
night	**knight** *(rank)*
nightengale	**night·in·gale**
nightime	**night·time**
nightmair	**night·mare**
niglect	**neg·lect**
nihalism	**ni·hil·ism**
nikname	**nick·name**

WRONG	RIGHT
nikotine	**nic·o·tine**
nilon	**ny·lon**
nimbley	**nim·bly**
nimph	**nymph**
ninconpoop	**nin·com·poop**
ninje	**nin·ja**
ninteen	**nine·teen**
nintieth	**nine·ti·eth**
ninty	**nine·ty**
nior	**noir**
niped	**nipped**
nippel	**nip·ple**
nitch	**niche**
nitragen	**ni·tro·gen**
nitraglycerin	**ni·tro·glyc·er·in**
nitrait	**ni·trate**
nitrick	**ni·tric**
nitroglisserin	**ni·tro·glyc·er·in**
nittie-grittie	**nit·ty-grit·ty**
nitting	**knit·ting**
nittwit	**nit·wit**
niusance	**nui·sance**
nives	**knives**
Noa	**No·ah**
nobby	**knob·by**
nobel	**no·ble**
nobeler	**no·bler**
nobelman	**no·ble·man**
nobillity	**no·bil·i·ty**
Noble	**No·bel** (prize)
nobley	**no·bly**
nock	**knock** (rap)

WRONG	RIGHT
nockout	**knock·out**
nockwurst	**knack·wurst**
nocternal	**noc·tur·nal**
nodjule	**nod·ule**
Noell	**No·el**
noisally	**nois·i·ly**
noisey	**noisy**
noissome	**noi·some**
nomanee	**nom·i·nee**
nome	**gnome** (small being)
nominaly	**nom·i·nal·ly**
nominnation	**nom·i·na·tion**
nommad	**no·mad**
nomminally	**nom·i·nal·ly**
nommination	**nom·i·na·tion**
nomminee	**nom·i·nee**
non	**none**
noncense	**non·sense**
nonchallance	**non·cha·lance**
noncomittal	**non·com·mit·tal**
nonconformest	**non·con·form·ist**
nondiscript	**non·de·script**
nonpariel	**non·pa·reil**
nonpartesan	**non·par·ti·san**
nonpluss	**non·plus**
nonprofet	**non·prof·it**
nonsence	**non·sense**
nonsensecal	**non·sen·si·cal**

WRONG	RIGHT
non sequiter	non se·qui·tur
nonshalance	non·cha·lance
nontheless	none·the·less
nonuclear	non·nu·cle·ar
noodel	noo·dle
noogat	nou·gat *(confection)*
nooter	neu·ter
nootrient	nu·tri·ent
nootritionally	nutri·tion·al·ly
nootritous	nutri·tious
Nordick	Nor·dic
norishment	nour·ish·ment
normallity	nor·mal·i·ty
normallize	nor·mal·ize
normalsy	nor·mal·cy
normelly	nor·mal·ly
northurn	north·ern
northword	north·ward
Norwejian	Nor·we·gian
nostallgia	nos·tal·gia
nostrel	nos·tril
notabley	no·ta·bly
notafication	noti·fi·ca·tion
notariety	no·to·ri·e·ty
notarrize	no·ta·rize
noteably	no·ta·bly
notefy	no·ti·fy
noteriety	no·to·ri·e·ty
noterize	no·ta·rize
notery	no·ta·ry

WRONG	RIGHT
noticably	notice·a·bly
notical	nau·ti·cal
noticeing	no·tic·ing
notifacation	noti·fi·ca·tion
notoriaty	no·to·ri·e·ty
notorrious	no·to·ri·ous
notted	knot·ted
notworthy	note·wor·thy
nougat	nug·get *(lump)*
nouveau rich	nou·veau riche
novellet	nov·el·ette
novellist	nov·el·ist
novilty	nov·el·ty
nowere	no·where
noxous	nox·ious
nozle	noz·zle
nu	gnu
nuckle	knuck·le
nucleas	nu·cle·us
nucular	nu·cle·ar
nuculus	nu·cle·us
nudety	nu·di·ty
nudgeing	nudg·ing
nuence	nu·ance
nueral	neu·ral
nueron	neu·ron
nueroscience	neu·ro·sci·ence
nuerosis	neu·ro·sis *(sing.)*
nueter	neu·ter
nuetral	neu·tral
nuetron	neu·tron
nugget	nou·gat *(confection)*

WRONG	RIGHT	WRONG	RIGHT
nuggit	**nug·get** (*lump*)	nuritis	**neu·ri·tis**
nuging	**nudg·ing**	nurology	**neu·rol·o·gy**
nuisence	**nui·sance**	nurrosis	**neu·ro·sis** (*sing.*)
nukleer	**nu·cle·ar**	nurrotic	**neu·rot·ic**
nukleus	**nu·cle·us**	nurseing	**nurs·ing**
nulify	**nul·li·fy**	nursmaid	**nurse·maid**
num	**numb**	nursrey	**nurs·ery**
numarel	**nu·mer·al**	nusance	**nui·sance**
numbor	**num·ber**	nute	**newt**
numerater	**nu·mer·a·tor**	nuter	**neu·ter**
numerrical	**nu·mer·i·cal**	nutreant	**nu·tri·ent**
numerus	**nu·mer·ous**	nutricious	**nutri·tious**
nummerical	**nu·mer·i·cal**	nutritionaly	
nummskull	**num·skull**		**nutri·tion·al·ly**
nuptual	**nup·tial**	nutron	**neu·tron**
nurchure	**nur·ture**	nuveau riche	
nurd	**nerd**		**nou·veau riche**
nurishment		nylong	**ny·lon**
	nour·ish·ment	nymf	**nymph**

152

O

WRONG	RIGHT
oad	**ode**
oakan	**oak·en**
oar	**ore** *(mineral)*
oases	**oa·sis** *(sing.)*
oasis	**oa·ses** *(pl.)*
oatmeel	**oat·meal**
obalisk	**ob·e·lisk**
obasance	**obei·sance**
obay	**obey**
obbelisk	**ob·e·lisk**
obbese	**obese**
obbituary	**obit·u·ary**
obbligatory	**ob·lig·a·to·ry**
obblivion	**ob·liv·i·on**
obece	**obese**
obediance	**obe·di·ence**
obediant	**obe·di·ent**
obeisence	**obei·sance**
obeyance	**abey·ance**
obeysance	**obei·sance**
obichuary	**obit·u·ary**
objeck	**ob·ject**
objecktion	**ob·jec·tion**
objectionible	
	ob·jec·tion·a·ble
objectivety	**ob·jec·tiv·i·ty**
oblagation	**ob·li·ga·tion**
obleke	**ob·lique**

WRONG	RIGHT
obligeing	**oblig·ing**
obligetory	**ob·lig·a·to·ry**
oblije	**oblige**
oblitterate	**ob·lit·er·ate**
obliveon	**ob·liv·i·on**
obliveous	**ob·liv·i·ous**
obnoctious	**ob·nox·ious**
obow	**oboe**
obsalescent	**ob·so·les·cent**
obsalete	**ob·so·lete**
obscenaty	**ob·scen·i·ty**
obscuraty	**ob·scu·ri·ty**
obseckwies	**ob·se·quies**
obsene	**ob·scene**
obsenity	**ob·scen·i·ty**
obsequius	**ob·se·qui·ous**
observence	**ob·serv·ance**
observent	**ob·serv·ant**
observible	**ob·serv·a·ble**
observitory	
	ob·serv·a·to·ry
obsesion	**ob·ses·sion**
obsesive	**ob·ses·sive**
obsidean	**ob·sid·i·an**
obsiquies	**ob·se·quies**
obsolescense	
	ob·so·les·cence
obsolessent	**ob·so·les·cent**

153

WRONG	RIGHT
obstanately	...**ob·sti·nate·ly**
obstatrician	...**ob·ste·tri·cian**
obstetricks	........**ob·stet·rics**
obstickle	.............**ob·sta·cle**
obstinasy	.........**ob·sti·na·cy**
obstinatly	.......**ob·sti·nate·ly**
obstruck	...............**ob·struct**
obstrucktion	...**ob·struc·tion**
obsurvation	....
	...............**ob·ser·va·tion**
obtane	....................**ob·tain**
obtoose	....................**ob·tuse**
obtrussive	.........**ob·tru·sive**
obveate	.............**ob·vi·ate**
obveous	...............**ob·vi·ous**
obvurse	...................**ob·verse**
obzervable	......**ob·serv·a·ble**
obzervation	...**ob·ser·va·tion**
occasionly	....
	...............**oc·ca·sion·al·ly**
occassion	.............**oc·ca·sion**
occelot	.....................**oce·lot**
occidentel	........**oc·ci·den·tal**
occular	.....................**oc·u·lar**
occupansy	.......**oc·cu·pan·cy**
occupent	............**oc·cu·pant**
occupie	.................**oc·cu·py**
occured	...............**oc·curred**
occuring	............**oc·cur·ring**
occurrance	......**oc·cur·rence**
oceanagraphy	....
	...........**oce·an·og·ra·phy**
oceanick	...............**oce·an·ic**
ocellot	...................**oce·lot**
ocian	........................**ocean**

WRONG	RIGHT
ocktagon	...............**oc·ta·gon**
ocktane	...................**oc·tane**
Ocktober	...............**Oc·to·ber**
ocktopus	..............**oc·to·pus**
oclock	.......................**o'clock**
oclusion	.............**oc·clu·sion**
ocra	...............................**okra**
ocsidental	........**oc·ci·den·tal**
ocsillate	...............**os·cil·late**
octain	.....................**oc·tane**
octapus	.............**oc·to·pus**
octive	.......................**oc·tave**
octogon	...............**oc·ta·gon**
oculer	....................**oc·u·lar**
ocult	..........................**oc·cult**
ocupancy	........**oc·cu·pan·cy**
ocupant	..............**oc·cu·pant**
ocupational	....
	...............**oc·cu·pa·tion·al**
ocupy	....................**oc·cu·py**
ocurred	...............**oc·curred**
ocurrence	........**oc·cur·rence**
ocurring	.............**oc·cur·ring**
o da cologne	....
	...........**eau de Co·logne**
oddaty	....................**odd·i·ty**
oddometer	.......**odom·e·ter**
oddyssey	...............**od·ys·sey**
odeous	....................**odi·ous**
oder	.............................**odor**
oderus	.................**odor·ous**
Odisseus	............**Odys·se·us**
odissey	.............**od·ys·sey**
odity	........................**odd·i·ty**
odius	.......................**odi·ous**

WRONG	RIGHT	WRONG	RIGHT
odrous	**odor·ous**	oister	**oys·ter**
Odyseus	**Odys·se·us**	oke	**oak** (tree)
odyssy	**od·ys·sey**	oker	**ocher**
Oedapus	**Oed·i·pus**	okre	**okra**
ofal	**of·fal**	olagarchy	**ol·i·gar·chy**
ofe	**oaf**	oldin	**old·en**
ofend	**of·fend**	oleomargerine	
ofense	**of·fense**		**ole·o·mar·ga·rine**
ofensive	**of·fen·sive**	olfactry	**ol·fac·to·ry**
ofer	**of·fer**	oligarky	**ol·i·gar·chy**
ofering	**of·fer·ing**	Olimpics	**Olym·pics**
offace	**of·fice**	oliomargarine	
offel	**of·fal**		**ole·o·mar·ga·rine**
offen	**of·ten**	ollfactory	**ol·fac·to·ry**
offerring	**of·fer·ing**	olligarchy	**ol·i·gar·chy**
officiery	**of·fi·ci·ary**	ollive	**ol·ive**
officius	**of·fi·cious**	ol-timer	**old-tim·er**
offiser	**of·fi·cer**	Olympicks	**Olym·pics**
offishal	**of·fi·cial**	ombudzman	
offishiary	**of·fi·ci·ary**		**om·buds·man**
offishiate	**of·fi·ci·ate**	ome	**ohm**
oficer	**of·fi·cer**	omellet	**om·e·let**
oficial	**of·fi·cial**	omenous	**om·i·nous**
oficiary	**of·fi·ci·ary**	omin	**omen**
oficiate	**of·fi·ci·ate**	omision	**omis·sion**
oficious	**of·fi·cious**	omiting	**omit·ting**
ofing	**off·ing**	omlet	**om·e·let**
ofset	**off·set**	ommen	**omen**
oftin	**of·ten**	omminous	**om·i·nous**
oger	**ogre**	ommision	**omis·sion**
oggled	**ogled**	omnabus	**om·ni·bus**
ohem	**ohm**	omnipitence	
oiller	**oil·er**		**om·nip·o·tence**
oilly	**oily**	omnipotant	
ointmint	**oint·ment**		**om·nip·o·tent**

WRONG	RIGHT
omnisciance	om·nis·cience
omnisciant	om·nis·cient
omniverous	om·niv·o·rous
onamatopoeia	on·o·mat·o·poe·ia
oncore	en·core
one	won (pt. of win)
onerus	on·er·ous
oness	one·ness (unity)
oness	onus (burden)
onesself	one·self
onian	on·ion
onix	on·yx
onley	on·ly
onomatapoeia	on·o·mat·o·poe·ia
onorous	on·er·ous
on route	en route
onse	once
onsemble	en·sem·ble
onslot	on·slaught
ontourage	en·tou·rage
ontray	en·tree
onvoy	en·voy
onword	on·ward
onyon	on·ion
oozo	ou·zo
opake	opaque
opalessent	opal·es·cent
opasity	opac·i·ty
opeate	opi·ate
opel	opal
openner	open·er

WRONG	RIGHT
openning	open·ing
operater	op·er·a·tor
operatick	op·er·at·ic
operationel	op·er·a·tion·al
operent	op·er·ant
opereta	op·er·et·ta
operible	op·er·a·ble
opes	opus
opeum	opi·um
ophthamology	oph·thal·mol·o·gy
opiam	opi·um
opin	open
opinian	opin·ion
opinionnated	opin·ion·at·ed
oponent	op·po·nent
oportune	op·por·tune
oportunism	op·por·tun·ism
oportunity	op·por·tu·ni·ty
oposite	op·po·site
opossition	op·po·si·tion
opp	opt
oppalescent	opal·es·cent
oppaque	opaque
oppen	open
oppera	op·era
opperant	op·er·ant
opperate	op·er·ate
opperational	op·er·a·tion·al
opperetta	op·er·et·ta
oppertune	op·por·tune

WRONG	RIGHT	WRONG	RIGHT

oppertunity..................................
...............**op·por·tu·ni·ty**
oppinion ....**opin·ion**
opponant ....**op·po·nent**
opportuneism ....
.............**op·por·tun·ism**
opposeable ......**op·pos·a·ble**
opposeing ....**op·pos·ing**
opposission ....**op·po·si·tion**
opposite..............**op·po·site**
oppossum ....**opos·sum**
oppresed............**op·pressed**
oppresion ....**op·pres·sion**
oppresser...........**op·pres·sor**
opprobrius ...**op·pro·bri·ous**
oppulent...............**op·u·lent**
opra ....**op·era**
oprable ....**op·er·a·ble**
opratic ....**op·er·at·ic**
oprative ....**op·er·a·tive**
opressed ....**op·pressed**
opression ....**op·pres·sion**
oprobrious ...**op·pro·bri·ous**
opsional...............**op·tion·al**
optacal ....**op·ti·cal**
optamal ....**op·ti·mal**
optamism ....**op·ti·mism**
optamistic........**op·ti·mis·tic**
opthalmology ....
.........**oph·thal·mol·o·gy**
optick.....................**op·tic**
opticle ....**op·ti·cal**
optimel ....**op·ti·mal**
optimistick........**op·ti·mis·tic**
optimizm ....**op·ti·mism**

optionel...............**op·tion·al**
optitian ....**op·ti·cian**
optomatrist...**op·tom·e·trist**
optomology ....
.........**oph·thal·mol·o·gy**
opulant.................**op·u·lent**
or ....**oar** *(paddle)*
or ....**ore** *(mineral)*
oracal....................**or·a·cle**
    (wise person)
orafice ....**or·i·fice**
oragin ....**or·i·gin**
oral ....**au·ral** *(of the ear)*
orangatan ....**orang·u·tan**
orateing.................**orat·ing**
orater ....**or·a·tor**
oratoricle ....**ora·tor·i·cal**
orbet......................**or·bit**
orcesstra.............**or·ches·tra**
orched...................**or·chid**
orcherd ....**or·chard**
orchestrel ....**or·ches·tral**
orchistra............**or·ches·tra**
orcid ....**or·chid**
ordanal ....**or·di·nal**
ordanance.........**or·di·nance**
    (regulation)
ordanarily........**or·di·nar·i·ly**
ordanary.............**or·di·nary**
ordanation ......**or·di·na·tion**
ordane ....**or·dain**
ordeel ....**or·deal**
orderley ....**or·der·ly**
ordinance ....**ord·nance**
    (military weapons)

WRONG	RIGHT	WRONG	RIGHT
ordinaraly........or·di·nar·i·ly	origanal ....orig·i·nal
ordnance ....or·di·nance	origen ....or·i·gin
(regulation)	origenate ....orig·i·nate
ordnarily ....or·di·nar·i·ly	originallity......orig·i·nal·i·ty
ordnary ....or·di·nary	originaly ....orig·i·nal·ly
ordnation........or·di·na·tion	originel ....orig·i·nal
ordnence ....ord·nance	Origon ....Or·e·gon
(military weapons)	orjiastic ....or·gi·as·tic
ore ....oar *(paddle)*	orjy ....or·gy
ore ....or *(conj.)*	ornamint...........or·na·ment
ore d'oeuvre	ornry ....or·nery
...............hors d'oeu·vre	orphanege ....or·phan·age
oregeno ....oreg·a·no	orphen ....or·phan
oreintal ....ori·en·tal	orrangutang .....orang·u·tan
oreintate............ori·en·tate	orratorical........ora·tor·i·cal
orel.........oral *(of the mouth)*	orregano ....oreg·a·no
orenge ....or·ange	orthadontist ....
orfan.......................or·phan	...............or·tho·don·tist
organazation	orthadox ....or·tho·dox
...............or·gan·i·za·tion	orthapedics...or·tho·pe·dics
organick................or·gan·ic	oscilate ....os·cil·late
organizeing ....or·gan·iz·ing	oscillater............os·cil·la·tor
organizm ....or·gan·ism	oseanic ....oce·an·ic
orgazm ....or·gasm	oselot ....oce·lot
orgeastic ....or·gi·as·tic	oshean.......................ocean
orgen ....or·gan	osmossis ....os·mo·sis
orgendy ....or·gan·dy	ossafy ....os·si·fy
orgenism............or·gan·ism	ossillate ....os·cil·late
orgenization........................	osstensible ....os·ten·si·ble
...............or·gan·i·za·tion	osstentatious ....
orgiastick............or·gi·as·tic	...............os·ten·ta·tious
oriantal ....ori·en·tal	osteapath ....os·te·o·path
oriantate ....ori·en·tate	ostensable........os·ten·si·ble
oricle...or·a·cle *(wise person)*	ostentatius ....
oriface ....or·i·fice	...............os·ten·ta·tious

158

WRONG	RIGHT	WRONG	RIGHT
ostiopath	**os·te·o·path**	overrought	**over·wrought**
ostrasize	**os·tra·cize**	overule	**over·rule**
ostritch	**os·trich**	overun	**over·run**
otemeal	**oat·meal**	overwelm	**over·whelm**
oter	**ot·ter**	overy	**ova·ry**
othe	**oath**	oveture	**over·ture**
Ottowa	**Ot·ta·wa**	ovewlation	**ovu·la·tion**
ouht	**ought**	ovin	**ov·en**
oul	**owl**	ovry	**ova·ry**
ounse	**ounce**	ovuler	**ovu·lar**
outragious	**out·ra·geous**	ovullation	**ovu·la·tion**
outriger	**out·rig·ger**	ovurt	**overt**
outter	**out·er**	oweing	**ow·ing**
outting	**out·ing**	owllish	**owl·ish**
outword	**out·ward**	ownce	**ounce**
ouze	**ooze**	ownly	**on·ly**
ovature	**over·ture**	owst	**oust**
ovel	**oval**	owter	**out·er**
overals	**over·alls**	oxedation	**ox·i·da·tion**
overate	**over·rate**	oxferd	**ox·ford**
	(rate too highly)	oxidental	**oc·ci·den·tal**
overawd	**over·awed**	oxigen	**ox·y·gen**
overbering	**over·bear·ing**	oxydation	**ox·i·da·tion**
overbord	**over·board**	oze	**ooze**
overchure	**over·ture**	ozmosis	**os·mo·sis**
overlaping	**over·lap·ping**	ozzone	**ozone**

P

WRONG	RIGHT	WRONG	RIGHT
pacefier	**pac·i·fi·er**	paletable	**pal·at·a·ble**
pacefist	**pac·i·fist**	palette	**pal·ate**
pachiderm	**pach·y·derm**		*(roof of mouth)*
pack	**pact** *(agreement)*	palette	**pal·let**
packedge	**pack·age**		*(bed; platform)*
packyderm	**pach·y·derm**	Palistine	**Pal·es·tine**
paddel	**pad·dle**	pallace	**pal·a·ce**
paddeling	**pad·dling**	paller	**pal·lor**
paddy	**pat·ty** *(cake)*	Pallestine	**Pal·es·tine**
padock	**pad·dock**	pallet	**pal·ate**
pageantrey	**pag·eant·ry**		*(roof of mouth)*
pagen	**pa·gan**	palletible	**pal·at·a·ble**
pagenation	**pag·i·na·tion**	pallette	**pal·ette**
pagent	**pag·eant**		*(paint board)*
pail	**pale** *(white)*	pallsy	**pal·sy**
pain	**pane** *(window)*	palmestry	**palm·is·try**
painfull	**pain·ful**	palpatate	**pal·pi·tate**
pair	**pare** *(trim)*	palpible	**pal·pa·ble**
pair	**pear** *(fruit)*	palsey	**pal·sy**
pairody	**par·o·dy**	paltrey	**pal·try** *(trifling)*
pajammas	**pa·ja·mas**	paltry	**poul·try** *(fowls)*
Pakestan	**Pa·ki·stan**	pamflit	**pam·phlet**
palacial	**pa·la·tial**	panarama	**pan·o·ra·ma**
palate	**pal·let**	pancrias	**pan·cre·as**
	(bed; platform)	pane	**pain** *(hurt)*
palate	**pal·ette**	paned	**panned** *(pt. of pan)*
	(paint board)	panellist	**pan·el·ist**
pale	**pail** *(bucket)*	paniking	**pan·ick·ing**

160

WRONG	RIGHT	WRONG	RIGHT
pannel	**pan·el**	paridise	**par·a·dise**
pansie	**pan·sy**	paridox	**par·a·dox**
pantamine	**pa·to·mime**	pariffin	**par·af·fin**
paper-maché		parigon	**par·a·gon**
	pa·pier-mâ·ché	parikeet	**par·a·keet**
pappal	**pa·pal**	parimount	**par·a·mount**
pappaya	**pa·pa·ya**	parinoia	**par·a·noia**
papreka	**pa·pri·ka**	parish	**per·ish** *(die)*
paradice	**par·a·dise**	parishute	**par·a·chute**
paradime	**par·a·digm**	parisol	**par·a·sol**
parady	**par·o·dy**	paritrooper	**par·a·troop·er**
parafin	**par·af·fin**	parkay	**par·quet**
paralel	**par·al·lel**	parlay	**par·ley** *(confer)*
paralize	**par·a·lyze**	parler	**par·lor**
parallysis	**pa·ral·y·sis**	parley	**par·lay** *(bet)*
parameter	**pe·rim·e·ter**	parliment	**par·lia·ment**
	(outside edge)	parocheal	**pa·ro·chi·al**
paraphenalia		parolled	**pa·roled**
	par·a·pher·na·lia	parot	**par·rot**
parden	**par·don**	parrable	**par·a·ble**
pare	**pair** *(two)*	parrachute	**par·a·chute**
pare	**pear** *(fruit)*	parrade	**pa·rade**
pareble	**par·a·ble**	parradox	**par·a·dox**
paredigm	**par·a·digm**	parragon	**par·a·gon**
parefenalia		parragraph	**par·a·graph**
	par·a·pher·na·lia	parrakeet	**par·a·keet**
paregaric	**par·e·gor·ic**	parralel	**par·al·lel**
paregraph	**par·a·graph**	parralysis	**pa·ral·y·sis**
Pareguay	**Par·a·guay**	parralyze	**par·a·lyze**
parentheses		parrameter	**pa·ram·e·ter**
	pa·ren·the·sis *(sing.)*		*(math constant; limit)*
parenthesis		parramount	**par·a·mount**
	pa·ren·the·ses *(pl.)*	parranoia	**par·a·noia**
paresite	**par·a·site**	parraphrase	**par·a·phrase**
parfay	**par·fait**	parrasol	**par·a·sol**

| --- | --- | --- | --- |

WRONG	RIGHT	WRONG	RIGHT
parrental	**pa·ren·tal**	passible	**pass·a·ble**
parret	**par·rot**	passifier	**pac·i·fi·er**
parrity	**par·i·ty**	passifist	**pac·i·fist**
parsel	**par·cel**	passionite	**pas·sion·ate**
parsen	**par·son**	passtel	**pas·tel**
parsly	**pars·ley**	passteurize	**pas·teur·ize**
partecle	**par·ti·cle**	passtime	**pas·time**
partesan	**par·ti·san**	passtrami	**pas·tra·mi**
partiallity	**par·ti·al·i·ty**	past	**passed** *(pt. of pass)*
partialy	**par·tial·ly**	paster	**pas·tor** *(clergy)*
participial	**par·ti·ci·ple** *(n.)*	paster	**pas·ture** *(field)*
participle		pasteral	**pas·to·ral**
	par·ti·cip·i·al *(adj.)*	pastesh	**pas·tiche**
particuler	**par·tic·u·lar**	pastor	**pas·ture** *(field)*
partime	**part·time**	pastrey	**pas·try**
partisipant	**par·tic·i·pant**	pastural	**pas·to·ral**
partisipeal		pasture	**pas·tor** *(clergy)*
	par·ti·cip·i·al *(adj.)*	pastureize	**pas·teur·ize**
partisiple	**par·ti·ci·ple** *(n.)*	patassium	**po·tas·si·um**
partrige	**par·tridge**	pateo	**pa·tio**
paruse	**pe·ruse**	patern	**pat·tern**
pasable	**pass·a·ble**	paternize	**pa·tron·ize**
pasage	**pas·sage**	pathas	**pa·thos**
pasay	**pas·sé**	pathelogical	
Pasedena	**Pas·a·de·na**		**path·o·log·i·cal**
pasemaker	**pace·mak·er**	pathelogist	**pa·thol·o·gist**
pasenger	**pas·sen·ger**	pathollogical	
Pasific	**Pa·cif·ic**		**path·o·log·i·cal**
pasionnate	**pas·sion·ate**	patience	**pa·tients**
pasive	**pas·sive**		*(pl. of patient)*
pasport	**pass·port**	patients	**pa·tience**
passanger	**pas·sen·ger**		*(endurance)*
passed	**past** *(over; beyond)*	patition	**pe·ti·tion**
passege	**pas·sage**	patrearch	**pa·tri·arch**
passeve	**pas·sive**	patren	**pa·tron**

WRONG	RIGHT
patriat	**pa·tri·ot**
patrinage	**pa·tron·age**
patroleum	**pe·tro·le·um**
patroling	**pa·trol·ling**
patronnage	**pa·tron·age**
patronnize	**pa·tron·ize**
pattent	**pat·ent**
patternal	**pa·ter·nal**
pattriotic	**pa·tri·ot·ic**
patturn	**pat·tern**
patty	**pad·dy** (rice)
paun	**pawn**
paverty	**pov·er·ty**
pavillion	**pa·vil·ion**
payible	**pay·a·ble**
peacan	**pe·can**
peace	**piece** (part)
peacefull	**peace·ful**
peacemeal	**piece·meal**
peak	**peek** (glance)
peak	**pique** (offend)
peal	**peel** (skin)
peany	**pe·o·ny**
pear	**pair** (two)
pear	**pare** (trim)
pearce	**pierce**
pearl	**purl** (stitch)
peasantrey	**peas·ant·ry**
peasent	**peas·ant**
peble	**peb·ble**
pecon	**pe·can**
peculierity	**pecu·li·ar·i·ty**
pedagree	**ped·i·gree**
pedal	**ped·dle** (sell)
peddeler	**ped·dler** (seller)

WRONG	RIGHT
peddestal	**ped·es·tal**
peddestrian	**pe·des·tri·an**
peddle	**ped·al** (foot lever)
pedeatrician	**pe·di·a·tri·cian**
pedistal	**ped·es·tal**
peech	**peach**
peecock	**pea·cock**
peek	**peak** (summit)
peek	**pique** (offend)
peel	**peal** (a ringing)
peenut	**pea·nut**
peeple	**peo·ple**
peer	**pier** (structure)
peice	**piece** (part)
peir	**pier** (structure)
peirce	**pierce**
pejoritive	**pejo·ra·tive**
pelet	**pel·let**
pellican	**pel·i·can**
pellit	**pel·let**
pelvas	**pel·vis**
penacillin	**pen·i·cil·lin**
pena colada	**pi·ña co·la·da**
penall	**pe·nal**
penallize	**pe·nal·ize**
penant	**pen·nant**
penatentiary	**pen·i·ten·tia·ry**
pencel	**pen·cil** (writing instrument)
penchent	**pen·chant**
pendullum	**pen·du·lum**
pengwin	**pen·guin**
penicilin	**pen·i·cil·lin**

WRONG	RIGHT
penitentiery .... **pen·i·ten·tia·ry**	
penitration ...**pen·e·tra·tion**	
pennalize............**pe·nal·ize**	
pennalty ....**pen·al·ty**	
pennance ....**pen·ance**	
pennent................**pen·nant**	
pennetration .... **pen·e·tra·tion**	
pennicillin.........**pen·i·cil·lin**	
penninsula ......**pen·in·su·la**	
Pennsilvania .... **Penn·syl·va·nia**	
pensave ....**pen·sive**	
Pentacostal ....**Pen·te·cos·tal**	
pentamiter ....**pen·tam·e·ter**	
Pentatuch ....**Pen·ta·teuch**	
pentigon ....**pen·ta·gon**	
pention ....**pen·sion**	
peonie ....**pe·o·ny**	
pepermint......**pep·per·mint**	
peragoric ....**par·e·gor·ic**	
perascope ....**per·i·scope**	
peratrooper .... **par·a·troop·er**	
percarious ....**pre·car·i·ous**	
percaution ......**pre·cau·tion**	
percedure ....**pro·ce·dure**	
perceed......**pro·ceed** (go on)	
perceiveable...**per·ceiv·a·ble**	
perceptably ....**per·cep·ti·bly**	
percession ....**pre·ces·sion** (precedence)	
percession ....**pro·ces·sion** (parade)	

WRONG	RIGHT
perchase ....**pur·chase**	
percieve ....**per·ceive**	
percipitation .... **pre·cip·i·ta·tion**	
percise ......**pre·cise** (definite)	
percision...........**pre·ci·sion**	
perclaim...........**pro·claim**	
perclude ....**pre·clude**	
percocious ....**pre·co·cious**	
percollator......**per·co·la·tor**	
percure ....**pro·cure**	
percursor ....**pre·cur·sor**	
percushion.......**per·cus·sion**	
perdicament .... **pre·dic·a·ment**	
perdiction..........**pre·dic·tion**	
perdigious........**pro·di·gious**	
perdominant...................... **pre·dom·i·nant**	
perducer ....**pro·duc·er**	
perduction ......**pro·duc·tion**	
perelous...............**per·il·ous**	
perenial............**per·en·ni·al**	
perenthesis ......**pa·ren·the·sis** (sing.)	
perfectable......**per·fect·i·ble**	
perferate.............**per·fo·rate**	
perfess ....**pro·fess**	
perfessional .... **pro·fes·sion·al**	
perficient...........**pro·fi·cient**	
performence....................... **per·form·ance**	
perfusion ....**pro·fu·sion**	
pergatory ....**pur·ga·to·ry**	

WRONG	RIGHT
pergressive	**pro·gres·sive**
perhibit	**pro·hib·it**
peridontist	
	per·i·o·don·tist
perifery	**pe·riph·ery**
perillous	**per·il·ous**
perimedic	**par·a·med·ic**
perimeter	**pa·ram·e·ter**
	(math constant)
perinoia	**par·a·noia**
perioddical	**pe·ri·od·i·cal**
peripharel	**pe·riph·er·al**
periphary	**pe·riph·ery**
perish	**par·ish**
	(church district)
perjection	**pro·jec·tion**
perjector	**pro·jec·tor**
perjery	**per·ju·ry**
perjorative	**pejo·ra·tive**
perkalator	**per·co·la·tor**
perl	**pearl** *(gem)*
perl	**purl** *(stitch)*
perliminary	**pre·lim·i·nary**
permenant	**per·ma·nent**
permiable	**per·me·a·ble**
permiate	**per·me·ate**
perminent	**per·ma·nent**
permisive	**per·mis·sive**
permissable	**per·mis·si·ble**
permited	**per·mit·ted**
permmutation	
	per·mu·ta·tion
pernounce	**pro·nounce**
pernunciation	
	pro·nun·ci·a·tion

WRONG	RIGHT
perochial	**pa·ro·chi·al**
perogative	**pre·rog·a·tive**
peroggi	**pi·ro·gi**
peroled	**pa·roled**
perpatrate	**per·pe·trate**
perpellant	**pro·pel·lant**
perpendiculer	
	per·pen·dic·u·lar
perpertrate	**per·pe·trate**
perpettuate	
	per·pet·u·ate
perpetualy	**per·pet·u·al·ly**
perpindicular	
	per·pen·dic·u·lar
perplexaty	**per·plex·i·ty**
perponderance	
	per·pon·der·ance
perportionate	
	pro·por·tion·ate
perposely	**pur·pose·ly**
perposterous	
	pre·pos·ter·ous
perquisite	**pre·req·ui·site**
	(requirement)
perrenial	**per·en·ni·al**
perrimeter	**pe·rim·e·ter**
	(boundary)
perripheral	**pe·riph·er·al**
perriscope	**per·i·scope**
perroxide	**per·ox·ide**
persacute	**per·se·cute**
	(harass)
persaverence	
	per·se·ver·ance
per-say	**per se**

WRONG	RIGHT	WRONG	RIGHT
perscribe	**pre·scribe**	perspective	**pro·spec·tive**
	(order)		*(expected)*
perscribe	**pro·scribe**	persperation	
	(forbid)		**per·spi·ra·tion**
perscription	**pre·scrip·tion**	persuassive	**per·sua·sive**
persecute	**pros·e·cute**	persuation	**per·sua·sion**
	(legal term)	persuede	**per·suade**
persent	**per·cent**	persuit	**pur·suit**
persentable	**pre·sent·a·ble**	persume	**pre·sume**
persentament		persumption	
	pre·sen·ti·ment		**pre·sump·tion**
	(foreboding)	persumptuous	
perseptibly	**per·cep·ti·bly**		**pre·sump·tu·ous**
perseption	**per·cep·tion**	pertanent	**per·ti·nent**
perserve	**pre·serve**	pertector	**pro·tec·tor**
perserverance		pertend	**por·tend**
	per·se·ver·ance		*(foreshadow)*
persistance	**per·sist·ence**	pertend	**pre·tend**
personafication			*(simulate)*
	per·son·i·fi·ca·tion	pertentious	**pre·ten·tious**
personal	**per·son·nel**	perterb	**per·turb**
	(employees)	participant	**par·tic·i·pant**
personallity	**per·son·al·i·ty**	particular	**par·tic·u·lar**
personel	**per·son·al**	pertition	**par·ti·tion**
	(private)	pervailing	**pre·vail·ing**
personel	**per·son·nel**	pervassive	**per·va·sive**
	(employees)	pervertion	**per·ver·sion**
personible	**per·son·a·ble**	pervurse	**per·verse**
personnage	**per·son·age**	pesant	**peas·ant**
personnality		pessamism	**pes·si·mism**
	per·son·al·i·ty	pestalence	**pes·ti·lence**
personnel	**per·son·al**	peta	**pi·ta**
	(private)	pete moss	**peat moss**
perspectave	**per·spec·tive**	petigree	**ped·i·gree**
	(view)	petle	**pet·al**

WRONG	RIGHT	WRONG	RIGHT
petoonia	**pe·tu·nia**	phisically	**phys·i·cal·ly**
petrachemical		phisiology	**phys·i·ol·o·gy**
	pet·ro·chem·i·cal	phlem	**phlegm**
petrefied	**pet·ri·fied**	phobea	**pho·bia**
petrollium	**pe·tro·le·um**	phonegraph	
pettiecoat	**pet·ti·coat**		**pho·no·graph**
pettition	**pe·ti·tion**	phoney	**pho·ny**
peuter	**pew·ter**	phonnetic	**pho·net·ic**
phantem	**phan·tom**	phosfate	**phos·phate**
pharmeceutical		phosforescence	
	phar·ma·ceu·ti·cal		**phos·pho·res·cence**
pharmecy	**phar·ma·cy**	phosforus	**phos·pho·rus**
Pharoh	**Phar·aoh**	phosphoresence	
(Egyptian ruler)			**phos·pho·res·cence**
phase	**faze** *(disturb)*	photoes	**pho·tos**
phaze	**phase** *(stage)*	photogennic	
phenomenan			**pho·to·gen·ic**
	phe·nom·e·non	photografer	
phenomenon			**pho·tog·ra·pher**
	phe·nom·e·na *(pl.)*	photosinthesis	
phenominal			**pho·to·syn·the·sis**
	phe·nom·e·nal	phylo	**phyl·lo**
Pheonix	**Phoe·nix**	physicion	**phy·si·cian**
Pheraoh	**Phar·aoh**	physicly	**phys·i·cal·ly**
(Egyptian ruler)		physiollogy	**phys·i·ol·o·gy**
pheseant	**pheas·ant**	pianeer	**pi·o·neer**
philbert	**fil·bert**	piannist	**pi·an·ist**
Philedelphia		pianoes	**pi·an·os**
	Phil·a·del·phia	piaty	**pi·e·ty**
philharmonnic		pican	**pe·can**
	phil·har·mon·ic	piceyune	**pic·a·yune**
Philipines	**Phil·ip·pines**	picher	**pitch·er**
phillanthropist		*(hurler; container)*	
	phi·lan·thro·pist	pichfork	**pitch·fork**
philosipher	**phi·los·o·pher**	pickel	**pick·le**

167

WRONG	RIGHT
pickeling	**pick·ling**
picknic	**pic·nic**
pickyune	**pic·a·yune**
picnik	**pic·nic**
picniking	**pic·nick·ing**
picollo	**pic·co·lo**
pictoral	**pic·to·ri·al**
picturresque	**pic·tur·esque**
picuniary	**pe·cu·ni·ary**
pidgeon	**pi·geon** (bird)
piece	**peace** (serenity)
pier	**peer** (equal; look)
piggon	**pi·geon** (bird)
pigmie	**pyg·my**
pijamas	**pa·ja·mas**
pikaxe	**pick·ax**
piknic	**pic·nic**
pilage	**pil·lage**
pilar	**pil·lar**
pilet	**pi·lot**
pilgrem	**pil·grim**
pilgrimege	**pil·grim·age**
pillege	**pil·lage**
piller	**pil·lar**
pillgrim	**pil·grim**
pilow	**pil·low**
pimmento	**pi·men·to**
pimpel	**pim·ple**
pinacle	**pin·na·cle** (acme)
pinacle	**pi·noch·le** (card game)
pina collada	**pi·ña co·la·da**
pinapple	**pine·ap·ple**

WRONG	RIGHT
pinnacle	**pi·noch·le** (card game)
pinnicle	**pin·na·cle** (acme)
pinyata	**pi·ña·ta**
pipeing	**pip·ing**
pipline	**pipe·line**
piracey	**pi·ra·cy**
piramid	**pyr·a·mid**
pire	**pyre**
piriodical	**pe·ri·od·i·cal**
piroette	**pir·ou·ette**
pirothechnics	**py·ro·tech·nics**
Pisees	**Pis·ces**
pistashio	**pis·ta·chio**
pistel	**pis·tol** (firearm)
pistol	**pis·til** (part of flower)
pistun	**pis·ton**
pitcher	**pic·ture** (likeness)
pithetic	**pa·thet·ic**
pithey	**pithy**
pithon	**py·thon**
pitta	**pi·ta**
pittence	**pit·tance**
pituetary	**pi·tu·i·tary**
pitunia	**pe·tu·nia**
pityless	**pit·i·less**
pius	**pi·ous**
pivetal	**piv·ot·al**
pizzaria	**piz·ze·ria**
placcard	**plac·ard**
placed	**plac·id** (calm)
placibo	**pla·ce·bo**
placque	**plaque**
plad	**plaid**

WRONG	RIGHT	WRONG	RIGHT
plage	**plague**	plentious	**plen·te·ous**
plagerism	**pla·gia·rism**	pleseant	**pleas·ant**
plain	**plane**	plethera	**pleth·o·ra**
	(airplane; surface)	pleurasy	**pleu·ri·sy**
plaintif	**plain·tiff**	plieing	**ply·ing**
plait	**plate** *(dish)*	plient	**pli·ant**
plancton	**plank·ton**	plite	**plight**
plane	**plain** *(simple)*	ploted	**plot·ted**
planed	**planned**	pluerisy	**pleu·ri·sy**
	(pt. of plan)	plum	**plumb**
plannet	**plan·et**		*(to test; a lead weight)*
plantiff	**plain·tiff**	plumb	**plum** *(fruit)*
plasebo	**pla·ce·bo**	plummer	**plumb·er**
plasenta	**pla·cen·ta**	plumming	**plumb·ing**
plassid	**plac·id** *(calm)*	plungeing	**plung·ing**
plasster	**plas·ter**	plurallity	**plu·ral·i·ty**
plastec	**plas·tic**	plurel	**plu·ral**
plate	**plait** *(braid)*	plurisy	**pleu·ri·sy**
plateu	**pla·teau**	plyable	**pli·a·ble**
platnum	**plat·i·num**	plyers	**pli·ers**
platonnic	**pla·ton·ic**	Plymuth	**Ply·mouth**
platteau	**pla·teau**	pnuematic	**pneu·mat·ic**
plattypus	**plat·y·pus**	pnuemonia	**pneu·mo·nia**
plausable	**plau·si·ble**	poched	**poached**
playwrite	**play·wright**	pockit	**pock·et**
plazma	**plas·ma**	podeum	**po·di·um**
plazza	**pla·za**	poetecal	**po·et·i·cal**
pleasantrey	**pleas·ant·ry**	pogoda	**pa·go·da**
pleasent	**pleas·ant**	poinant	**poign·ant**
pleasurible	**pleas·ur·a·ble**	poinsetta	**poin·set·tia**
plee	**plea**	poisenous	**poi·son·ous**
pleed	**plead**	Polanesian	**Pol·y·ne·sian**
pleet	**pleat**	polarazation	
plege	**pledge**		**polar·i·za·tion**
plentaful	**plen·ti·ful**	polatician	**pol·i·ti·cian**

WRONG	RIGHT	WRONG	RIGHT
pole	**poll** *(vote)*	polyunsaterated	**pol·y·un·sat·u·rat·ed**
polecy	**pol·i·cy**	pome	**po·em** *(verse)*
polen	**pol·len**	pomegranite	**pome·gran·ate**
poler	**po·lar** *(of the poles)*	pomel	**pom·mel**
polerization	**polar·i·za·tion**	pompus	**pom·pous** *(pretentious)*
poligamy	**po·lyg·a·my**	ponch	**paunch**
poligraph	**pol·y·graph**	pontifacate	**pon·tif·i·cate**
polimer	**pol·y·mer**	pooberty	**pu·ber·ty**
polip	**pol·yp**	poodel	**poo·dle**
politacal	**po·lit·i·cal**	poper	**pau·per**
politically	**pol·i·tic·ly** *(prudently)*	poplar	**pop·u·lar** *(common)*
politicing	**pol·i·tick·ing**	popler	**pop·lar** *(tree)*
politicion	**pol·i·ti·cian**	popourri	**pot·pour·ri**
politicly	**po·lit·i·cal·ly** *(in a political manner)*	populace	**pop·u·lous** *(crowded)*
poll	**pole** *(rod)*	popular	**pop·lar** *(tree)*
pollice	**po·lice**	popularety	**pop·u·lar·i·ty**
pollicy	**pol·i·cy**	populer	**pop·u·lar** *(common)*
pollin	**pol·len**	populous	**pop·u·lace** *(the people)*
pollish	**pol·ish**	porcelin	**por·ce·lain**
pollite	**po·lite**	porcipine	**por·cu·pine**
pollitical	**po·lit·i·cal**	pore	**pour** *(flow)*
pollup	**pol·yp**	porfolio	**port·fo·lio**
pollutent	**pol·lu·tant**	poridge	**por·ridge**
pollyester	**pol·y·es·ter**	porkupine	**por·cu·pine**
Pollynesian	**Pol·y·ne·sian**	pornogerphy	**por·nog·ra·phy**
poltry	**poul·try** *(fowls)*	porpous	**por·poise**
polutant	**pol·lu·tant**	porrage	**por·ridge**
polyesther	**pol·y·es·ter**	porselain	**por·ce·lain**
polyethelene	**pol·y·eth·yl·ene**		
polygemy	**po·lyg·a·my**		

170

WRONG	**RIGHT**	WRONG	**RIGHT**
portant	**por·tent** *(omen)*	poting	**pot·ting**
Porta Rico	**Puer·to Ri·co**	potpoorri	**pot·pour·ri**
portel	**por·tal**	pottary	**pot·tery**
portend	**por·tent** *(omen)*	pottasium	**po·tas·si·um**
portent	**por·tend**	pouder	**pow·der**
	(foreshadow)	poultrey	**poul·try** *(fowls)*
portfollio	**port·fo·lio**	poultry	**pal·try** *(trifling)*
portible	**port·a·ble**	pour	**pore**
portraid	**por·trayed**		*(opening; ponder)*
portret	**por·trait**	povarty	**pov·er·ty**
posative	**pos·i·tive**	powncing	**pounc·ing**
poschulate	**pos·tu·late**	powt	**pout**
poschumous		pracee	**pré·cis** *(summary)*
	post·hu·mous	practecal	**prac·ti·cal**
posession	**pos·ses·sion**	practiceing	**prac·tic·ing**
posessive	**pos·ses·sive**	practicianer	**prac·ti·tion·er**
posibility	**pos·si·bil·i·ty**	practicly	**prac·ti·cal·ly**
posible	**pos·si·ble**	pragmattic	**prag·mat·ic**
pospone	**post·pone**	praisworthy	
possably	**pos·si·bly**		**praise·wor·thy**
posscript	**post·script**	prarie	**prai·rie**
possebility	**pos·si·bil·i·ty**	praun	**prawn**
possesive	**pos·ses·sive**	pray	**prey** *(victim)*
possition	**po·si·tion**	prean	**preen**
postege	**post·age**	precapice	**prec·i·pice**
posteraty	**pos·ter·i·ty**	precarius	**pre·car·i·ous**
posthumus	**post·hu·mous**	precedance	**prec·e·dence**
post-mortum			*(priority)*
	post·mor·tem	precedence	**pre·ced·ent**
postoolate	**pos·tu·late**		*(example)*
postumous	**post·hu·mous**	preceed	**pre·cede**
potant	**po·tent**		*(come before)*
potatos	**po·ta·toes** *(pl.)*	preceedence	**prec·e·dence**
potensial	**po·ten·tial**		*(priority)*
potery	**pot·tery**	precense	**pres·ence**

WRONG	RIGHT
precession	**pro·ces·sion** *(parade)*
precice	**pre·cise** *(definite)*
precipatation	**pre·cip·i·ta·tion**
precipiece	**prec·i·pice**
precise	**pré·cis** *(summary)*
precission	**pre·ci·sion**
precius	**pre·cious**
preconseption	**pre·con·cep·tion**
precosious	**pre·co·cious**
precurser	**pre·cur·sor**
predacate	**pred·i·cate**
predater	**pred·a·tor**
predesessor	**pred·e·ces·sor**
predesposed	**pre·dis·posed**
predicsion	**pre·dic·tion**
predicument	**pre·dic·a·ment**
predillection	**pre·di·lec·tion**
preditor	**pred·a·tor**
predjudice	**prej·u·dice**
predomanent	**pre·dom·i·nant**
preech	**preach**
preemanant	**pre·em·i·nent**
prefabercate	**pre·fab·ri·cate**
preferance	**pref·er·ence**
prefered	**pre·ferred**
preferible	**pref·er·a·ble**

WRONG	RIGHT
preferrential	**pref·er·en·tial**
prefertory	**pref·a·to·ry**
prefface	**pref·ace**
preffered	**pre·ferred**
prefferential	**pref·er·en·tial**
pregnent	**preg·nant**
preisthood	**priest·hood**
prejidace	**prej·u·dice**
prelimanary	**pre·lim·i·nary**
prellude	**prel·ude**
premanition	**pre·mo·ni·tion**
premedetated	**pre·med·i·tat·ed**
premeir	**pre·mier** *(first; prime minister)*
premeire	**pre·mière** *(first performance)*
premenstral	**pre·men·stru·al**
premerital	**pre·mar·i·tal**
premeum	**pre·mi·um**
premiere	**pre·mier** *(first; prime minister)*
preminent	**pre·em·i·nent**
premmise	**prem·ise**
prempt	**pre·empt**
preocuppied	**pre·oc·cu·pied**
prepair	**pre·pare**
prepatory	**prep·a·ra·to·ry**
preperation	**prep·a·ra·tion**
prepisition	**prep·o·si·tion**

WRONG	RIGHT
preponderence	**pre·pon·der·ance**
prepostorous	**pre·pos·ter·ous**
prepposition	**prep·o·si·tion**
prerequesite	**pre·req·ui·site** *(requirement)*
prerequisite	**per·qui·site** *(privilege)*
prerie	**prai·rie**
prerogitive	**pre·rog·a·tive**
presadency	**pres·i·den·cy**
presancę	**pres·ence**
Presbiterian	**Pres·by·te·ri·an**
prescribe	**pro·scribe** *(forbid)*
prescriptian	**pre·scrip·tion**
presede	**pre·cede** *(come before)*
presedence	**prec·e·dence** *(priority)*
presedent	**pre·ced·ent** *(example)*
presentible	**pre·sent·a·ble**
presentment	**pre·sen·ti·ment** *(foreboding)*
presept	**pre·cept**
presidancy	**pres·i·den·cy**
presinct	**pre·cinct**
presious	**pre·cious**

WRONG	RIGHT
presipitation	**pre·cip·i·ta·tion**
presise	**pre·cise** *(definite)*
presision	**pre·ci·sion**
prespective	**pro·spec·tive** *(expected)*
prespiration	**per·spi·ra·tion**
pressage	**pres·age**
pressence	**pres·ence**
presservative	**pre·ser·va·tive**
pressidency	**pres·i·den·cy**
pressipice	**prec·i·pice**
prestegious	**pres·ti·gious**
prestiege	**pres·tige**
presumtion	**pre·sump·tion**
presumtuous	**pre·sump·tu·ous**
presure	**pres·sure**
pretensious	**pre·ten·tious**
pretention	**pre·ten·sion**
pretex	**pre·text**
pretsel	**pret·zel**
prevaling	**pre·vail·ing**
prevelant	**prev·a·lent**
preveous	**pre·vi·ous**
preversion	**per·ver·sion**
prey	**pray** *(implore)*
prickley	**prick·ly**
prier	**pri·or** *(earlier)*
primative	**prim·i·tive**
primerily	**pri·ma·ri·ly**
primery	**pri·ma·ry**

WRONG	RIGHT	WRONG	RIGHT
primevil	**pri·me·val**	procter	**proc·tor**
primmitive	**prim·i·tive**	prodduct	**prod·uct**
principal	**prin·ci·ple**	prodegal	**prod·i·gal**
	(basic rule)	prodege	**pro·té·gé**
principle	**prin·ci·pal** *(chief)*		*(one helped by another)*
princley	**prince·ly**	prodigee	**prod·i·gy**
prior	**pri·er**		*(genius)*
	(one who pries)	prodigias	**pro·di·gious**
priorrity	**pri·or·i·ty**	producktion	**pro·duc·tion**
prisem	**prism**	produser	**pro·duc·er**
prisen	**pris·on**	profain	**pro·fane**
prisonner	**pris·on·er**	profannity	**pro·fan·i·ty**
privecy	**pri·va·cy**	profecy	**proph·e·cy** *(n.)*
privelage	**priv·i·lege**	profesional	**pro·fes·sion·al**
privite	**pri·vate**	professer	**pro·fes·sor**
privitize	**pri·va·tize**	profesy	**proph·e·sy** *(v.)*
prizm	**prism**	proffess	**pro·fess**
probabillity	**prob·a·bil·i·ty**	proffessor	**pro·fes·sor**
probbably	**prob·a·bly**	proffet	**proph·et**
probbation	**pro·ba·tion**		*(one who predicts)*
probibility	**prob·a·bil·i·ty**	profficient	**pro·fi·cient**
probibly	**prob·a·bly**	proffile	**pro·file**
problimatic	**prob·lem·at·ic**	proffit	**prof·it** *(gain)*
procede	**pro·ceed** *(go on)*	proffusion	**pro·fu·sion**
proceed	**pre·cede**	proficiant	**pro·fi·cient**
	(come before)	profillactic	**pro·phy·lac·tic**
proceedure	**pro·ce·dure**	profit	**proph·et**
procession	**pre·ces·sion**		*(one who predicts)*
	(precedence)	profitible	**prof·it·a·ble**
proclame	**pro·claim**	profuzion	**pro·fu·sion**
proclimation		prognoses	**prog·no·sis**
	proc·la·ma·tion		*(sing.)*
procrasstinate		prognosis	**prog·no·ses** *(pl.)*
	pro·cras·ti·nate	prognostecation	
procriation	**pro·cre·a·tion**		**prog·nos·ti·ca·tion**

WRONG	RIGHT	WRONG	RIGHT
programmible ....pro·gram·ma·ble		propigate..........prop·a·gate	
programor ....pro·gram·mer		propoganda...prop·a·ganda	
progresive.......pro·gres·sive		proponant ....pro·po·nent	
progriss ....prog·ress		proportionnate ....pro·por·tion·ate	
prohabition ...pro·hi·bi·tion		proposel ....pro·pos·al	
projeck...................proj·ect		proppeller ....pro·pel·ler	
projecter.............pro·jec·tor		propper ....prop·er	
prolifferate ......pro·lif·er·ate		propperty...........prop·er·ty	
proliffic ....pro·lif·ic		propponent .....pro·po·nent	
prolitariate ......pro·le·tar·iat		propposition ....prop·o·si·tion	
prolliferate ......pro·lif·er·ate		propriatery ....pro·pri·e·tary	
prologe ....pro·logue		proprieter ....pro·pri·e·tor	
prominade .....prom·e·nade		propullsion ......pro·pul·sion	
prominance ...prom·i·nence		prosayic ....pro·sa·ic	
promiscuety ....prom·is·cu·i·ty		proscribe ....pre·scribe *(order)*	
promiscuos...........................pro·mis·cu·ous		prosecute...........per·se·cute *(harass)*	
promissing........prom·is·ing		prosecuter.......pros·e·cu·tor	
promp ....prompt		proselitize ....pros·e·lyt·ize	
pronounciation...................pro·nun·ci·a·tion		prosessed ....proc·essed	
pronounse ....pro·nounce		prosession........pro·ces·sion *(parade)*	
proove ....prove		prosicute ....pros·e·cute *(legal term)*	
propasition....prop·o·si·tion		prosicution ...pros·e·cu·tion	
propelent ....pro·pel·lant		prosletyze ....pros·e·lyt·ize	
propellor ....pro·pel·ler		prosparity........pros·per·i·ty	
propencity ......pro·pen·si·ty		prosparous ....pros·per·ous	
prophallactic ....pro·phy·lac·tic		prospecter.......pros·pec·tor	
prophecy......proph·e·sy *(v.)*		prospective .....per·spec·tive *(view)*	
prophesy .....proph·e·cy *(n.)*		prosperrity.......pros·per·i·ty	
prophet ....prof·it *(gain)*			
propicious ....pro·pi·tious			

WRONG	RIGHT	WRONG	RIGHT
prossecution ....pros·e·cu·tion		pruriant ....pru·ri·ent	
prossetics ....pros·thet·tics		pseudanim .....pseu·do·nym	
prosspect..............pros·pect		psiche ..psy·che *(mind; soul)*	
prostate ...pros·trate *(prone)*		psichedelic ....psy·che·del·ic	
prostatute..........pros·ti·tute		psichiatrist.....psy·chi·a·trist	
prostheesis.......pros·the·sis		psichic ....psy·chic	
prostrate ...pros·tate *(gland)*		psichological...................... ....psy·cho·log·i·cal	
protaganist....pro·tag·o·nist			
protan ....pro·ton		psichosis ....psy·cho·ses *(pl.)*	
protaplasm .....pro·to·plasm		psichosis ....psy·cho·sis *(sing.)*	
protatype ....pro·to·type		psolm ....psalm	
protecol ....pro·to·col		psorriasis ....pso·ri·a·sis	
protecter ....pro·tec·tor		psuedonym ....pseu·do·nym	
protein ....pro·te·an *(changeable)*		psycapath.......psy·cho·path	
protien ....pro·tein *(substance)*		psych ...psy·che *(mind; soul)*	
Protistant ....Prot·es·tant		psychadelic ....psy·che·del·ic	
protocall..............pro·to·col			
protracter ....pro·trac·tor		psyche......................psych *(excite; outwit)*	
protrussion ......pro·tru·sion		psychec ....psy·chic	
protuberence...................... ....pro·tu·ber·ance		psychoanallysis...................... ....psy·cho·a·nal·y·sis	
provance ....prov·ince		psychobable ....psy·cho·bab·ble	
provedence .....prov·i·dence			
proverbeal ....pro·ver·bi·al		psychollogy ...psy·chol·o·gy	
provication...pro·vo·ca·tion		psychologecal ....psy·cho·log·i·cal	
providance......prov·i·dence			
provintial ....pro·vin·cial		psychosamatic ....psy·cho·so·mat·ic	
provocitive....pro·voc·a·tive			
prowel....................prowl		psychoses...........psy·cho·sis *(sing.)*	
proxide ....per·ox·ide		psychotheripy...................... ....psy·cho·ther·apy	
proximaty ....prox·im·i·ty			
prudance.............pru·dence		psyciatrist ......psy·chi·a·trist	

WRONG	RIGHT
psycoanalysis	psy·cho·a·nal·y·sis
psycological	psy·cho·log·i·cal
psycotic	psy·chot·ic
pteradactyl	pter·o·dac·tyl
pubarty	pu·ber·ty
pubec	pu·bic
publec	pub·lic
publecation	pub·li·ca·tion
publesher	pub·lish·er
publisity	pub·lic·i·ty
puding	pud·ding
pudle	pud·dle
puker	puck·er *(purse lips)*
pullmonary	pul·mo·nary
pullpit	pul·pit
pullsate	pul·sate
pullverize	pul·ver·ize
pully	pul·ley
pulmenary	pul·mo·nary
pulpet	pul·pit
pulvarize	pul·ver·ize
pumise	pum·ice
pumkin	pump·kin
punative	pu·ni·tive
punctuetion	punc·tu·a·tion
punctule	punc·tu·al
puneshment	pun·ish·ment
puney	pu·ny
pungant	pun·gent
punkin	pump·kin
punktual	punc·tu·al

WRONG	RIGHT
punktuation	punc·tu·a·tion
punkture	punc·ture
punnishment	pun·ish·ment
punnitive	pu·ni·tive
pupel	pu·pil
puppit	pup·pet
puray	pu·rée
purcent	per·cent
purception	per·cep·tion
purchace	pur·chase
purcolator	per·co·la·tor
purcussion	per·cus·sion
puré	pu·rée
purefication	puri·fi·ca·tion
pureley	pure·ly
Puretan	Pu·ri·tan
purety	pu·ri·ty
purfectible	per·fect·i·ble
purforate	per·fo·rate
performance	per·form·ance
purgery	per·ju·ry
purgetory	pur·ga·to·ry
purient	pru·ri·ent
purifecation	puri·fi·ca·tion
puritannical	puri·tan·i·cal
purl	pearl *(gem)*
purmeate	per·me·ate
purmutation	per·mu·ta·tion
purpel	pur·ple
purpendicular	per·pen·dic·u·lar

WRONG	RIGHT	WRONG	RIGHT
purplexity	**per·plex·i·ty**	putred	**pu·trid**
purposly	**pur·pose·ly**	puttie	**put·ty**
pursute	**pur·suit**	puzzeling	**puz·zling**
purterb	**per·turb**	pweblo	**pueb·lo**
puss	**pus** (*matter*)	pyremid	**pyr·a·mid**
pusstule	**pus·tule**	pyrotecnics	**py·ro·tech·nics**
put	**putt** (*golf stroke*)	pythan	**py·thon**

Q

WRONG	RIGHT	WRONG	RIGHT
qeue	**queue** *(line)*	quandry	**quan·da·ry**
qiche	**quiche**	quanitative	**quan·ti·ta·tive**
Quaalood	**Quaa·lude**	quanity	**quan·ti·ty**
quackary	**quack·ery**	quantafy	**quan·ti·fy**
quadralateral		quante	**quaint**
	quad·ri·lat·er·al	quantety	**quan·ti·ty**
quadraplegic		quantom	**quan·tum**
	quad·ri·ple·gic	quarel	**quar·rel**
quadratick	**quad·rat·ic**	quarrantine	**quar·an·tine**
quadrent	**quad·rant**	quarterley	**quar·ter·ly**
quadrilion	**quad·ril·lion**	quartor	**quar·ter**
quadrillateral		quarts	**quartz** *(mineral)*
	quad·ri·lat·er·al	quarulous	**quer·u·lous**
quadriplejic		quarum	**quo·rum**
	quad·ri·ple·gic	quary	**quar·ry** *(prey; hole)*
quadrupel	**quad·ru·ple**	quazar	**qua·sar**
quadruplette	**quad·ru·plet**	quazi	**qua·si**
quafe	**quaff**	que	**queue** *(line)*
quagmier	**quag·mire**	quear	**queer**
qualafication		queazy	**quea·sy**
	qual·i·fi·ca·tion	Quebeck	**Que·bec**
quale	**quail** *(bird; cower)*	queche	**quiche**
qualety	**qual·i·ty**	queery	**que·ry**
quallified	**qual·i·fied**	queesy	**quea·sy**
quallitative	**qual·i·ta·tive**	queiscent	**qui·es·cent**
quallity	**qual·i·ty**	quel	**quell**
Qualude	**Quaa·lude**	quentessential	
quam	**qualm**		**quin·tes·sen·tial**

179

WRONG	RIGHT	WRONG	RIGHT
queralous	**quer·u·lous**	quintissential	
querk	**quirk**		**quin·tes·sen·tial**
quesstion	**ques·tion**	quints	**quince** *(tree)*
questionaire		quintupplet	**quin·tu·plet**
	ques·tion·naire	quiry	**que·ry**
questionible		quisine	**cui·sine**
	ques·tion·a·ble	quite	**qui·et** *(silence)*
quesy	**quea·sy**	quiting	**quit·ting**
quey	**quay** *(wharf)*	quivver	**quiv·er**
quible	**quib·ble**	quixatic	**quix·ot·ic**
quicksotic	**quix·ot·ic**	quizical	**quiz·zi·cal**
quiessent	**qui·es·cent**	quorentine	**quar·an·tine**
quiet	**quite** *(entirely)*	quorril	**quar·rel**
quiettude	**qui·e·tude**	quorry	**quar·ry**
quillt	**quilt**	quort	**quart**
quinesential		quorter	**quar·ter**
	quin·tes·sen·tial	quortet	**quar·tet**
quinnine	**qui·nine**	quoteable	**quot·a·ble**
quintilion	**quin·til·lion**	quotiant	**quo·tient**

180

R

WRONG	RIGHT
rabbel	**rab·ble**
rabbenical	**rab·bin·i·cal**
rabbet	**rab·bit** *(animal)*
rabbid	**rab·id**
rabbie	**rab·bi**
rabbies	**ra·bies** *(disease)*
rabed	**rab·id**
rabellion	**re·bel·lion**
rabi	**rab·bi**
rabinical	**rab·bin·i·cal**
rabit	**rab·bit** *(animal)*
rable	**rab·ble**
racey	**racy**
rachet	**ratch·et**
racizm	**rac·ism**
rackit	**rack·et**
raconter	**rac·on·teur**
racous	**rau·cous**
radacal	**rad·i·cal** *(extreme)*
raddar	**ra·dar**
raddial	**ra·di·al**
raddically	**rad·i·cal·ly**
raddio	**ra·dio**
raddish	**rad·ish**
rade	**raid**
radeal	**ra·di·al**
radeating	**ra·di·at·ing**
radeo	**ra·dio**

WRONG	RIGHT
radeoactive	**ra·di·o·ac·tive**
radeology	**ra·di·ol·o·gy**
radeus	**ra·di·us**
radiactive	**ra·di·o·ac·tive**
radialogy	**ra·di·ol·o·gy**
radiateing	**ra·di·at·ing**
radiater	**ra·di·a·tor**
radicaly	**rad·i·cal·ly**
radicle	**rad·i·cal** *(extreme)*
radience	**ra·di·ance**
raffel	**raf·fle**
raffter	**raft·er**
raged	**rag·ged** *(tattered)*
rageing	**rag·ing**
raggoo	**ra·gout**
raglen	**rag·lan**
ragou	**ra·gout**
railling	**rail·ing**
railrode	**rail·road**
rain	**reign** *(rule)*
rain	**rein** *(a leather strap)*
raindeer	**rein·deer**
raise	**raze** *(demolish)*
raisen	**rai·sin**
rak	**rack** *(framework)*
rak	**wrack** *(torment)*
rakeing	**rak·ing**
rakket	**racket**

WRONG	RIGHT
rale	**rail**
ralley	**ral·ly**
ramafication	**ram·i·fi·ca·tion**
rambeling	**ram·bling**
ramblor	**ram·bler**
rambunktious	**ram·bunc·tious**
ramedial	**re·me·di·al**
rammification	**ram·i·fi·ca·tion**
rammpage	**ram·page**
rampent	**ramp·ant**
ramshakle	**ram·shack·le**
rancer	**ran·cor**
randezvous	**ren·dez·vous**
rane	**reign** *(rule)*
rane	**rein** *(a leather strap)*
ranewal	**re·new·al**
rangeing	**rang·ing**
rangey	**rangy**
rangle	**wran·gle**
rankor	**ran·cor**
ransak	**ran·sack**
ransid	**ran·cid**
ransome	**ran·som**
rap	**wrap** *(cover)*
rapchure	**rap·ture**
rapiar	**ra·pi·er**
raping	**rap·ping** *(tapping)*
raport	**rap·port** *(harmony)*
raport	**re·port** *(an account)*
rappid	**rap·id**

WRONG	RIGHT
rappidity	**ra·pid·i·ty**
rappier	**ra·pi·er**
rappist	**rap·ist**
rappor	**rap·port** *(harmony)*
rapprochment	**rap·proche·ment**
rapsody	**rhap·so·dy**
rapter	**rap·tor**
raquetball	**rac·quet·ball**
rarafy	**rar·e·fy**
rarety	**rar·i·ty**
rarly	**rare·ly**
rascel	**ras·cal**
rase	**race** *(contest)*
rase	**raise** *(lift)*
rase	**raze** *(demolish)*
rashal	**ra·cial**
rasin	**rai·sin**
rasism	**rac·ism**
raskal	**ras·cal**
rassberry	**rasp·ber·ry**
rassion	**ra·tion**
ratan	**rat·tan**
ratchit	**ratch·et**
ratefy	**rat·i·fy**
rateing	**rat·ing**
rateo	**ra·tio**
rath	**wrath** *(rage)*
ratial	**ra·cial**
rational	**ra·tion·a·le** *(explanation)*
rationallize	**ration·al·ize**
rationel	**ra·tion·al** *(reasoning)*

WRONG	RIGHT	WRONG	RIGHT
ratle	**rat·tle**	reaf	**reef**
ratlesnake	**rat·tle·snake**	reajustment	
ratten	**rat·tan**		**re·ad·just·ment**
rattify	**rat·i·fy**	reak	**reek** *(smell)*
rattion	**ra·tion**	real	**reel** *(whirl; spool)*
rattional	**ra·tion·al**	realaty	**re·al·i·ty** *(fact)*
	(reasoning)	realine	**re·a·lign**
rattleling	**rat·tling**	realistick	**re·al·is·tic**
rattlsnake	**rat·tle·snake**	reality	**re·al·ty** *(real estate)*
raucus	**rau·cous**	reallign	**re·a·lign**
raunchey	**raun·chy**	reallism	**re·al·ism**
ravageing	**rav·ag·ing**	reallistic	**re·al·is·tic**
ravanous	**rav·e·nous**	reallity	**re·al·i·ty** *(fact)*
ravege	**rav·age**	reallization	**real·i·za·tion**
raveing	**rav·ing**	realstate	**real es·tate**
ravene	**ra·vine**	realty	**re·al·i·ty** *(fact)*
ravenus	**rav·e·nous**	realy	**re·al·ly**
raveoli	**ra·vi·o·li**	reancarnation	
ravle	**rav·el**		**re·in·car·na·tion**
ravvish	**rav·ish**	rearange	**re·ar·range**
rawide	**raw·hide**	rearrangment	
rayan	**ray·on**		**re·ar·range·ment**
raze	**raise** *(lift)*	reasen	**rea·son**
razer	**ra·zor**	reasonible	**rea·son·a·ble**
razzberry	**rasp·ber·ry**	reath	**wreath** *(a band)*
reacktionary		reathe	**wreathe**
	re·ac·tion·ary		*(to encircle)*
reactavate	**re·ac·ti·vate**	reazon	**rea·son**
reacter	**re·ac·tor**	rebait	**re·bate**
reactionery	**re·ac·tion·ary**	rebbel	**reb·el**
read	**reed** *(plant)*	rebbellious	**re·bel·lious**
readilly	**read·i·ly**	rebbuttal	**re·but·tal**
readjusment		rebeling	**reb·el·ling**
	re·ad·just·ment	rebelion	**re·bel·lion**
readyness	**read·i·ness**	rebelious	**re·bel·lious**

WRONG	RIGHT
reble	**reb·el**
rebownd	**re·bound**
rebutal	**re·but·tal**
recalsitrant	**re·cal·ci·trant**
recampense	**rec·om·pense**
recanize	**rec·og·nize**
recannoiter	**rec·on·noi·ter**
recapitchulation	**re·ca·pit·u·la·tion**
reccognise	**rec·og·nize**
reccognition	**rec·og·ni·tion**
reccolect	**rec·ol·lect**
reccommend	**rec·om·mend**
recconciliation	**rec·on·cil·i·a·tion**
recconning	**reck·on·ing**
receed	**re·cede**
receiveable	**re·ceiv·a·ble**
recent	**re·sent** *(feel a hurt)*
recepe	**rec·i·pe**
recepter	**re·cep·tor**
recepticle	**re·cep·ta·cle**
recerd	**rec·ord**
recesion	**re·ces·sion**
receve	**re·ceive**
rech	**retch** *(vomit)*
reciept	**re·ceipt**
recieve	**re·ceive**
recint	**re·cent** *(new)*
recipiant	**re·cip·i·ent**
recipracal	**re·cip·ro·cal**
recipracate	**re·cip·ro·cate**
recitel	**re·cit·al**

WRONG	RIGHT
reck	**wreck**
reckening	**reck·on·ing**
reckoncilible	**rec·on·cil·a·ble**
reckord	**rec·ord**
reckreational	**rec·re·a·tion·al**
recktify	**rec·ti·fy**
recktitude	**rec·ti·tude**
reclaimation	**rec·la·ma·tion**
reclame	**re·claim**
reclineing	**re·clin·ing**
recloose	**rec·luse**
recoarse	**re·course**
recognizence	**re·cog·ni·zance**
recognizible	**rec·og·niz·a·ble**
recolleck	**rec·ol·lect**
recomend	**rec·om·mend**
recompence	**rec·om·pense**
reconaissance	**re·con·nais·sance**
reconcileable	**rec·on·cil·a·ble**
reconcilliation	**rec·on·cil·i·a·tion**
reconnaisance	**re·con·nais·sance**
reconoiter	**rec·on·noi·ter**
reconsiliation	**rec·on·cil·i·a·tion**
reconstatute	**re·con·sti·tute**

WRONG	RIGHT	WRONG	RIGHT
reconstrucktion		redundency......................	
...........**re·con·struc·tion**		...............**re·dun·dan·cy**	
recoop....................**re·coup**		redundent ....**re·dun·dant**	
recooperate.....**re·cu·per·ate**		redusing..............**re·duc·ing**	
recorse ....**re·course**		reed..........**read** (*understand*)	
recoverey.............**re·cov·ery**		reek ....**wreak** (*inflict*)	
recquirement		reel ....**real** (*actual*)	
...............**re·quire·ment**		reelly ....**re·al·ly**	
recquisite ....**req·ui·site**		reem ....**ream**	
recquisition ....**req·ui·si·tion**		reemburse ....**re·im·burse**	
recreationel		reencarnation	
...............**rec·re·a·tion·al**		...........**re·in·car·na·tion**	
recrute ....**re·cruit**		reenforcement	
rectafy.....................**rec·ti·fy**		...........**re·in·force·ment**	
rectanguler ....**rec·tan·gu·lar**		reep ....**reap**	
rectatude ....**rec·ti·tude**		reeson........................**rea·son**	
rectel ....**rec·tal**		refecktory ....**re·fec·to·ry**	
recter ....**rec·tor**		referal ....**re·fer·ral**	
rectery ....**rec·to·ry**		referance ....**ref·er·ence**	
recuparate.......**re·cu·per·ate**		refered ....**re·ferred**	
recurence ....**re·cur·rence**		referindum....**ref·er·en·dum**	
recuring..............**re·cur·ring**		refering ....**re·fer·ring**	
recurrance.......**re·cur·rence**		referrel....................**re·fer·ral**	
recykle ....**re·cy·cle**		refferee ....**ref·er·ee**	
red ....**read** (*pt. of read*)		refference...........**ref·er·ence**	
reddolent ....**red·o·lent**		refferendum	
reddy.........................**ready**		...............**ref·er·en·dum**	
redeam....................**re·deem**		refferring ....**re·fer·ring**	
redemtion ......**re·demp·tion**		reffuge ....**ref·uge**	
rediculous..........**ridic·u·lous**		reffugee...............**ref·u·gee**	
redolant............**red·o·lent**		reffuse ....**ref·use** (*trash*)	
redondancy......................		refinary....................**re·fin·ery**	
...............**re·dun·dan·cy**		refinment........**re·fine·ment**	
reduceing............**re·duc·ing**		refleck ....**re·flect**	
reducktion.........**re·duc·tion**		reflecks......**re·flex** (*response*)	

185

WRONG	RIGHT	WRONG	RIGHT
reflecktion	**re·flec·tion**	regualation	**reg·u·la·tion**
refoose	**re·fuse** (decline)	reguard	**re·gard**
reformitory		regulater	**reg·u·la·tor**
	re·form·a·to·ry	reguler	**reg·u·lar**
refracktion	**re·frac·tion**	regurjitation	
refrane	**re·frain**		**re·gur·gi·ta·tion**
refrence	**ref·er·ence**	reguvenate	**re·ju·ve·nate**
refreshmint	**re·fresh·ment**	rehabillitate	
refridgerator			**re·ha·bil·i·tate**
	re·frig·er·a·tor	rehearsel	**re·hears·al**
refun	**re·fund**	reign	
refusel	**re·fus·al**		**rein** (a leather strap)
refuze	**re·fuse** (decline)	reimberse	**re·im·burse**
regae	**reg·gae**	rein	**reign** (rule)
regail	**re·gale** (entertain)	reinforcemint	
regale	**re·gal** (royal)		**re·in·force·ment**
regallia	**re·ga·lia**	reitarate	**re·it·er·ate**
regamen	**reg·i·men**	rejeck	**re·ject**
regament	**reg·i·ment**	rejency	**re·gen·cy**
regel	**re·gal** (royal)	rejenerate	**re·gen·er·ate**
regeme	**re·gime**	rejent	**re·gent**
regenarate	**re·gen·er·ate**	rejime	**re·gime**
regergitation		rejimen	**reg·i·men**
	re·gur·gi·ta·tion	rejiment	**reg·i·ment**
regester	**reg·is·ter**	rejister	**reg·is·ter**
reggay	**reg·gae**	rejoiceing	**re·joic·ing**
regimint	**reg·i·ment**	rejoiner	**re·join·der**
regin	**re·gion**	rejoyce	**re·joice**
reginal	**re·gion·al**	rejuvanate	**re·ju·ve·nate**
regincy	**re·gen·cy**	reke	**reek** (smell)
regint	**re·gent**	rekless	**reck·less**
regionel	**re·gion·al**	rekluse	**rec·luse**
regon	**re·gion**	reknowned	**re·nowned**
regresion	**re·gres·sion**	relacks	**re·lax**
regretable	**re·gret·ta·ble**	relagate	**rel·e·gate**

WRONG	RIGHT	WRONG	RIGHT
relaid	**re·layed** *(conveyed)*	remembrence	**re·mem·brance**
relateing	**re·lat·ing**	remenisce	**rem·i·nisce**
relativaty	**rel·a·tiv·i·ty**	remine	**re·mind**
relavant	**rel·e·vant**	reminisence	**rem·i·nis·cence**
releese	**re·lease**	reminiss	**rem·i·nisce**
releif	**re·lief** *(n.)*	remision	**re·mis·sion**
releive	**re·lieve** *(v.)*	remitance	**re·mit·tance**
relevent	**rel·e·vant**	remminisce	**rem·i·nisce**
relick	**rel·ic**	remminiscene	**rem·i·nis·cence**
relie	**re·ly**	remnent	**rem·nant**
relieable	**re·li·a·ble**	remourse	**re·morse**
relient	**re·li·ant**	removeable	**re·mov·a·ble**
religin	**re·li·gion**	removel	**re·mov·al**
religous	**re·li·gious**	ren	**wren**
relization	**real·i·za·tion**	renagade	**ren·e·gade**
rellative	**rel·a·tive**	renaissence	**ren·ais·sance**
rellativity	**rel·a·tiv·i·ty**	renavate	**ren·o·vate**
rellegate	**rel·e·gate**	rench	**wrench**
rellentless	**re·lent·less**	rendavous	**ren·dez·vous**
rellevant	**rel·e·vant**	rendring	**ren·der·ing**
rellic	**rel·ic**	renewel	**re·new·al**
relligion	**re·li·gion**	renig	**re·nege**
relligious	**re·li·gious**	rennaissance	**ren·ais·sance**
rellinquish	**re·lin·quish**	rennegade	**ren·e·gade**
rellish	**rel·ish**	rennovate	**ren·o·vate**
relluctance	**re·luc·tance**	renouned	**re·nowned**
relm	**realm**	renownce	**re·nounce**
reluctently	**re·luc·tant·ly**	rentel	**rent·al**
relyable	**re·li·a·ble**	renumeration	**re·mu·ner·a·tion**
remady	**rem·e·dy**	renunsiation	**re·nun·ci·a·tion**
remander	**re·main·der**		
remane	**re·main**		
remann	**re·mand**		
remarkible	**re·mark·a·ble**		
remedeal	**re·me·di·al**		

187

WRONG	RIGHT	WRONG	RIGHT
repare	**re·pair**	reppetition	**rep·e·ti·tion**
repayed	**re·paid**	repport	
repeel	**re·peal**		**re·port** *(an account)*
repeet	**re·peat**	reppresent	**rep·re·sent**
repeling	**re·pel·ling**	reppudiate	**re·pu·di·ate**
repell	**re·pel** *(drive back)*	repputation	**rep·u·ta·tion**
repellant	**re·pel·lent**	reprabate	**rep·ro·bate**
repentent	**re·pent·ant**	repraduce	**re·pro·duce**
reperations	**rep·a·ra·tions**	reprahensible	
repercusion			**rep·re·hen·si·ble**
	re·per·cus·sion	repramand	**rep·ri·mand**
repersent	**rep·re·sent**	reprasentative	
repertoiar	**rep·er·toire**		**rep·re·sent·a·tive**
repete	**re·peat**	reprehensable	
repetitius	**rep·e·ti·tious**		**rep·re·hen·si·ble**
repetoire	**rep·er·toire**	repreive	**re·prieve**
repetory	**rep·er·to·ry**	represe	**re·prise**
repettitive	**re·pet·i·tive**	represion	**re·pres·sion**
repitition	**rep·e·ti·tion**	repriman	**rep·ri·mand**
repititious	**rep·e·ti·tious**	reprizal	**re·pris·al**
replaca	**rep·li·ca**	reprize	**re·prise**
replacment	**re·place·ment**	reproche	**re·proach**
repleat	**re·plete**	reproduse	**re·pro·duce**
replennish	**re·plen·ish**	reptle	**rep·tile**
replie	**re·ply**	republick	**re·pub·lic**
reposatory	**re·pos·i·to·ry**	repudeate	**re·pu·di·ate**
reposession		repugnent	**re·pug·nant**
	re·pos·ses·sion	repullsive	**re·pul·sive**
repparations		requasition	**req·ui·si·tion**
	rep·a·ra·tions	requess	**re·quest**
reppartee	**rep·ar·tee**	requierment	
reppel	**re·pel** *(drive back)*		**re·quire·ment**
reppercussion		requiset	**req·ui·site**
	re·per·cus·sion	resadue	**res·i·due**
reppertory	**rep·er·to·ry**	resaleable	**re·sal·a·ble**

188

WRONG	RIGHT	WRONG	RIGHT
resalution	**res·o·lu·tion**	resistor	**re·sist·er**
résamé	**ré·su·mé**		*(one who resists)*
rescend	**re·scind**	resital	**re·cit·al**
rescusitator	**re·sus·ci·ta·tor**	resitation	**rec·i·ta·tion**
resede	**re·cede**	resonater	**res·o·na·tor**
resedential	**res·i·den·tial**	resonence	**res·o·nance**
resegnation	**res·ig·na·tion**	resorceful	**re·source·ful**
reseipt	**re·ceipt**	resownding	**re·sound·ing**
reseive	**re·ceive**	respand	**re·spond**
resemblence		respeck	**re·spect**
	re·sem·blance	respectible	**re·spect·a·ble**
resent	**re·cent** *(new)*	resperation	**res·pi·ra·tion**
reseptacle	**re·cep·ta·cle**	respirater	**res·pi·ra·tor**
reseption	**re·cep·tion**	respit	**res·pite**
reseptor	**re·cep·tor**	resplendant	**re·splend·ent**
reserch	**re·search**	responsability	
resergent	**re·sur·gent**		**re·spon·si·bil·i·ty**
reserrection		responsable	**re·spon·si·ble**
	res·ur·rec·tion	respratory	**res·pi·ra·to·ry**
resess	**re·cess**	resservation	
resession	**re·ces·sion**		**res·er·va·tion**
resevoir	**res·er·voir**	restaration	**res·to·ra·tion**
residancy	**res·i·den·cy**	restatution	**res·ti·tu·tion**
residencial	**res·i·den·tial**	resterant	**res·tau·rant**
residew	**res·i·due**	restle	**wres·tle**
resiliance	**re·sil·ience**	restrant	**re·straint**
resind	**re·scind**	restrant	**res·tau·rant**
resine	**re·sign**	restrick	**re·strict**
resipe	**rec·i·pe**	resultent	**re·sult·ant**
resipient	**re·cip·i·ent**	résumae	**ré·su·mé**
resiprocal	**re·cip·ro·cal**	resumtion	**re·sump·tion**
resiprocate	**re·cip·ro·cate**	resurection	**res·ur·rec·tion**
resistence	**re·sist·ance**	resurgant	**re·sur·gent**
resister	**re·sis·tor**	resussitator	**re·sus·ci·ta·tor**
	(electrical device)	resycle	**re·cy·cle**

WRONG	RIGHT	WRONG	RIGHT
retale	**re·tail**	revelry	**rev·er·ie**
retalliate	**re·tal·i·ate**		*(daydream)*
retane	**re·tain**	revelry	**re·veil·le**
retanue	**ret·i·nue**		*(bugle call)*
retch	**wretch**	reverance	**rev·er·ence**
	(miserable person)	reverbarate	**re·ver·ber·ate**
retecence	**ret·i·cence**	reversable	**re·vers·i·ble**
retension	**re·ten·tion**	revery	**rev·el·ry** *(festivity)*
retern	**re·turn**	revery	**rev·er·ie**
retisence	**ret·i·cence**		*(daydream)*
retna	**ret·i·na**	revinge	**re·venge**
retorical	**rhe·tor·i·cal**	revission	**re·vi·sion**
retrabution	**ret·ri·bu·tion**	revivel	**re·viv·al**
retrack	**re·tract**	revize	**re·vise**
retraspect	**ret·ro·spect**	revolutionery	
retreet	**re·treat**		**rev·o·lu·tion·ary**
retreival	**re·triev·al**	revolveing	**re·volv·ing**
retrospeck	**ret·ro·spect**	revrence	**rev·er·ence**
retticence	**ret·i·cence**	revullsion	**re·vul·sion**
rettina	**ret·i·na**	rezentment	**re·sent·ment**
rettinue	**ret·i·nue**	rezervation	**res·er·va·tion**
rettribution	**ret·ri·bu·tion**	rezervoir	**res·er·voir**
reumatic	**rheu·mat·ic**	rezide	**re·side**
revalation	**rev·e·la·tion**	rezidency	**res·i·den·cy**
revalutionary		rezidential	**res·i·den·tial**
	rev·o·lu·tion·ary	rezidual	**re·sid·u·al**
revanue	**rev·e·nue**	rezidue	**res·i·due**
reveer	**re·vere**	rezign	**re·sign**
reveiw	**re·view** *(survey)*	rezignation	**res·ig·na·tion**
reveiw	**re·vue**	rezin	**res·in**
	(musical show)	rezistance	**re·sist·ance**
revellation	**rev·e·la·tion**	rezolution	**res·o·lu·tion**
revelle	**re·veil·le**	rezolved	**re·solved**
	(bugle call)	rezonance	**res·o·nance**
revellry	**rev·el·ry** *(festivity)*	rezonator	**res·o·na·tor**

WRONG	RIGHT	WRONG	RIGHT
rezort	**re·sort**	ridress	**re·dress**
rezounding	**re·sound·ing**	riducing	**re·duc·ing**
rezultant	**re·sult·ant**	riduction	**re·duc·tion**
rezumption	**re·sump·tion**	riduplication	
rhapsady	**rhap·so·dy**		**re·du·pli·ca·tion**
rhetoricle	**rhe·tor·i·cal**	rie	**rye** *(grain)*
rheumatick	**rheu·mat·ic**	riffle	**ri·fle** *(gun)*
rhime	**rhyme** *(verse)*	rifle	**rif·fle** *(shuffle)*
rhinoseros	**rhi·noc·er·os**	riformatory	
rhithm	**rhythm**		**re·form·a·to·ry**
rhodadendron		rifrigerator	**re·frig·er·a·tor**
	rho·do·den·dron	rifute	**re·fute**
rhyme	**rime** *(frost)*	rigalia	**re·ga·lia**
rhythem	**rhythm**	rigamaroll	**rig·ma·role**
rhythymical	**rhyth·mi·cal**	rige	**ridge**
ribben	**rib·bon**	rigerous	**rig·or·ous**
ricachet	**ric·o·chet**	riggatoni	**ri·ga·to·ni**
riceptacle	**re·cep·ta·cle**	rigger	**rig·or** *(hardship)*
riciprocate	**re·cip·ro·cate**	riggle	**wrig·gle**
ricital	**re·cit·al**	right	**rite** *(ritual)*
ricketts	**rick·ets**	right	**write** *(inscribe)*
ricognizance		rightous	**right·eous**
	re·cog·ni·zance	riging	**rig·ging**
ricoshet	**ric·o·chet**	rigor	**rig·ger** *(one who rigs)*
ricruit	**re·cruit**	rigorus	**rig·or·ous**
ridacule	**rid·i·cule**	rigression	**re·gres·sion**
riddel	**rid·dle**	rigurgitation	
riddence	**rid·dance**		**re·gur·gi·ta·tion**
riddicule	**rid·i·cule**	rilationship	**re·la·tion·ship**
rideem	**re·deem**	rilease	**re·lease**
rideing	**rid·ing**	rilentless	**re·lent·less**
ridemption	**re·demp·tion**	rilief	**re·lief** *(n.)*
ridgid	**rig·id**	rilieve	**re·lieve** *(v.)*
ridickulous	**ridic·u·lous**	rimand	**re·mand**
ridle	**rid·dle**	rimember	**re·mem·ber**

WRONG	RIGHT	WRONG	RIGHT
rimiss	**re·miss**	rivoke	**re·voke**
rimission	**re·mis·sion**	rivolt	**re·volt**
rimuneration		rivue	**re·vue** *(musical show)*
	re·mu·ner·a·tion	rivulsion	**re·vul·sion**
rine	**rind**	robbin	**rob·in**
rinege	**re·nege**	robbot	**ro·bot**
rinestone	**rhine·stone**	roben	**rob·in**
ring	**wring** *(twist)*	robery	**rob·bery**
rinoceros	**rhi·noc·eros**	roche	**roach**
riotus	**ri·ot·ous**	rockit	**rock·et**
riplenish	**re·plen·ish**	rodant	**ro·dent**
ripository	**re·pos·i·to·ry**	rodao	**ro·deo**
riprisal	**re·pris·al**	rododendron	
ripugnant	**re·pug·nant**		**rho·do·den·dron**
ripulsive	**re·pul·sive**	roge	**rogue**
riscind	**re·scind**	roil	**roy·al** *(regal)*
risentment	**re·sent·ment**	role	**roll** *(turn)*
risidual	**re·sid·u·al**	roler	**roll·er**
riskey	**risky** *(dangerous)*	roll	**role** *(an actor's part)*
risky	**ris·qué** *(indecent)*	romane	**ro·maine**
risourceful	**re·source·ful**	romanse	**ro·mance**
rispond	**re·spond**	rome	**roam**
risponsible	**re·spon·si·ble**	rommantic	**ro·man·tic**
ritchual	**rit·u·al**	ronchy	**raun·chy**
rite	**right** *(correct)*	rondezvous	**ren·dez·vous**
rite	**write** *(inscribe)*	rone	**roan**
rithe	**writhe**	roomate	**room·mate**
rithm	**rhythm**	roomor	**room·er** *(lodger)*
ritort	**re·tort**	root	**route** *(way)*
ritten	**writ·ten**	rootabaga	**ru·ta·ba·ga**
rivallry	**ri·val·ry**	rosery	**ro·sa·ry**
rivelry	**ri·val·ry**	rosey	**rosy**
riverberate	**re·ver·ber·ate**	rost	**roast**
rivision	**re·vi·sion**	roten	**rot·ten**
rivit	**riv·et**	rotery	**ro·ta·ry**

WRONG	RIGHT	WRONG	RIGHT
rotiserie	**rotis·serie**	ruff	**rough** *(not smooth)*
rotonda	**ro·tun·da**	ruffage	**rough·age**
Rotweiler	**Rott·weil·er**	rufian	**ruf·fi·an**
roudy	**row·dy**	rufle	**ruf·fle**
rouff	**rough** *(not smooth)*	ruge	**rouge**
roughege	**rough·age**	rulette	**rou·lette**
rouje	**rouge**	rumage	**rum·mage**
roulet	**rou·lette**	rumanant	**ru·mi·nant**
rout	**route** *(way)*	rumatic	**rheu·mat·ic**
route	**root** *(source)*	rumenate	**ru·mi·nate**
route	**rout** *(defeat)*	rumer	**ru·mor** *(gossip)*
routene	**rou·tine**	ruminent	**ru·mi·nant**
row	**roe** *(fish eggs)*	rummege	**rum·mage**
rowse	**rouse**	rung	**wrung**
rowst	**roust**		*(pt. of wring)*
rowt	**rout** *(defeat)*	runing	**run·ning**
royal	**roil** *(stir up)*	rupchure	**rup·ture**
royel	**roy·al** *(regal)*	rurel	**ru·ral**
royelty	**roy·al·ty**	ruset	**rus·set**
rozin	**ros·in**	russle	**rus·tle**
rubarb	**rhu·barb**	rutine	**rou·tine**
rubbry	**rub·bery**	ruttabaga	**ru·ta·ba·ga**
rubela	**ru·bel·la**	rutter	**rud·der**
ruber	**rub·ber**	ruze	**ruse**
rubey	**ru·by**	rye	**wry** *(twisted; ironic)*
rubish	**rub·bish**	ryme	**rime** *(frost)*
rudamentary		ryme	**rhyme** *(verse)*
	rudi·men·ta·ry	rythm	**rhythm**
rudy	**rud·dy**	rythmical	**rhyth·mi·cal**

S

WRONG	RIGHT	WRONG	RIGHT
sabattical	**sab·bat·i·cal**	sadesm	**sad·ism**
Sabbeth	**Sab·bath**	saduce	**se·duce**
sabbotage	**sab·o·tage**	saence	**sé·ance**
sabboteur	**sab·o·teur**	safegaurd	**safe·guard**
sabor	**sa·ber**	saffari	**sa·fa·ri**
saboter	**sab·o·teur**	safire	**sap·phire**
saccarine	**sac·cha·rine**	saflower	**saf·flow·er**
	(too sweet)	safron	**saf·fron**
sacerfice	**sac·ri·fice**	safty	**safe·ty**
sacerficial	**sac·ri·fi·cial**	sagga	**sa·ga**
sacerligous	**sac·ri·le·gious**	Saggitarius	**Sag·it·tar·i·us**
sacharine	**sac·cha·rin**	Sahera	**Sa·ha·ra**
	(sugar substitute)	saidism	**sad·ism**
sachel	**satch·el**	saige	**sage**
sacheration	**sat·u·ra·tion**	sail	**sale**
sack	**sac** *(organic pouch)*		*(business exchange)*
sackroiliac	**sa·cro·il·i·ac**	sailer	**sail·or** *(person)*
sacraficial	**sac·ri·fi·cial**	sailor	**sail·er** *(boat)*
sacrefice	**sac·ri·fice**	sakred	**sa·cred**
sacrelige	**sac·ri·lege**	salary	**cel·e·ry** *(vegetable)*
sacreligious	**sac·ri·le·gious**	salavate	**sal·i·vate**
sacrement	**sac·ra·ment**	sale	**sail** *(boat's canvas)*
sacrid	**sa·cred**	salemn	**sol·emn**
sacrine	**sac·cha·rine**	saliant	**sa·lient**
	(too sweet)	sallad	**sal·ad**
sacroilliac	**sa·cro·il·i·ac**	sallamander	**sal·a·man·der**
saddeling	**sad·dling**	sallami	**sa·la·mi**
saddistic	**sa·dis·tic**	sallary	**sal·a·ry** *(pay)*

194

WRONG	RIGHT	WRONG	RIGHT
sallient	**sa·lient**	saphire	**sap·phire**
salline	**sa·line**	saprano	**so·pra·no**
salliva	**sa·li·va**	Sarasen	**Sar·a·cen**
sallivate	**sal·i·vate**	sarcasem	**sar·casm**
sallon	**sa·lon**	sarcasticly	**sar·cas·ti·cal·ly**
salloon	**sa·loon**	sarcofagus	**sar·coph·a·gus**
sallutation	**sal·u·ta·tion**	sardene	**sar·dine**
sallute	**sa·lute**	sardonnic	**sar·don·ic**
salm	**psalm**	sargeant	**ser·geant**
salman	**salm·on**	saringe	**sy·ringe**
salow	**sal·low**	sarkastically	
salstice	**sol·stice**		**sar·cas·ti·cal·ly**
saltsellar	**salt·cel·lar**	sarkophagus	
salution	**so·lu·tion**		**sar·coph·a·gus**
salvege	**sal·vage**	Sarracen	**Sar·a·cen**
samantics	**se·man·tics**	sarri	**sa·ri** *(Hindu garment)*
sammon	**salm·on**	sarsparilla	**sar·sa·pa·ril·la**
samorai	**sam·u·rai**	sasafras	**sas·sa·fras**
sampeling	**sam·pling**	sashay	**sa·chet**
sanatarium	**san·i·tar·i·um**		*(perfumed powder)*
sanatation	**san·i·ta·tion**	sashiate	**sa·ti·ate**
sanctefied	**sanc·ti·fied**	sasparilla	**sar·sa·pa·ril·la**
sanctuery	**sanc·tu·ary**	satannic	**sa·tan·ic**
San Deigo	**San Di·e·go**	satchle	**satch·el**
sandle	**san·dal**	satelite	**sat·el·lite**
Sandskrit	**San·skrit**	saten	**sat·in** *(fabric)*
sandwitch	**sand·wich**	sater	**sat·yr** *(deity)*
sanetary	**san·i·tary**	Saterday	**Sat·ur·day**
sanety	**san·i·ty**	saterize	**sat·i·rize**
sangwin	**san·guine**	Satern	**Sat·urn**
saniterium	**san·i·tar·i·um**	satesfaction	**sat·is·fac·tion**
sanktion	**sanc·tion**	Satin	**Sa·tan** *(devil)*
sannitation	**san·i·ta·tion**	satisfactery	**sat·is·fac·to·ry**
Sanscrit	**San·skrit**	sattanic	**sa·tan·ic**
sanwich	**sand·wich**	sattelite	**sat·el·lite**

WRONG	RIGHT	WRONG	RIGHT
sattin	**sat·in** (fabric)	scalion	**scal·lion**
sattire	**sat·ire** (ridicule)	scallap	**scal·lop**
sattyr	**sat·yr** (deity)	scalled	**scald** (burn)
saturration	**sat·u·ra·tion**	scalpul	**scal·pel**
saucey	**sau·cy**	scandallize	**scan·dal·ize**
sauercraut	**sau·er·kraut**	Scandanavia	
saught	**sought**		**Scan·di·na·via**
saunna	**sau·na**	scandel	**scan·dal**
saurkraut	**sau·er·kraut**	scandilous	**scan·dal·ous**
sause	**sauce**	scaner	**scan·ner**
sausege	**sau·sage**	scaning	**scan·ning**
sauser	**sau·cer**	scapgoat	**scape·goat**
sautté	**sau·té**	scarceley	**scarce·ly**
savagrey	**sav·age·ry**	scarcety	**scar·ci·ty**
save	**salve** (ointment)	scared	**scarred** (marred)
savege	**sav·age**	scarey	**scary**
saveing	**sav·ing**	scarlit	**scar·let**
saver	**sa·vor** (taste or smell)	scarred	**scared** (frightened)
saver	**sav·ior** (rescuer)	scarsely	**scarce·ly**
savery	**sa·vory**	scarsity	**scar·ci·ty**
savier	**sav·ior** (rescuer)	scatering	**scat·ter·ing**
savier	**sav·er**	scatheing	**scath·ing**
	(keeper; one who saves)	scavinger	**scav·eng·er**
savoir-fair	**sa·voir-faire**	sceen	**scene** (location)
savor	**sav·ior** (rescuer)	scematic	**sche·mat·ic**
savor	**sav·er**	scemed	**schemed**
	(keeper; one who saves)	scenary	**sce·nery**
savuar-faire	**sa·voir-faire**	scennario	**sce·nar·io**
savy	**sav·vy**	scent	**cent** (money)
saxaphone	**sax·o·phone**	scent	**sent** (pt. of send)
Saxen	**Sax·on**	scepticle	**skep·ti·cal**
sayed	**said**	sceptor	**scep·ter**
scafold	**scaf·fold**	scewer	**skew·er**
scaleing	**scal·ing**	schedual	**sched·ule**
scaley	**scaly**	schedulling	**sched·ul·ing**

WRONG	RIGHT	WRONG	RIGHT
scheemed	**schemed**	scrachy	**scratchy**
schitsophrenia		scragly	**scrag·gly**
	schiz·o·phre·nia	scrambeling	**scram·bling**
schnopps	**schnapps**	scraped	**scrapped**
schnouzer	**schnau·zer**		*(discarded)*
scholer	**schol·ar**	scrapped	**scraped** *(rubbed)*
schollastic	**scho·las·tic**	scraul	**scrawl**
schoolling	**school·ing**	scrauny	**scraw·ny**
sciense	**sci·ence**	screach	**screech**
scientiffic	**sci·en·tif·ic**	screeming	**scream·ing**
scimmed	**skimmed**	scribling	**scrib·bling**
scimpy	**skimpy**	scrimage	**scrim·mage**
scintilate	**scin·til·late**	scrip	**script** *(manuscript)*
scirmish	**skir·mish**	scripcher	**scrip·ture**
scism	**schism**	script	**scrip** *(certificate)*
scismatic	**schis·mat·ic**	scrole	**scroll**
scisors	**scis·sors**	scroopulous	**scru·pu·lous**
scithe	**scythe**	scrootinize	**scru·ti·nize**
scizophrenia		scrownge	**scrounge**
	schiz·o·phre·nia	scrubed	**scrubbed**
sclirosis	**scle·ro·sis**	scrupullous	**scru·pu·lous**
scoch	**scotch**	scrutenize	**scru·ti·nize**
scolar	**schol·ar**	scruteny	**scru·ti·ny**
scolastic	**scho·las·tic**	scuad	**squad**
scooling	**school·ing**	scufle	**scuf·fle**
scooner	**schoon·er**	scull	**skull** *(head)*
scoreing	**scor·ing**	sculpcher	**sculp·ture**
scornfull	**scorn·ful**	sculpter	**sculp·tor**
Scorpeo	**Scor·pio**	scunk	**skunk**
scorpeon	**scor·pi·on**	scurge	**scourge**
Scotish	**Scot·tish**	scurilous	**scur·ril·ous**
scoul	**scowl**	scurvey	**scur·vy**
scower	**scour**	scury	**scur·ry**
scowndrel	**scoun·drel**	scutle	**scut·tle**
scowt	**scout**	scyth	**scythe**

WRONG	RIGHT
sea	**see** *(perceive)*
seady	**seedy**
sealent	**seal·ant**
sealing	**ceil·ing** *(overhead covering)*
seam	**seem** *(appear)*
seamly	**seem·ly**
seamstriss	**seam·stress**
seapage	**seep·age**
sear	**seer** *(prophet)*
seasaw	**see·saw**
seasen	**sea·son**
seasening	**sea·son·ing**
Seatle	**Se·at·tle**
Sebtember	**Sep·tem·ber**
seccede	**se·cede** *(withdraw)*
seccessive	**suc·ces·sive**
seccular	**sec·u·lar**
seceed	**se·cede** *(withdraw)*
secertary	**sec·re·tary**
seclussion	**se·clu·sion**
secondery	**sec·ond·ary**
secracy	**se·cre·cy**
secratary	**sec·re·tary**
secrative	**se·cre·tive**
secreet	**se·crete**
secreetion	**se·cre·tion**
secresy	**se·cre·cy**
secs	**sects** *(factions)*
secter	**sec·tor**
seculer	**sec·u·lar**
secullarize	**sec·u·lar·ize**
secundary	**sec·ond·ary**
securety	**se·cu·ri·ty**
sed	**said**

WRONG	RIGHT
sedament	**sed·i·ment**
sedantary	**sed·en·tary**
sedar	**ce·dar**
seddan	**se·dan**
seddation	**se·da·tion**
seddative	**sed·a·tive**
sedductive	**se·duc·tive**
sede	**cede** *(give up)*
sedentery	**sed·en·tary**
sedimant	**sed·i·ment**
seditive	**sed·a·tive**
seductave	**se·duc·tive**
see	**sea** *(body of water)*
seed	**cede** *(give up)*
seege	**siege**
seem	**seam** *(line)*
seemstress	**seam·stress**
seemy	**seamy**
seen	**scene** *(location)*
seenile	**se·nile**
seepege	**seep·age**
seequel	**se·quel**
seequin	**se·quin**
seer	**sear** *(burn)*
seeth	**seethe**
seeting	**seat·ing**
segmint	**seg·ment**
segragation	**seg·re·ga·tion**
seige	**siege**
seirra	**si·er·ra**
seismagraph	**seis·mo·graph**
seive	**sieve**
seizeing	**seiz·ing**
sekoia	**se·quoia**

WRONG	**RIGHT**	WRONG	**RIGHT**
sekts	**sects** *(factions)*	sensasional	**sen·sa·tion·al**
seldum	**sel·dom**	sensative	**sen·si·tive**
selectave	**se·lec·tive**	sensativity	**sen·si·tiv·i·ty**
self-concious		sensatize	**sen·si·tize**
	self-con·scious	sensery	**sen·so·ry**
self-rightious		sensitivaty	**sen·si·tiv·i·ty**
	self-right·eous	sensor	**cen·sor** *(prohibiter)*
sell	**cell** *(room)*	sensuallity	**sen·su·al·i·ty**
sellar	**sell·er** *(vendor)*	sensuas	**sen·su·ous**
sellection	**se·lec·tion**	sensule	**sen·su·al**
sellective	**se·lec·tive**	sensus	**cen·sus**
seller	**cel·lar** *(basement)*	sent	**cent** *(money)*
seltser	**selt·zer**	sent	**scent** *(smell)*
semafore	**sem·a·phore**	sentamental	
semalina	**sem·o·li·na**		**sen·ti·men·tal**
semanary	**sem·i·nary**	sentement	**sen·ti·ment**
sembelance	**sem·blance**	sentense	**sen·tence**
semenal	**sem·i·nal**	sentinnel	**sen·ti·nel**
Semetic	**Se·mit·ic**	sentrey	**sen·try**
seminery	**sem·i·nary**	sentury	**cen·tu·ry**
semmantics	**se·man·tics**	separration	**sep·a·ra·tion**
semmester	**se·mes·ter**	seperable	**sep·a·ra·ble**
semmicolon	**sem·i·co·lon**	seperate	**sep·a·rate**
semminary	**sem·i·nary**	seperation	**sep·a·ra·tion**
Semmitic	**Se·mit·ic**	Septembar	**Sep·tem·ber**
senario	**sce·nar·io**	septer	**scep·ter**
senater	**sen·a·tor**	seqoia	**se·quoia**
senatoreal	**sen·a·to·ri·al**	sequal	**se·quel**
sence	**sense**	sequance	**se·quence**
senier	**sen·ior**	sequen	**se·quin**
sennator	**sen·a·tor**	seranade	**ser·e·nade**
sennile	**se·nile**	serch	**search**
senority	**sen·ior·i·ty**	sercharge	**sur·charge**
sensability	**sen·si·bil·i·ty**	serenety	**se·ren·i·ty**
sensable	**sen·si·ble**	serf	**surf** *(waves)*

WRONG	RIGHT	WRONG	RIGHT
serface	**sur·face**	sessian	**ses·sion** *(meeting)*
serfboard	**surf·board**	session	**ces·sion**
serge	**surge**		*(a giving up)*
	(sudden increase; wave)	sesspool	**cess·pool**
sergent	**ser·geant**	setteler	**set·tler**
sergeon	**sur·geon**	settlement	**set·tle·ment**
sergery	**sur·gery**	seudonym	**pseu·do·nym**
sergical	**sur·gi·cal**	sevanth	**sev·enth**
serial	**ce·re·al** *(grain)*	sevarel	**sev·er·al**
seriusness	**seri·ous·ness**	sevarence	**sev·er·ance**
serloin	**sir·loin**	severity	**se·ver·i·ty**
serly	**sur·ly** *(rude)*	seveer	**se·vere**
serman	**ser·mon**	seventeith	**sev·en·ti·eth**
sermise	**sur·mise**	severrity	**se·ver·i·ty**
serpant	**ser·pent**	sevinteen	**sev·en·teen**
serpassed	**sur·passed**	sevral	**sev·er·al**
serplus	**sur·plus** *(excess)*	sevrance	**sev·er·ance**
serreal	**sur·real** *(fantastic)*	sevver	**sev·er**
serrenade	**ser·e·nade**	sew	**sow** *(plant)*
serrene	**se·rene** *(calm)*	sew	**sue** *(prosecute)*
serenity	**se·ren·ity**	sewege	**sew·age**
serrogate	**sur·ro·gate**	sexey	**sexy**
serrum	**se·rum**	sextent	**sex·tant**
sertax	**sur·tax**	sexuallity	**sex·u·al·i·ty**
servace	**serv·ice**	sfere	**sphere**
servatude	**ser·vi·tude**	shabbie	**shab·by**
serveillance	**sur·veil·lance**	Shablis	**Cha·blis**
servent	**serv·ant**	shackeled	**shack·led**
servial	**ser·vile**	shaddow	**shad·ow**
servicable	**serv·ice·a·ble**	shadey	**shady**
servise	**serv·ice**	shaggie	**shag·gy**
servival	**sur·viv·al**	shakey	**shaky**
sesami	**ses·a·me**	shakled	**shack·led**
sesede	**se·cede** *(withdraw)*	Shakspeare	**Shake·speare**
sessame	**ses·a·me**	shalet	**cha·let**

WRONG	RIGHT
shalot	**shal·lot** *(onion)*
shalow	**shal·low** *(not deep)*
shambels	**sham·bles**
shamful	**shame·ful**
shamois	**cham·ois**
shampane	**cham·pagne** *(wine)*
shampo	**sham·poo**
shandelier	**chan·de·lier**
Shanghi	**Shang·hai**
shantey	**shan·ty** *(shack)*
shantie	**chan·tey** *(song)*
shapliness	**shape·li·ness**
sharade	**cha·rade**
shassis	**chas·sis**
shateau	**châ·teau**
shater	**shat·ter**
shaul	**shawl**
shear	**sheer** *(thin; steep)*
sheathe	**sheath** *(n.)*
sheef	**sheaf**
sheek	**sheik** *(Arab chief)*
sheer	**shear** *(clip)*
sheeth	**sheath** *(n.)*
sheeth	**sheathe** *(v.)*
shef	**chef** *(cook)*
sheik	**chic** *(fashionable)*
sheild	**shield**
sheperd	**shep·herd**
sherbert	**sher·bet**
sherif	**sher·iff** *(law officer)*
sherrie	**sher·ry**
shicanery	**chi·can·ery**
shiek	**sheik** *(Arab chief)*

WRONG	RIGHT
shiling	**shil·ling**
shillac	**shel·lac**
shimer	**shim·mer**
shiney	**shiny**
shingel	**shin·gle**
shining	**shin·ning** *(climbing)*
shinning	**shin·ing** *(radiant)*
shiped	**shipped**
shirtail	**shirt·tail**
shivver	**shiv·er**
shlock	**schlock**
shmorgasbord	**smor·gas·bord**
shnapps	**schnapps**
shnauzer	**schnau·zer**
shnitzel	**schnit·zel**
shody	**shod·dy**
sholder	**shoul·der**
shoot	**chute** *(trough)*
shortning	**short·en·ing**
shovinism	**chau·vin·ism**
showey	**showy**
shrapnle	**shrap·nel**
shreek	**shriek**
shreud	**shrewd**
shrinkege	**shrink·age**
shrivvel	**shriv·el**
shrowd	**shroud**
shrubery	**shrub·bery**
shufled	**shuf·fled**
shulder	**shoul·der**
shurbit	**sher·bet**
shurely	**sure·ly** *(certainly)*

WRONG	RIGHT	WRONG	RIGHT
shurk	**shirk**	silacone	**sil·i·cone**
shuter	**shut·ter**		*(compound)*
shutteling	**shut·tling**	silantro	**ci·lan·tro**
shuvel	**shov·el**	silecon	**sil·i·con** *(element)*
shyed	**shied**	silense	**si·lence**
Siammese	**Si·a·mese**	silhuette	**sil·hou·ette**
siatica	**sci·at·i·ca**	silia	**cil·ia**
sibbeling	**sib·ling**	silkan	**silk·en**
Sibiria	**Si·ber·ia**	sillabic	**syl·lab·ic**
sicada	**ci·ca·da**	sillable	**syl·la·ble**
sicamore	**syc·a·more**	sillabus	**syl·la·bus**
sick	**sic** *(set upon; incite)*	sillica	**sil·i·ca**
sickel	**sick·le**	sillicon	**sil·i·con** *(element)*
siclusion	**se·clu·sion**	sillicone	**sil·i·cone**
sidition	**se·di·tion**		*(compound)*
siduce	**se·duce**	sillogism	**syl·lo·gism**
sience	**sci·ence**	sillos	**si·los**
sientific	**sci·en·tif·ic**	sillouette	**sil·hou·ette**
siera	**si·er·ra**	siloes	**si·los**
siesmograph		silverey	**sil·very**
	seis·mo·graph	simbiotic	**sym·bi·ot·ic**
siethe	**seethe**	simbol	**sym·bol** *(mark)*
siezing	**seiz·ing**	simbolism	**sym·bol·ism**
siezure	**sei·zure**	simbollize	**sym·bol·ize**
siffilis	**syph·i·lis**	simean	**sim·i·an**
sifon	**si·phon**	simeltaneous	
sight	**cite** *(quote)*		**simul·ta·ne·ous**
sight	**site** *(location)*	simer	**sim·mer**
sightseing	**sight·see·ing**	simfony	**sym·pho·ny**
sign	**sine** *(ratio)*	similation	**sim·u·la·tion**
signat	**sig·net**	similer	**sim·i·lar**
signefy	**sig·ni·fy**	simmetrical	**sym·met·ri·cal**
signel	**sig·nal**	simmetry	**sym·me·try**
signeture	**sig·na·ture**	simmian	**sim·i·an**
significanse	**sig·nif·i·cance**	simmulation	**sim·u·la·tion**

WRONG	RIGHT	WRONG	RIGHT
simpathetic	sym·pa·thet·ic	sinnister	sin·is·ter
simpathy	sym·pa·thy	sinnopses	syn·op·ses *(pl.)*
simpelton	sim·ple·ton	sinnuous	sin·u·ous
simphonic	sym·phon·ic	sinonym	syn·o·nym
simplefy	sim·pli·fy	sinopsis	syn·op·sis *(sing.)*
simplicety	sim·plic·i·ty	sinous	si·nus
simposium	sym·po·si·um	sinserely	sin·cere·ly
simptom	symp·tom	sinserity	sin·cer·i·ty
simular	sim·i·lar	sintax	syn·tax
simulater	sim·u·la·tor	sinthesis	syn·the·sis *(sing.)*
simultanious	simul·ta·ne·ous	sinthetic	syn·thet·ic
		sintillate	scin·til·late
sinagogue	syn·a·gogue	sinue	sin·ew
sincerly	sin·cere·ly	sion	sci·on
sincerrity	sin·cer·i·ty	siphen	si·phon
sinchronize	syn·chro·nize	siphilis	syph·i·lis
sinchronous	syn·chro·nous	sircharge	sur·charge
		sirene	se·rene *(calm)*
sincopation	syn·co·pa·tion	Siria	Syr·ia
sinder	cin·der	sirial	se·ri·al *(in a series)*
sindicate	syn·di·cate	sirin	si·ren
sindrome	syn·drome	siringe	sy·ringe
sine	sign *(signal)*	sirly	sur·ly *(rude)*
sinester	sin·is·ter	sirmon	ser·mon
sinfuel	syn·fu·el	sirname	sur·name
sinfull	sin·ful	sirpent	ser·pent
singeling	sin·gling	sirrup	syr·up
singing	singe·ing	sirtax	sur·tax
	(burning)	sirum	se·rum
singuler	sin·gu·lar	sism	schism
sink	sync *(synchronize)*	sissors	scis·sors
sinkronize	syn·chro·nize	sistem	sys·tem
sinnew	sin·ew	sistematic	sys·tem·at·ic
		sistern	cis·tern
		sitation	ci·ta·tion

WRONG	RIGHT	WRONG	RIGHT
site	**cite** *(quote)*	skiped	**skipped**
site	**sight** *(vision)*	skoff	**scoff**
sither	**zith·er**	skooner	**schoon·er**
siting	**sit·ting** *(prp. of sit)*	skooter	**scoot·er**
sittuation	**sit·u·a·tion**	skope	**scope**
siutcase	**suit·case**	skorch	**scorch**
sixteith	**six·ti·eth**	skorpion	**scor·pi·on**
sizeing	**siz·ing**	skotch	**scotch**
sizemograph		skowl	**scowl**
	seis·mo·graph	skrawny	**scraw·ny**
sizmatic	**schis·mat·ic**	skreen	**screen**
sizzeling	**siz·zling**	skrimp	**scrimp**
skab	**scab**	skroll	**scroll**
skain	**skein**	skuba	**scu·ba**
skald	**scald** *(burn)*	skuff	**scuff**
skallion	**scal·lion**	skull	**scull** *(oar; boat)*
skalp	**scalp**	skulptor	**sculp·tor**
skamper	**scam·per**	skum	**scum**
Skandinavia		skurmish	**skir·mish**
	Scan·di·na·via	skwid	**squid**
skanty	**scanty**	skwint	**squint**
skathing	**scath·ing**	skyskraper	**sky·scrap·er**
skavenger	**scav·eng·er**	slalem	**sla·lom**
skech	**sketch**	slandorous	**slan·der·ous**
skedule	**sched·ule**	slaternly	**slat·tern·ly**
skee	**ski**	slath	**sloth**
skeing	**ski·ing**	slaugter	**slaugh·ter**
skeleten	**skel·e·ton**	slavvery	**slav·ery**
skeptacism	**skep·ti·cism**	Slavvic	**Slav·ic**
skeptecal	**skep·ti·cal**	slay	**sleigh** *(vehicle)*
skewar	**skew·er**	sleak	**sleek**
skien	**skein**	sleat	**sleet**
skilfull	**skill·ful**	sleave	**sleeve**
skimpie	**skimpy**		*(arm covering)*
sking	**ski·ing**	sleazie	**slea·zy**

WRONG	RIGHT
sleepally	**sleep·i·ly**
sleevless	**sleeve·less**
sleezy	**slea·zy**
slege	**sledge**
sleight	**slight** *(thin)*
sley	**slay** *(kill)*
sliceing	**slic·ing**
sliegh	**sleigh** *(vehicle)*
slight	**sleight** *(dexterity)*
slimey	**slimy**
sliped	**slipped**
slipry	**slip·pery**
slising	**slic·ing**
slite	**sleight** *(dexterity)*
slithary	**slith·ery**
slo	**sloe** *(fruit)*
slober	**slob·ber**
slogen	**slo·gan**
slolom	**sla·lom**
slooth	**sleuth**
slopy	**slop·py**
sloted	**slot·ted**
slothe	**sloth**
slou	**slough**
sloughter	**slaugh·ter**
slovvenly	**slov·en·ly**
slow	**sloe** *(fruit)*
sluce	**sluice**
sludje	**sludge**
slueth	**sleuth**
sluf	**slough**
slugard	**slug·gard**
slugish	**slug·gish**
slurr	**slur**
smaterring	**smat·ter·ing**

WRONG	RIGHT
smeer	**smear**
smely	**smelly**
smerch	**smirch**
smerk	**smirk**
smokey	**smoky** *(of smoke)*
smollder	**smol·der**
smootch	**smooch**
smorgasboard	**smor·gas·bord**
smuggeling	**smug·gling**
smurch	**smirch**
smurk	**smirk**
smuther	**smoth·er**
snach	**snatch**
snair	**snare**
snakey	**snaky**
snappie	**snap·py**
sneeky	**sneaky**
snich	**snitch**
sniffeling	**snif·fling**
sniped	**snipped** *(cut)*
snivling	**sniv·el·ing**
snoball	**snow·ball**
snobery	**snob·bery**
snorkle	**snor·kel**
snowey	**snowy**
snuggeling	**snug·gling**
so	**sew** *(stitch)*
so	**sow** *(plant)*
soar	**sore** *(painful)*
soberiety	**so·bri·e·ty**
socable	**so·cia·ble**
sociallism	**so·cial·ism**
sociallize	**so·cial·ize**

WRONG	RIGHT	WRONG	RIGHT
sociological ....so·ci·o·log·i·cal		solilequy ....so·lil·o·quy	
socialy ....so·cial·ly		solisitor ....so·lic·i·tor	
sociaty................so·ci·e·ty		sollace ....sol·ace	
sociologecal........................ ....so·ci·o·log·i·cal		sollar.........................so·lar	
socker.......................soc·cer		sollemn ....sol·emn	
sockit ....sock·et		sollicitor ....so·lic·i·tor	
Socrites ....Soc·ra·tes		sollid ......sol·id *(substantial)*	
sodda ....so·da		solliloquy............so·lil·o·quy	
sodder..sol·der *(metal alloy)*		sollitaire ....sol·i·taire	
sodeum ....so·di·um		sollitary ....sol·i·tary	
soffa ....so·fa		sollitude ....sol·i·tude	
soffener..............sof·ten·er		Sollomon ....Sol·o·mon	
sofistication ....sophis·ti·ca·tion		sollution ....so·lu·tion	
sofistry ....soph·is·try		solstise ....sol·stice	
sofomore ....soph·o·more		solumn ....sol·emn	
softner ....sof·ten·er		solvant...................sol·vent	
sojurn....................so·journ		sombody ....some·body	
solase.......................sol·ace		sombraro ....som·bre·ro	
solatude...............sol·i·tude		somersalt ....som·er·sault	
solder ....sol·dier *(person in army)*		sonec.......................son·ic	
sole ....soul *(spirit)*		sonnar.....................so·nar	
soled ....sol·id *(substantial)*		sonnata ....so·na·ta	
soledarity ....sol·i·dar·i·ty		sonnic ....son·ic	
soler..........................so·lar		sonnit.....................son·net	
soletaire...............sol·i·taire		sonnit.....................son·net	
soletary................sol·i·tary		sooflé......................souf·flé	
soley.......................sole·ly		sooth ....soothe *(make calm)*	
solice ....sol·ace		soovenir ....sou·ve·nir	
soliciter ....so·lic·i·tor		sophestry............soph·is·try	
solidefy ....so·lid·i·fy		sophistecation.................... ....sophis·ti·ca·tion	
soliderity ....sol·i·dar·i·ty		sophmore ....soph·o·more	
		sopranno ....so·pra·no	
		sorcary...................sor·cery	
		sorce ....source	
		sorceror ....sor·cer·er	

206

WRONG	RIGHT
sord	**sword** (weapon)
sorded	**sor·did**
sore	**soar** (fly)
soriasis	**pso·ri·a·sis**
sorley	**sore·ly**
sorow	**sor·row**
sorrority	**so·ror·i·ty**
sorry	**sa·ri** (Hindu garment)
sorserer	**sor·cer·er**
sorsery	**sor·cery**
sosiable	**so·cia·ble**
sosialism	**so·cial·ism**
sosially	**so·cial·ly**
sosiety	**so·ci·e·ty**
soterne	**sau·terne**
souflé	**souf·flé**
soul	**sole** (single; bottom)
sourkraut	**sau·er·kraut**
sourse	**source**
southren	**south·ern**
southword	**south·ward**
souvanir	**sou·ve·nir**
Soux	**Sioux**
soviat	**so·vi·et**
sovreign	**sov·er·eign**
sow	**sew** (stitch)
sowse	**souse**
spachula	**spat·u·la**
spacial	**spa·tial**
spacific	**spe·cif·ic**
spacifically	**spe·cif·i·cal·ly**
spacous	**spa·cious**
spade	**spayed** (pt. of spay)
spagetti	**spa·ghet·ti**
spangeled	**span·gled**

WRONG	RIGHT
spanniel	**span·iel**
Spannish	**Span·ish**
sparce	**sparse**
sparibs	**spare·ribs**
sparing	**spar·ring** (boxing)
sparkeler	**spar·kler**
sparow	**spar·row**
sparr	**spar**
sparring	**spar·ing** (saving)
spasem	**spasm**
spasious	**spa·cious**
spasmoddic	**spas·mod·ic**
spaun	**spawn**
spazm	**spasm**
speach	**speech**
speccify	**spec·i·fy**
specculation	**spec·u·la·tion**
specefication	**spec·i·fi·ca·tion**
specemin	**spec·i·men**
speciallist	**spe·cial·ist**
speciallize	**spe·cial·ize**
specie	**spe·cies** (variety)
speciel	**spe·cial**
specielty	**spe·cial·ty**
species	**spe·cie** (coin)
specifecation	**spec·i·fi·ca·tion**
speciffic	**spe·cif·ic**
specificly	**spe·cif·i·cal·ly**
speckeled	**speck·led**
speckter	**spec·ter**
spectacel	**spec·ta·cle**
spectater	**spec·ta·tor**

WRONG	RIGHT	WRONG	RIGHT
specteral	**spec·tral**	spinich	**spin·ach**
specticle	**spec·ta·cle**	spinnoff	**spin·off**
spector	**spec·ter**	spiratual	**spir·it·u·al**
spectrem	**spec·trum**	spirel	**spi·ral**
speculitive	**spec·u·la·tive**	spiret	**spir·it**
specullation	**spec·u·la·tion**	spiritted	**spir·it·ed**
spedometer	**speed·om·e·ter**	spirituallity	**spir·it·u·al·i·ty**
speek	**speak**	spiritule	**spir·it·u·al**
speer	**spear**	spirral	**spi·ral**
speermint	**spear·mint**	spirrit	**spir·it**
spekled	**speck·led**	spitefull	**spite·ful**
spektrum	**spec·trum**	splean	**spleen**
spelbound	**spell·bound**	splended	**splen·did**
speradic	**spo·rad·ic**	splender	**splen·dor**
spern	**spurn**	sploch	**splotch**
sperrow	**spar·row**	spoillage	**spoil·age**
spert	**spurt**	spoilling	**spoil·ing**
spesial	**spe·cial**	spongey	**spon·gy**
spesialize	**spe·cial·ize**	sponser	**spon·sor**
spesify	**spec·i·fy**	spontanious	**spon·ta·ne·ous**
spesimen	**spec·i·men**	sponteneity	**spon·ta·ne·i·ty**
sphear	**sphere**	sporradic	**spo·rad·ic**
spheracle	**spher·i·cal**	spoted	**spot·ted**
sphynx	**sphinx**	spoutted	**spout·ed**
spicey	**spicy**	spowse	**spouse**
spicket	**spig·ot**	spralled	**sprawled**
spidary	**spi·dery**	spraned	**sprained**
spiggot	**spig·ot**	sprauled	**sprawled**
spimoni	**spu·mo·ni**	spred	**spread**
spindel	**spin·dle**	spredsheet	**spread·sheet**
spindely	**spin·dly**	sprinkeling	**sprin·kling**
spinel	**spi·nal** *(of the spine)*	spritely	**spright·ly**
spiney	**spiny**	sprowt	**sprout**

208

| --- | --- | --- | --- |
spue	**spew**	staff	**staph** *(bacterium)*
spummoni	**spu·mo·ni**	stagerring	**stag·ger·ing**
spunge	**sponge**	stagey	**stagy**
spured	**spurred**	stagnent	**stag·nant**
spurm	**sperm**	staid	**stayed** *(pt. of stay)*
spurrious	**spu·ri·ous**	staidium	**sta·di·um**
sputer	**sput·ter**	stail	**stale**
spyre	**spire**	stailmate	**stale·mate**
squable	**squab·ble**	stair	**stare** *(gaze)*
squadren	**squad·ron**	staive	**stave**
squallid	**squal·id**	stake	**steak** *(meat slice)*
squallor	**squal·or**	stalacmite	**sta·lag·mite**
squauk	**squawk**		*(lime deposit on floor)*
squeek	**squeak**	stalagtite	**sta·lac·tite**
squeel	**squeal**		*(lime deposit from roof)*
squeemish	**squeam·ish**	stalid	**stol·id** *(impassive)*
squeltch	**squelch**	stalion	**stal·lion**
squerm	**squirm**	stallactite	**sta·lac·tite**
squerrel	**squir·rel**		*(lime deposit from roof)*
squert	**squirt**	stallagmite	**sta·lag·mite**
squigly	**squig·gly**		*(lime deposit on floor)*
squirel	**squir·rel**	stallwart	**stal·wart**
squonder	**squan·der**	stalmate	**stale·mate**
squosh	**squash**	stamena	**stam·i·na**
squot	**squat**	stamerer	**stam·mer·er**
stabed	**stabbed**	stamin	**sta·men**
stabel	**sta·ble**	stammina	**stam·i·na**
stabillity	**sta·bil·i·ty**	stampeed	**stam·pede**
stabillize	**sta·bi·lize**	stanby	**stand·by**
stableize	**sta·bi·lize**	standerd	**stand·ard**
stacatto	**stac·ca·to**	standerdize	**stand·ard·ize**
stachure	**stat·ure**	stansa	**stan·za**
stackade	**stock·ade**	stanse	**stance**
stacking	**stock·ing** *(sock)*	stanstill	**stand·still**
stadeum	**sta·di·um**	stapel	**sta·ple**

WRONG	RIGHT	WRONG	RIGHT
stapeling	**sta·pling**	steap	**steep**
stappler	**sta·pler**	steaple	**stee·ple**
stare	**stair** *(step)*	stear	**steer**
stared	**starred**	stearage	**steer·age**
	(marked with a star)	sted	**stead** *(place)*
stareo	**ster·eo**	stedy	**steady**
starred	**stared** *(pt. of stare)*	steed	**stead** *(place)*
startch	**starch**	steel	**steal** *(rob)*
starteling	**star·tling**	steem	**steam**
stary	**star·ry**	steepel	**stee·ple**
statastition	**stat·is·ti·cian**	stegasaurus	**steg·o·sau·rus**
statchute	**stat·ute**	steller	**stel·lar**
statick	**stat·ic**	stelthy	**stealthy**
stationary	**sta·tion·ery**	stennographer	
	(writing materials)		**ste·nog·ra·pher**
stationery	**sta·tion·ary**	stensil	**sten·cil**
	(still)	stentch	**stench**
statis	**sta·tus**	step	**steppe** *(plain)*
statly	**state·ly**	steral	**ster·ile**
stattic	**stat·ic**	steralize	**ster·i·lize**
stattistics	**sta·tis·tics**	sterdy	**stur·dy**
stattue	**stat·ue**	stereofonic	
statture	**stat·ure**		**ster·e·o·phon·ic**
stattutory	**stat·u·to·ry**	stereotipe	**ster·e·o·type**
statuery	**stat·u·ary**	sterillization	
statueske	**stat·u·esque**		**ster·i·li·za·tion**
statuet	**stat·u·ette**	sterio	**ster·eo**
stauk	**stalk** *(stem)*	steriotype	**ster·e·o·type**
staul	**stall**	sterness	**stern·ness**
staut	**stout**	sterreo	**ster·eo**
stawnch	**staunch**	sterreophonic	
stayed	**staid** *(sober)*		**ster·e·o·phon·ic**
stead	**steed** *(horse)*	sterreotype	**ster·e·o·type**
steak	**stake** *(post; share)*	sterrile	**ster·ile**
steal	**steel** *(metal)*	stethiscope	**steth·o·scope**

WRONG	RIGHT
steword	**stew·ard**
stewerdess	**stew·ard·ess**
stiched	**stitched**
stie	**sty**
stien	**stein**
stifen	**stiff·en**
stifness	**stiff·ness**
stigmatism	**astig·ma·tism** *(lens distortion)*
stigme	**stig·ma**
stigmitism	**stig·ma·tism** *(condition of normal lens)*
stikler	**stick·ler**
stile	**style** *(manner)*
stilletto	**sti·let·to**
stilus	**sty·lus**
stimie	**sty·mie**
stimmulate	**stim·u·late**
stimulas	**stim·u·lus**
stimulent	**stim·u·lant**
stine	**stein**
stingey	**stin·gy**
stipand	**sti·pend**
stipled	**stip·pled**
stippend	**sti·pend**
stippulation	**stip·u·la·tion**
stired	**stirred**
stirene	**sty·rene**
stirling	**ster·ling**
stirup	**stir·rup**
stlactite	**sta·lac·tite** *(lime deposit from roof)*
stlagmite	**sta·lag·mite** *(lime deposit on floor)*

WRONG	RIGHT
stock	**stalk** *(stem)*
stodgey	**stodgy** *(dull; unfashionable)*
stogey	**sto·gie** *(cigar)*
stokyard	**stock·yard**
stollen	**stol·en** *(pp. of steal)*
stollid	**stol·id** *(impassive)*
stomich	**stom·ach**
stonch	**staunch**
stoney	**stony**
stoped	**stopped**
storie	**sto·ry**
storrage	**stor·age**
stowe	**stow**
stowic	**sto·ic**
stowt	**stout**
stradling	**strad·dling**
straggeling	**strag·gling**
stragle	**strag·gle**
straight	**strait** *(narrow passage)*
straigten	**straight·en**
strait	**straight** *(even)*
straned	**strained**
strangel	**stran·gle**
strangellation	**stran·gu·la·tion**
strangness	**strange·ness**
stratagy	**strat·e·gy**
stratajem	**strat·a·gem**
strateegic	**stra·te·gic**
stratefy	**strat·i·fy**
stratigem	**strat·a·gem**
stratisphere	**strat·o·sphere**

WRONG	RIGHT
strattegy	**strat·e·gy**
strattify	**strat·i·fy**
strecher	**stretch·er**
streek	**streak**
streem	**stream**
streemlined	**stream·lined**
strennuous	**stren·u·ous**
strenthen	**strength·en**
strepp	**strep** *(bacterium)*
streusal	**streu·sel**
strick	**strict** *(rigid)*
stricly	**strict·ly**
stringant	**strin·gent**
strip	**strep** *(bacterium)*
striped	**stripped** *(pp. of strip)*
stripped	**striped** *(pp. of stripe)*
stroabe	**strobe**
stroginoff	**stro·ga·noff**
stroler	**stroll·er**
structurel	**struc·tur·al**
struesel	**streu·sel**
struggeling	**strug·gling**
stuard	**stew·ard**
stubborness	**stub·born·ness**
stuble	**stub·ble**
stucko	**stuc·co**
studant	**stu·dent**
studdied	**stud·ied**
studdious	**stu·di·ous**
studeing	**stud·y·ing**
studeous	**stu·di·ous**
studing	**stud·y·ing**

WRONG	RIGHT
stufy	**stuffy**
stumbeling	**stum·bling**
stuped	**stu·pid**
stuper	**stu·por**
stupidety	**stu·pid·i·ty**
stupify	**stu·pe·fy**
stuppendous	**stu·pen·dous**
stuppor	**stu·por**
sturling	**ster·ling**
sturred	**stirred**
sturrup	**stir·rup**
stuterring	**stut·ter·ing**
stylesh	**styl·ish**
styllus	**sty·lus**
styreen	**sty·rene**
subblimate	**sub·li·mate**
subblime	**sub·lime**
subbordinate	**sub·or·di·nate**
subburban	**sub·ur·ban**
subconsious	**sub·con·scious**
subdew	**sub·due**
subdude	**sub·dued**
suberban	**sub·ur·ban**
subgigate	**sub·ju·gate**
subjeck	**sub·ject**
subjegate	**sub·ju·gate**
subjektive	**sub·jec·tive**
sublemate	**sub·li·mate**
sublimmation	**sub·li·ma·tion**
sublimminal	**sub·lim·i·nal**
submerine	**sub·ma·rine**

WRONG	RIGHT	WRONG	RIGHT
submersable	**sub·mers·i·ble**	subteler	**sub·tler**
submision	**sub·mis·sion**	subtelty	**sub·tle·ty**
submisive	**sub·mis·sive**	subterranian	**sub·ter·ra·ne·an**
submited	**sub·mit·ted**	subturanean	**sub·ter·ra·ne·an**
submurge	**sub·merge**	subturfuge	**sub·ter·fuge**
submursion	**sub·mer·sion**	subversave	**sub·ver·sive**
suborddinate	**sub·or·di·nate**	succatash	**suc·co·tash**
subordenation	**sub·or·di·na·tion**	succede	**suc·ceed** *(follow; achieve)*
subpeena	**sub·poe·na**	succeed	**se·cede** *(withdraw)*
subplant	**sup·plant**	succesion	**suc·ces·sion**
subpoenied	**sub·poe·naed**	successer	**suc·ces·sor**
subsadize	**sub·si·dize**	succion	**suc·tion**
subsaquent	**sub·se·quent**	succulant	**suc·cu·lent**
subscribsion	**sub·scrip·tion**	succeed	**suc·ceed** *(follow; achieve)*
subsedy	**sub·si·dy**	suceptibility	**sus·cep·ti·bil·i·ty**
subserviant	**sub·ser·vi·ent**	sucess	**suc·cess**
subsidiery	**sub·sid·i·ary**	sucession	**suc·ces·sion**
subsiquant	**sub·se·quent**	sucessive	**suc·ces·sive**
subsistance	**sub·sist·ence**	sucessor	**suc·ces·sor**
subsitute	**sub·sti·tute**	suchure	**su·ture**
subsitution	**sub·sti·tu·tion**	suckeled	**suck·led**
substancial	**sub·stan·tial**	sucker	**suc·cor** *(help)*
substanciate	**sub·stan·ti·ate**	suckotash	**suc·co·tash**
substatute	**sub·sti·tute**	sucksion	**suc·tion**
substence	**sub·stance**	suckumb	**suc·cumb**
substetution	**sub·sti·tu·tion**	sucor	**suc·cor** *(help)*
subsurvient	**sub·ser·vi·ent**	sucroce	**su·crose**
subtel	**sub·tle**	sucsess	**suc·cess**

WRONG	RIGHT	WRONG	RIGHT
sucsinct	**suc·cinct**	sumarrize	**sum·ma·rize**
suculent	**suc·cu·lent**	sumary	**sum·ma·ry**
sucumb	**suc·cumb**		*(brief account)*
suecidal	**su·i·ci·dal**	sumbrero	**som·bre·ro**
suer	**sew·er**	sumed	**summed**
sufering	**suf·fer·ing**	sumer	**sum·mer**
sufferage	**suf·frage**	sumit	**sum·mit**
suffex	**suf·fix**	summen	**sum·mon**
sufficate	**suf·fo·cate**	summerize	**sum·ma·rize**
suffisiency	**sufficiency**	summersalt	**som·er·sault**
suffring	**suf·fer·ing**	summery	**sum·ma·ry**
sufice	**suf·fice**		*(brief account)*
suficiency	**suf·fi·cien·cy**	summet	**sum·mit**
sufix	**suf·fix**	sumon	**sum·mon**
sufocate	**suf·fo·cate**	sumptious	**sump·tu·ous**
sufrage	**suf·frage**	sunbath	**sun·bathe** *(v.)*
sufuse	**suf·fuse**	sunbathe	**sun·bath** *(n.)*
suger	**sug·ar**	sunbern	**sun·burn**
sugest	**sug·gest**	sunday	**sun·dae** *(dessert)*
sugestion	**sug·ges·tion**	sundile	**sun·di·al**
sugestive	**sug·ges·tive**	sundrey	**sun·dry**
suggary	**sug·ary**	sunkin	**sunk·en**
suisidal	**su·i·ci·dal**	suovenir	**sou·ve·nir**
suit	**su·et** *(fat)*	super	**sup·per** *(dinner)*
suit	**suite** *(apartment)*	superceed	**su·per·sede**
suite	**suit**	supercillious	
	(clothes; legal action)		**su·per·cil·i·ous**
suiter	**suit·or**	superempose	
suitible	**suit·a·ble**		**su·per·im·pose**
sulfer	**sul·fur**	supereority	**su·pe·ri·or·i·ty**
sullin	**sul·len**	superfishal	**su·per·fi·cial**
sullky	**sulky**	superflewas	**su·per·flu·ous**
sulpher	**sul·fur**	superintendant	
sulten	**sul·tan**		**su·per·in·tend·ent**
sultrey	**sul·try**	superletive	**su·per·la·tive**

214

WRONG	RIGHT	WRONG	RIGHT
supernateral		suppliment ....**sup·ple·ment**	
.............**su·per·nat·u·ral**		supposetory	
superseed ....**su·per·sede**		...............**sup·pos·i·to·ry**	
supersilious		suppossedly ...**sup·pos·ed·ly**	
.............**su·per·cil·i·ous**		suppremacy ....**su·prem·a·cy**	
supersonnic ....**su·per·son·ic**		suppreme ....**su·preme**	
supersticious		suppresion .....**sup·pres·sion**	
.............**su·per·sti·tious**		suppressent....**sup·pres·sant**	
superstission		supreem ....**su·preme**	
.............**su·per·sti·tion**		supremmacy ...**su·prem·a·cy**	
supervizer ....**su·per·vi·sor**		supress ....**sup·press**	
supirior ....**su·pe·ri·or**		supressant......**sup·pres·sant**	
suplamentary		suprise ....**sur·prise**	
..........**sup·ple·men·ta·ry**		supscription	
suplant ....**sup·plant**		................**sub·scrip·tion**	
suple ....**sup·ple**		supterfuge ....**sub·ter·fuge**	
suplement......**sup·ple·ment**		supurb ....**su·perb**	
suplication ...**sup·pli·ca·tion**		supurfluous ...**su·per·flu·ous**	
suply ....**sup·ply**		sureal ......**sur·real** *(fantastic)*	
supoena............**sub·poe·na**		surely ....**sur·ly** *(rude)*	
suport ....**sup·port**		surender ....**sur·ren·der**	
supose ....**sup·pose**		sureptitious	
suposedly ....**sup·pos·ed·ly**		...............**sur·rep·ti·tious**	
suposition ....**sup·po·si·tion**		surf ....**serf** *(slave)*	
supository....**sup·pos·i·to·ry**		surfbord.............**surf·board**	
suppel.....................**sup·ple**		surfice ....**sur·face**	
supper............**su·per** *(great)*		surfiet.....................**sur·feit**	
supperb ....**su·perb**		surge...............**serge** *(fabric)*	
supperficial......**su·per·fi·cial**		surgecal...............**sur·gi·cal**	
supperior ....**su·pe·ri·or**		surgen ....**sur·geon**	
supperlative....**su·per·la·tive**		surgury...................**sur·gery**	
supplication		surloin ....**sir·loin**	
................**sup·pli·ca·tion**		surly ....**sure·ly** *(certainly)*	
supplementery		surmize ....**sur·mise**	
..........**sup·ple·men·ta·ry**		suroggate ....**sur·ro·gate**	

215

WRONG	RIGHT	WRONG	RIGHT
suround	**sur·round**	sutle	**sub·tle**
suroundings		sutor	**suit·or**
	sur·round·ings	swade	**suede**
surpased	**sur·passed**	swadling	**swad·dling**
surplice	**sur·plus** *(excess)*	swager	**swag·ger**
surprize	**sur·prise**	swalow	**swal·low**
surreel	**sur·real** *(fantastic)*	swaped	**swapped**
surrendar	**sur·ren·der**	sward	**sword** *(weapon)*
surrepetitious		swated	**swat·ted**
	sur·rep·ti·tious	swath	**swathe** *(to wrap)*
surry	**sur·rey**	swave	**suave**
surtain	**cer·tain**	sweator	**sweat·er**
survay	**sur·vey**	sweepsteaks	**sweep·stakes**
surveilance	**sur·veil·lance**	sweet	**suite** *(apartment)*
surveyer	**sur·vey·or**	sweethart	**sweet·heart**
survile	**ser·vile**	sweetner	**sweet·en·er**
survivel	**sur·viv·al**	sweltring	**swel·ter·ing**
survix	**cer·vix**	swepped	**swept**
susceptable	**sus·cep·ti·ble**	swet	**sweat**
suseptability		swetter	**sweat·er**
	sus·cep·ti·bil·i·ty	swich	**switch**
suspeck	**sus·pect**	swieback	**zwie·back**
suspence	**sus·pense**	swiming	**swim·ming**
suspendors	**sus·pend·ers**	swindel	**swin·dle**
suspention	**sus·pen·sion**	swindeler	**swin·dler**
suspision	**sus·pi·cion**	Switserland	**Switz·er·land**
suspisious	**sus·pi·cious**	swivvle	**swiv·el**
susseptibility		swizel	**swiz·zle**
	sus·cep·ti·bil·i·ty	swolen	**swol·len**
susseptible	**sus·cep·ti·ble**	swollow	**swal·low**
sustane	**sus·tain**	sword	**sward** *(turf)*
sustinence	**sus·te·nance**	sworm	**swarm**
sutcase	**suit·case**	sworthy	**swarthy**
sutherly	**south·er·ly**	swoted	**swat·ted**
suthern	**south·ern**	swoth	**swath** *(strip)*

WRONG	RIGHT
swurl	**swirl**
swurve	**swerve**
syanide	**cy·a·nide**
sycemore	**syc·a·more**
syche	**psy·che**
	(mind; soul)
sychedelic	**psy·che·del·ic**
sychoanalysis	**psy·cho·a·nal·y·sis**
sychological	**psy·cho·log·i·cal**
sychoses	**psy·cho·ses** *(pl.)*
syclone	**cy·clone**
syfilis	**syph·i·lis**
sylabbic	**syl·lab·ic**
sylabbus	**syl·la·bus**
sylable	**syl·la·ble**
sylinder	**cyl·in·der**
sylogism	**syl·lo·gism**
symbalism	**sym·bol·ism**
symbelize	**sym·bol·ize**
symbeotic	**sym·bi·ot·ic**
symble	**sym·bol** *(mark)*
symbol	**cym·bal**
	(brass plate)
symbollic	**sym·bol·ic**
symetrical	**sym·met·ri·cal**
symfonic	**sym·phon·ic**
symmatry	**sym·me·try**
symmetrecal	**sym·met·ri·cal**

WRONG	RIGHT
sympethetic	**sym·pa·thet·ic**
sympethize	**sym·pa·thize**
sympethy	**sym·pa·thy**
symphany	**sym·pho·ny**
symposeum	**sym·po·si·um**
symptem	**symp·tom**
symptommatic	**symp·to·mat·ic**
synanym	**syn·o·nym**
synchopation	**syn·co·pa·tion**
syncronize	**syn·chro·nize**
syncronous	**syn·chro·nous**
syndecate	**syn·di·cate**
synical	**cyn·i·cal**
synogog	**syn·a·gogue**
synonimous	**syn·on·y·mous**
synopses	**syn·op·sis** *(sing.)*
synopsis	**syn·op·ses** *(pl.)*
synthasis	**syn·the·sis** *(sing.)*
synthettic	**syn·thet·ic**
synthises	**syn·the·ses** *(pl.)*
syphalis	**syph·i·lis**
syrringe	**sy·ringe**
syrrup	**syr·up**
systam	**sys·tem**
systemmatic	**sys·tem·at·ic**
sythe	**scythe**

T

| WRONG | RIGHT |

WRONG	RIGHT
tabacco	**to·bac·co**
tabbernacle	**tab·er·nac·le**
tabboo	**ta·boo**
tabercular	**tuber·cu·lar**
taberculosis	**tuber·cu·lo·sis**
tabernackle	**tab·er·nac·le**
tableu	**tab·leau**
tablit	**tab·let**
taboggan	**to·bog·gan**
tabooli	**tab·bou·leh**
tabuler	**tab·u·lar**
taburnacle	**tab·er·nac·le**
tacet	**tac·it** *(implied)*
tachameter	**tachom·e·ter**
tacitern	**tac·i·turn**
tack	**tact** *(sensitivity)*
tackel	**tack·le**
tackometer	**tachom·e·ter**
tacks	**tax** *(payment)*
tacticks	**tac·tics**
tactitian	**tac·ti·cian**
tactle	**tac·tile**
tae kwan do	**tae kwon do**
tafeta	**taf·fe·ta**
taffey	**taf·fy**
tagether	**to·geth·er**
tai kwon do	**tae kwon do**

WRONG	RIGHT
tail	**tale** *(story)*
tailer	**tai·lor** *(clothes maker)*
tailight	**tail·light**
tailling	**tail·ing**
takeing	**tak·ing**
tako	**ta·co**
Talahassee	**Tal·la·has·see**
talant	**tal·ent**
talasman	**tal·is·man** *(good luck charm)*
talcam	**tal·cum**
tale	**tail** *(rear end)*
talen	**tal·on**
talesman	**tal·is·man** *(good luck charm)*
talk	**talc** *(powder)*
Tallahasee	**Tal·la·has·see**
tallent	**tal·ent**
tallisman	**tal·is·man** *(good luck charm)*
tallon	**tal·on**
talow	**tal·low**
taly	**tal·ly**
tamahawk	**tom·a·hawk**
tamalle	**ta·ma·le**
tamato	**to·ma·to**
tamborine	**tam·bou·rine**

WRONG	RIGHT	WRONG	RIGHT
tammale	**ta·ma·le**	tarter	**tar·tar**
tamultuous	**tumul·tu·ous**	tasit	**tac·it** *(implied)*
tanalize	**tan·ta·lize**	tasiturn	**tac·i·turn**
tanamount	**tan·ta·mount**	tassle	**tas·sel**
tandum	**tan·dem**	tasteing	**tast·ing**
tangable	**tan·gi·ble**	tastey	**tasty**
tangalo	**tan·ge·lo**	taters	**tat·ters** *(rags)*
tangarine	**tan·ge·rine**	tatler	**tat·tler**
tanjelo	**tan·ge·lo**	tatoo	**tat·too**
tanjent	**tan·gent**	tattletail	**tat·tle·tale**
tanjerine	**tan·ge·rine**	taudry	**taw·dry**
tant	**taint**	taught	**taut** *(tight)*
tantallize	**tan·ta·lize**	tauny	**taw·ny**
tantemount	**tan·ta·mount**	Taurrus	**Tau·rus**
tantrem	**tan·trum**	taut	**taught**
tapastry	**tap·es·try**		*(pt. of teach)*
tapeing	**tap·ing**	tavurn	**tav·ern**
	(using tape)	tawney	**taw·ny**
tapeoca	**tap·i·o·ca**	tawt	**taut** *(tight)*
taper	**ta·pir** *(animal)*	taxadermy	**tax·i·der·my**
taping	**tap·ping** *(rapping)*	taxible	**tax·a·ble**
tapir	**ta·per** *(candle)*	taxie	**taxi**
tapography	**topog·ra·phy**	tea	**tee** *(ball-holder)*
tappestry	**tap·es·try**	team	**teem** *(be full of)*
taranchula	**ta·ran·tu·la**	teamate	**team·mate**
tardyness	**tar·di·ness**	tear	**tier** *(row)*
tarif	**tar·iff**	technicallity	
tarnesh	**tar·nish**		**tech·ni·cal·i·ty**
taro	**tar·ot** *(cards)*	technicke	**tech·nique**
tarot	**ta·ro** *(plant)*	technicle	**tech·ni·cal**
tarpaulen	**tar·pau·lin**	technitian	**tech·ni·cian**
tarrantula	**ta·ran·tu·la**	technolagical	
tarro	**ta·ro** *(plant)*		**tech·no·log·i·cal**
tarrot	**tar·ot** *(cards)*	tecknical	**tech·ni·cal**
tarten	**tar·tan**	tecknique	**tech·nique**

WRONG	RIGHT
tecknological.................... ....**tech·no·log·i·cal**	
tecnicality ....**tech·ni·cal·i·ty**	
tecnician ....**tech·ni·cian**	
tecnique.............**tech·nique**	
tedeous..................**te·di·ous**	
tee ....**tea** *(beverage)*	
teek............................**teak**	
teem ....**team** *(group)*	
teeth ......**teethe** *(grow teeth)*	
teethe .....**teeth** *(pl. of tooth)*	
telacast...................**tel·e·cast**	
telagram ....**tel·e·gram**	
telagraph ....**tel·e·graph**	
telaphone ....**tel·e·phone**	
telascope............**tel·e·scope**	
telathon ....**tel·e·thon**	
telavision ....**tel·e·vi·sion**	
telefone ....**tel·e·phone**	
telegraf ....**tel·e·graph**	
tellecast.................**tel·e·cast**	
telleconference ....**tel·e·con·fer·ence**	
tellegram ....**tel·e·gram**	
tellegraphy .....**te·leg·ra·phy**	
tellemarketing.................... ....**tel·e·mar·ket·ing**	
tellepathy ....**te·lep·a·thy**	
tellescope............**tel·e·scope**	
tellevangelist..................... ....**tel·e·van·ge·list**	
tellevision ....**tel·e·vi·sion**	
teltale ....**tell·tale**	
temarity..............**te·mer·i·ty**	
tempel ....**tem·ple**	

WRONG	RIGHT
temperal ....**tem·po·ral**	
temperary ....**tem·po·rary**	
temperchure...................... ....**tem·per·a·ture**	
temperence....**tem·per·ance**	
tempermental ....**tem·per·a·men·tal**	
tempestous........................ ....**tem·pes·tu·ous**	
tempist..................**tem·pest**	
tempora.....**tem·pu·ra** *(food)*	
temporery ....**tem·po·rary**	
tempra ......**tem·pera** *(paint)*	
tempral ....**tem·po·ral**	
tempramental ....**tem·per·a·men·tal**	
temprance .....**tem·per·ance**	
temprate ....**tem·per·ate**	
temprature...**tem·per·a·ture**	
temtation........**temp·ta·tion**	
tenacius ....**te·na·cious**	
tenacle ....**ten·ta·cle**	
tenament...........**ten·e·ment**	
tenasity ....**te·nac·i·ty**	
tenatious ....**te·na·cious**	
tenative ....**ten·ta·tive**	
tence.............................**tense**	
tendancy ....**tend·en·cy**	
tenden ....**ten·don**	
tendonitis ....**ten·di·ni·tis**	
tenent.....................**ten·ant**	
tener ....**ten·or** *(singer; meaning)*	
Tenessee ....**Ten·nes·see**	
tenible...................**ten·a·ble**	

WRONG	RIGHT	WRONG	RIGHT
tenis	**ten·nis**	termanology	
tenit	**ten·et**		**ter·mi·nol·o·gy**
tennable	**ten·a·ble**	terminel	**ter·mi·nal**
tenner	**ten·or**	termoil	**tur·moil**
	(singer; meaning)	ternip	**tur·nip**
tenner		terodactyl	**pter·o·dac·tyl**
	ten·ure *(time held)*	teror	**ter·ror**
Tennesee	**Ten·nes·see**	terot	**tar·ot** *(cards)*
tenor	**ten·ure** *(time held)*	terpentine	**tur·pen·tine**
tensle	**ten·sile** *(flexible)*	terquoise	**tur·quoise**
tenticle	**ten·ta·cle**	terrable	**ter·ri·ble**
tention	**ten·sion**	terrareum	**ter·rar·i·um**
tentitive	**ten·ta·tive**	terratorial	**ter·ri·to·ri·al**
tenuos	**ten·u·ous** *(slight)*	terrer	**ter·ror**
tenur	**ten·or**	terrice	**ter·race**
	(singer; meaning)	terriffic	**ter·rif·ic**
teppid	**tep·id**	terriyaki	**ter·i·ya·ki**
tequela	**te·qui·la**	terry	**tar·ry** *(linger)*
terace	**ter·race**	tershiary	**ter·ti·ary**
terain	**ter·rain**	tertle	**tur·tle**
terarium	**ter·rar·i·um**	teryaki	**ter·i·ya·ki**
terbine	**tur·bine**	testacle	**tes·ti·cle**
	(engine)	testafy	**tes·ti·fy**
terbulence	**tur·bu·lence**	testamonial	**tes·ti·mo·ni·al**
terce	**terse** *(concise)*	testamony	**tes·ti·mo·ny**
terestrial	**ter·res·tri·al**	testement	**tes·ta·ment**
terf	**turf**	testical	**tes·ti·cle**
terible	**ter·ri·ble**	tetnus	**tet·a·nus**
terier	**ter·ri·er**	Teusday	**Tues·day**
teriff	**tar·iff**	texbook	**text·book**
terific	**ter·rif·ic**	texchual	**tex·tu·al**
teritorial	**ter·ri·to·ri·al**	texchure	**tex·ture**
terkey	**tur·key**	textle	**tex·tile**
termanation		thach	**thatch**
	ter·mi·na·tion	than	**then** *(at that time)*

WRONG	RIGHT	WRONG	RIGHT
thankfull	**thank·ful**	thesarus	**the·sau·rus**
thealogian	**the·o·lo·gi·an**	theses	**the·sis** *(sing.)*
thealogy	**the·ol·o·gy**	thesis	**the·ses** *(pl.)*
thearem	**the·o·rem**	thesorus	**the·sau·rus**
theoretical	**the·o·ret·i·cal**	theyre	**they're** *(they are)*
theary	**the·o·ry**	they're	**their** *(poss.)*
theatricle	**the·at·ri·cal**	they're	**there** *(adv.)*
theem	**theme**	thickning	**thick·en·ing**
theeter	**the·a·ter**	thief	**thieve** *(v.)*
theif	**thief** *(n.)*	thieve	**thief** *(n.)*
their	**they're** *(they are)*	thievry	**thiev·ery**
their	**there** *(adv.)*	thimbel	**thim·ble**
theirs	**there's** *(there is)*	thime	**thyme** *(herb)*
theive	**thieve** *(v.)*	thiner	**thin·ner**
theivery	**thiev·ery**	thiroid	**thy·roid**
themomater		thirstey	**thirsty**
	ther·mom·e·ter	thirteith	**thir·ti·eth**
then	**than** *(conj.; prep.)*	thissel	**this·tle**
theologen	**the·o·lo·gi·an**	thorney	**thorny**
theraputic	**ther·a·peu·tic**	thorobred	**thor·ough·bred**
there	**their** *(poss.)*	thorou	**thor·ough**
there	**they're** *(they are)*		*(absolute)*
therem	**the·o·rem**	thorough	**through**
theres	**there's** *(there is)*		*(from end to end)*
there's	**theirs** *(poss.)*	thousanth	**thou·sandth**
theretical	**the·o·ret·i·cal**	thousend	**thou·sand**
therfore	**there·fore** *(hence)*	thout	**thought**
thermameter		thowsand	**thou·sand**
	ther·mom·e·ter	threatning	**threat·en·ing**
thermastat	**ther·mo·stat**	thred	**thread**
thermel	**ther·mal** *(of heat)*	threshhold	**thresh·old**
thermus	**ther·mos**	thret	**threat**
Thersday	**Thurs·day**	thretening	**threat·en·ing**
therteen	**thir·teen**	threw	**through**
therty	**thir·ty**		*(from end to end)*

WRONG	RIGHT	WRONG	RIGHT
thriler	**thrill·er**	timley	**time·ly**
throes	**throws** *(pitches)*	timmid	**tim·id**
throte	**throat**	tinacity	**te·nac·ity**
throtle	**throt·tle**	tingley	**tin·gly**
through	**threw**	tinje	**tinge**
	(pt. of throw)	tinkture	**tinc·ture**
through	**thor·ough**	tinsel	**ten·sile** *(flexible)*
	(absolute)	tinsle	**tin·sel**
throws	**throes**	tipe	**type**
	(spasm; struggle)	tiphoid	**ty·phoid**
thru	**threw** *(pt. of throw)*	tiphus	**ty·phus**
thum	**thumb**	tipical	**typ·i·cal**
thumtack	**thumb·tack**	tiquila	**te·qui·la**
thundring	**thun·der·ing**	tirannical	**tyran·ni·cal**
thursty	**thirsty**	tirannosaur	**ty·ran·no·saur**
thwort	**thwart**	tiranny	**tyr·an·ny**
tic	**tick** *(mite)*	tirant	**ty·rant**
tick	**tic** *(spasm)*	tiresum	**tire·some**
tickeling	**tick·ling**	tirrade	**ti·rade**
tickit	**tick·et**	tisshue	**tis·sue**
ticklesh	**tick·lish**	titaler	**tit·u·lar**
tidel	**tid·al** *(of tides)*	titchular	**tit·u·lar**
tidey	**ti·dy**	titen	**ti·tan**
tiecoon	**ty·coon**	tittillate	**tit·il·late**
tieing	**ty·ing**	to	**too** *(also; overly)*
tiephoon	**ty·phoon**	to	**two** *(number)*
tigger	**ti·ger**	tobbacco	**to·bac·co**
timber	**tim·bre**	tobogan	**to·bog·gan**
	(quality of sound)	todler	**tod·dler**
timbre	**tim·ber** *(wood)*	toe	**tow** *(pull)*
time	**thyme** *(herb)*	tofee	**tof·fee**
timed	**tim·id** *(shy)*	tofoo	**to·fu**
timeing	**tim·ing**	toillet	**toi·let**
timerity	**te·mer·i·ty**	tokan	**to·ken**
timerous	**tim·or·ous**	tole	**told** *(pt. of tell)*

223

WRONG	RIGHT
tole	**toll** (a tax)
tollerable	**tol·er·a·ble**
tollerance	**tol·er·ance**
tomatos	**to·ma·toes** (pl.)
tommahawk	**tom·a·hawk**
tommato	**to·ma·to**
tomorow	**to·mor·row**
tomstone	**tomb·stone**
tong	**tongue** (taste organ)
tonick	**ton·ic**
tonsilectomy	**ton·sil·lec·to·my**
tonsles	**ton·sils**
too	**to** (prep.)
too	**two** (number)
toomb	**tomb**
toomult	**tu·mult**
tootelage	**tu·te·lage**
toothake	**tooth·ache**
topagraphy	**topog·ra·phy**
tope	**taupe** (brownish gray)
topick	**top·ic**
tople	**top·ple**
torchure	**tor·ture**
torent	**tor·rent**
torential	**tor·ren·tial**
torid	**tor·rid**
torist	**tour·ist**
tork	**torque**
tormenter	**tor·men·tor**
tornament	**tour·na·ment**
torped	**tor·pid**
torper	**tor·por**
torreador	**tor·e·a·dor**
torrencial	**tor·ren·tial**

WRONG	RIGHT
torrint	**tor·rent**
torrpid	**tor·pid**
Torrus	**Tau·rus**
tortelini	**tor·tel·lini**
tortila	**tor·til·la**
tortion	**tor·sion**
tortuous	**tor·tur·ous** (causing pain)
torturous	**tor·tu·ous** (twisting)
tortus	**tor·toise**
totallitarian	**total·i·tar·i·an**
totaly	**to·tal·ly**
totel	**to·tal**
tottler	**tod·dler**
totum	**to·tem**
toupay	**tou·pee**
tournaquet	**tour·ni·quet**
tourniment	**tour·na·ment**
toussel	**tou·sle**
tow	**toe** (digit of a foot)
towelet	**tow·el·ette**
towle	**tow·el**
toword	**toward**
towring	**tow·er·ing**
towsle	**tou·sle**
towt	**tout** (praise)
toxec	**tox·ic**
toylet	**toi·let**
traceing	**trac·ing**
track	**tract** (area; pamphlet)
tracktable	**trac·ta·ble**
tracktion	**trac·tion**
tracter	**trac·tor**

WRONG	RIGHT	WRONG	RIGHT
tractible	**trac·ta·ble**	transmision **trans·mis·sion**	
traddition	**tra·di·tion**	transmiting	**trans·mit·ting**
tradeing	**trad·ing**	transparancy **trans·par·en·cy**	
trafic	**traf·fic**	transperent	**trans·par·ent**
tragec	**trag·ic**	transpertation **trans·por·ta·tion**	
tragidy	**trag·e·dy**	transsend	**tran·scend**
trailler	**trail·er**	transum	**tran·som**
traiter	**trai·tor**	transvurse	**trans·verse**
trajedy	**trag·e·dy**	tranzaction	**trans·ac·tion**
traktor	**trac·tor**	trappeze	**tra·peze**
trale	**trail**	trase	**trace**
traler	**trail·er**	trate	**trait**
trama	**trau·ma**	trator	**trai·tor**
trambone	**trom·bone**	traval	**trav·el** *(journey)*
tramendous	**tre·men·dous**	travel	**trav·ail** *(toil; agony)*
trampolene	**tram·po·line**	travisty	**trav·es·ty**
tranqualizer	**tran·quil·iz·er**	travurse	**trav·erse**
tranquel	**tran·quil**	treacherus	**treach·er·ous**
transaktion	**trans·ac·tion**	treasen	**trea·son**
transative	**tran·si·tive**	treaserer	**treas·ur·er**
transcrip	**tran·script**	treasurey	**treas·ury**
transe	**trance**	treatey	**trea·ty**
transeint	**tran·sient**	treatiss	**trea·tise**
transendental **tran·scen·den·tal**		treazure	**treas·ure** *(wealth)*
transet	**trans·it**	trecherous	**treach·er·ous**
transferance **trans·fer·ence**		treck	**trek**
transfered	**trans·ferred**	trecot	**tri·cot**
transfuzion	**trans·fu·sion**	tred	**tread**
transiant	**tran·sient**	treeson	**trea·son**
transision	**tran·si·tion**	trelis	**trel·lis**
transister	**tran·sis·tor**	tremalous	**trem·u·lous**
translater	**trans·la·tor**	trembel	**trem·ble**
translusent	**trans·lu·cent**		

WRONG	RIGHT
tremendus	**tre·men·dous**
tremer	**trem·or**
tremulus	**trem·u·lous**
trenchent	**trench·ant**
treo	**trio**
trepadation	**trep·i·da·tion**
tressel	**tres·tle**
tresspass	**tres·pass**
tresure	**treas·ure** *(wealth)*
tresurer	**treas·ur·er**
tretise	**trea·tise**
trey	**tray** *(flat receptacle)*
triangel	**tri·an·gle**
trianguler	**tri·an·gu·lar**
triathalon	**tri·ath·lon**
tribbulation	**trib·u·la·tion**
tribel	**trib·al**
tributery	**trib·u·tary**
tricerotops	**tri·cer·a·tops**
trickey	**tricky**
trico	**tri·cot**
triel	**tri·al**
trifekta	**tri·fec·ta**
trifel	**tri·fle**
triganometry	**trig·o·nom·e·try**
triger	**trig·ger**
trikle	**trick·le**
trilion	**tril·lion**
trillogy	**tril·o·gy**
triming	**trim·ming**
trinkit	**trin·ket**
trinnity	**trin·i·ty**
triping	**trip·ping**
triplacate	**trip·li·cate**

WRONG	RIGHT
triplit	**tri·plet**
tripple	**tri·ple**
triseratops	**tri·cer·a·tops**
trist	**tryst**
trisycle	**tri·cy·cle**
tritly	**trite·ly**
triumf	**tri·umph**
triumphent	**tri·um·phant**
triveal	**triv·i·al**
troff	**trough**
trofy	**tro·phy**
trogh	**trough**
trole	**troll**
troley	**trol·ley**
troop	**troupe** *(group of actors)*
trophey	**tro·phy**
tropicks	**trop·ics**
tropicle	**trop·i·cal**
troting	**trot·ting**
troubador	**trou·ba·dour**
troubble	**trou·ble**
troublesum	**trou·ble·some**
troule	**trow·el**
trounse	**trounce**
trouseau	**trous·seau**
trouzers	**trou·sers**
trowl	**trow·el**
trownce	**trounce**
trowsers	**trou·sers**
trowt	**trout**
trubadour	**trou·ba·dour**
truculant	**truc·u·lent**
trueism	**tru·ism**
truely	**tru·ly**

WRONG	RIGHT	WRONG	RIGHT
truent	**tru·ant**	turbine	**tur·ban**
truging	**trudg·ing**		*(head covering)*
trumpit	**trum·pet**	turbulance	**tur·bu·lence**
trunkate	**trun·cate**	turcoise	**tur·quoise**
truse	**truce**	turet	**tur·ret**
trusseau	**trous·seau**	turine	**tu·reen**
trustee	**trusty**	turist	**tour·ist**
	(dependable)	turky	**tur·key**
trusty	**trus·tee** *(manager)*	turm	**term**
trusworthy	**trust·wor·thy**	terminal	**ter·mi·nal**
truthfull	**truth·ful**	turmination	
trycicle	**tri·cy·cle**		**ter·mi·na·tion**
tryed	**tried**	turminology	
trypod	**tri·pod**		**ter·mi·nol·o·gy**
trys	**tries**	turn	**tern** *(bird)*
tuberculer	**tuber·cu·lar**	turnament	**tour·na·ment**
tubercullosis		turniquet	**tour·ni·quet**
	tuber·cu·lo·sis	turnup	**tur·nip**
tubuler	**tu·bu·lar**	turpintine	**tur·pen·tine**
tucksedo	**tux·e·do**	turquoize	**tur·quoise**
tuetion	**tu·i·tion**	turrit	**tur·ret**
tuff	**tough** *(strong)*	turse	**terse** *(concise)*
tuff	**tuft** *(clump)*	turtel	**tur·tle**
tuision	**tu·i·tion**	Tusday	**Tues·day**
tullip	**tu·lip**	Tuson	**Tuc·son**
tumbeling	**tum·bling**	tussel	**tus·sle**
tumer	**tu·mor**	tuter	**tu·tor**
tumulltuous	**tumul·tu·ous**	tutilage	**tu·te·lage**
tun	**ton** *(2000 lbs.)*	tutoreal	**tu·to·ri·al**
tunec	**tu·nic**	tuxido	**tuxedo**
tunel	**tun·nel**	twead	**tweed**
tungue	**tongue**	tweater	**tweet·er**
	(taste organ)	tweek	**tweak**
tupee	**tou·pee**	twelf	**twelfth**
turban	**tur·bine** *(engine)*	twerl	**twirl**

227

WRONG	RIGHT	WRONG	RIGHT
twich	**twitch**	typacal	**typ·i·cal**
twinje	**twinge**	typeriter	**type·writ·er**
twurl	**twirl**	typewritting	
tye	**tie**		**type·writ·ing**
tyfoid	**ty·phoid**	tyrade	**ti·rade**
tyfoon	**ty·phoon**	tyrany	**tyr·an·ny**
tyfus	**ty·phus**	tyrent	**ty·rant**
tykoon	**ty·coon**	tyrranical	**tyran·ni·cal**
tyme	**thyme** *(herb)*	tyrranosaur	**ty·ran·no·saur**

U

WRONG	RIGHT
ubickuitous	**ubiq·ui·tous**
udder	**ut·ter** *(speak)*
uder	**ud·der** *(milk gland)*
ukalele	**uku·le·le**
ulcerus	**ul·cer·ous**
ulltra	**ul·tra**
ulser	**ul·cer**
ulserous	**ul·cer·ous**
ultamate	**ul·ti·mate**
ultamatum	**ul·ti·ma·tum**
ulterier	**ul·te·ri·or**
ultrasanic	**ul·tra·son·ic**
ultravilet	**ul·tra·vi·o·let**
umbillical	**um·bil·i·cal**
umbrege	**um·brage**
umbrela	**um·brel·la**
umpier	**um·pire**
unabriged	**un·a·bridged**
unacorn	**uni·corn**
unacycle	**uni·cy·cle**
unafication	**uni·fi·ca·tion**
unalienable	**in·al·ien·a·ble**
unanamous	**unan·i·mous**
unason	**uni·son**
unatural	**un·nat·u·ral**
unaty	**uni·ty**
unaversal	**uni·ver·sal**
unaversity	**uni·ver·si·ty**

WRONG	RIGHT
uncanny	**un·can·ny**
unconshunable	**un·con·scion·a·ble**
uncuth	**un·couth**
undenyable	**un·de·ni·a·ble**
underite	**un·der·write**
underneth	**un·der·neath**
undiniable	**un·de·ni·a·ble**
undoutedly	**un·doubt·ed·ly**
undullate	**un·du·late**
undur	**un·der**
unecessarily	**un·nec·es·sar·i·ly**
unecessary	**un·nec·es·sary**
uneform	**uni·form**
unefy	**uni·fy**
uneque	**unique**
unerth	**un·earth**
unifacation	**uni·fi·ca·tion**
uniformaty	**uni·form·i·ty**
unike	**unique**
unisun	**uni·son**
unisycle	**uni·cy·cle**
uniteing	**unit·ing**
univursal	**uni·ver·sal**
univursity	**uni·ver·si·ty**
unkemt	**un·kempt**

229

WRONG	RIGHT
unkle	**un·cle**
unkouth	**un·couth**
unmaned	**un·manned**
unmentionibles .... **un·men·tion·a·bles**	
unmistakeable.................... **un·mis·tak·a·ble**	
unmitagated	**un·mit·i·gat·ed**
unnecessaryly .... **un·nec·es·sar·i·ly**	
unruley	**un·ruly**
unscrupulus .... **un·scru·pu·lous**	
untenible	**un·ten·a·ble**
untill	**un·til**
untye	**un·tie**
unwanted	**un·wont·ed** *(not usual)*
unwonted	**un·want·ed** *(not wanted)*
unyon	**on·ion**
upan	**up·on**
upbrade	**up·braid**
uper	**up·per**
upheval	**up·heav·al**
upolstery	**up·hol·stery**
upriseing	**up·ris·ing**
uprite	**up·right**
uprorious	**up·roar·i·ous**
upword	**up·ward**
uranal	**uri·nal**

WRONG	RIGHT
uraneum	**ura·ni·um**
Urannus	**Ura·nus**
urathane	**ure·thane**
urban	**ur·bane** *(refined)*
urbane	**ur·ban** *(of a city)*
urchen	**ur·chin**
uren	**urine**
urgincy	**ur·gen·cy**
urgint	**ur·gent**
urinel	**uri·nal**
urjency	**ur·gen·cy**
urmine	**er·mine**
urr	**err** *(be wrong)*
usefull	**use·ful**
usege	**us·age**
useing	**us·ing**
userp	**usurp**
ushur	**ush·er**
ussage	**us·age**
usualy	**usu·al·ly**
utensle	**uten·sil**
uteran	**uter·ine**
uterance	**ut·ter·ance**
utillitarian	**util·i·tar·i·an**
utillity	**util·i·ty**
utillize	**uti·lize**
utopea	**uto·pia**
utter	**ud·der** *(milk gland)*
utterence	**ut·ter·ance**
uturus	**uter·us**
uzually	**usu·al·ly**

V

WRONG	RIGHT	WRONG	RIGHT
vacansy	**va·can·cy**	valedictorion	
vacashun	**va·ca·tion**		**val·e·dic·to·ri·an**
vaccanate	**vac·ci·nate**	valence	**val·ance** *(curtain)*
vaccene	**vac·cine**	valer	**val·or**
vaccum	**vac·u·um**	valese	**va·lise**
vacency	**va·can·cy**	valey	**val·ley**
vacent	**va·cant**	validaty	**va·lid·i·ty**
vacilate	**vac·il·late**	valient	**val·iant**
vacine	**vac·cine**	valit	**val·et**
vacksinate	**vac·ci·nate**	valition	**vo·li·tion**
vadeville	**vaude·ville**	vallance	**val·ance** *(curtain)*
vage	**vague**	valledictorian	
vagery	**va·gary**		**val·e·dic·to·ri·an**
vagibond	**vag·a·bond**	vallentine	**val·en·tine**
vagrent	**va·grant**	vallet	**val·et**
vain	**vane** *(blade)*	valley	**vol·ley**
vain	**vein**		*(discharge; ball return)*
	(blood vessel)	valliant	**val·iant**
vajina	**va·gi·na**	vallid	**val·id**
valadate	**val·i·date**	vallidate	**val·i·date**
valadictorian		vallidity	**va·lid·i·ty**
	val·e·dic·to·ri·an	vallise	**va·lise**
valance	**va·lence**	valluable	**val·u·a·ble**
	(chemistry term)	vallue	**val·ue**
valantine	**val·en·tine**	vally	**val·ley**
valay	**val·et**	valt	**vault**
vale	**veil** *(screen)*	valu	**val·ue**
valed	**val·id**	valueable	**val·u·a·ble**

WRONG	RIGHT
valume	**vol·ume**
valuminous	**volu·mi·nous**
valuntary	**vol·un·tary**
valunteer	**vol·un·teer**
vanaty	**van·i·ty**
vandelism	**van·dal·ism**
vane	**vain** (conceited)
vane	**vein** (blood vessel)
vaneer	**ve·neer**
vangard	**van·guard**
vanila	**va·nil·la**
vankuish	**van·quish**
vannish	**van·ish**
vantege	**van·tage**
vaped	**vap·id**
vaper	**va·por**
vaperizer	**va·por·iz·er**
varanda	**ve·ran·da**
vareable	**var·i·a·ble**
vareagated	**var·i·e·gat·ed**
vareation	**var·i·a·tion**
varecose	**var·i·cose**
vareous	**var·i·ous**
variaty	**va·ri·e·ty**
varient	**var·i·ant**
varius	**var·i·ous**
varnnish	**var·nish**
varsaty	**var·si·ty**
vary	**very** (exceedingly)
varyed	**var·ied**
vasal	**vas·sal** (subordinate)
vasaline	**vas·e·line**
vasculer	**vas·cu·lar**
vasecktomy	**vas·ec·to·my**
vaselene	**vas·e·line**

WRONG	RIGHT
vasillate	**vac·il·late**
vass	**vast** (great)
vassal	**ves·sel** (container)
vassel	**vas·sal** (subordinate)
Vattican	**Vat·i·can**
vaudville	**vaude·ville**
vaxine	**vac·cine**
vaze	**vase**
veamently	**vehe·ment·ly**
vear	**veer**
vecter	**vec·tor**
veel	**veal**
vegatarian	**veg·e·tar·i·an**
vegatate	**veg·e·tate**
vegtable	**veg·e·ta·ble**
vehementley	
	vehe·ment·ly
vehical	**ve·hi·cle**
vehiculer	**ve·hic·u·lar**
vehimently	**vehe·ment·ly**
veicle	**ve·hi·cle**
veil	**vale** (valley)
vein	**vain** (conceited)
vein	**vane** (blade)
veinglorious	
	vain·glo·ri·ous
veiw	**view**
vejetable	**veg·e·ta·ble**
vejetarian	**veg·e·tar·i·an**
vejetate	**veg·e·tate**
velacity	**ve·loc·i·ty**
vellour	**ve·lour**
velosity	**ve·loc·i·ty**
velum	**vel·lum** (paper)
velvit	**vel·vet**

WRONG	RIGHT	WRONG	RIGHT
venal	**ve·ni·al** *(excusable)*	verbel	**ver·bal**
venarate	**ven·er·ate**	verdent	**ver·dant**
venchure	**ven·ture**	verdick	**ver·dict**
vendeta	**ven·det·ta**	verginal	**vir·gin·al**
venel	**ve·nal** *(corrupt)*	verginity	**vir·gin·i·ty**
venemous	**ven·om·ous**	Vergo	**Vir·go**
venerial	**ve·ne·re·al**	veriable	**var·i·a·ble**
venerible	**ven·er·a·ble**	veriant	**var·i·ant**
Venetion	**Ve·ne·tian**	veriation	**var·i·a·tion**
venew	**ven·ue**	vericose	**var·i·cose**
vengefull	**venge·ful**	veriegated	**var·i·e·gat·ed**
vengence	**venge·ance**	veriety	**va·ri·e·ty**
venial	**ve·nal** *(corrupt)*	verifyable	**ver·i·fi·a·ble**
venilate	**ven·ti·late**	verile	**vir·ile**
venire	**ve·neer**	verious	**var·i·ous**
venireal	**ve·ne·re·al**	verismillitude	
vennison	**ven·i·son**		**ver·i·si·mil·i·tude**
ventalate	**ven·ti·late**	veritible	**ver·i·ta·ble**
ventillator	**ven·ti·la·tor**	vermacelli	**ver·mi·celli**
ventrical	**ven·tri·cle**	vermen	**ver·min**
ventrilloquist		vermillion	**ver·mil·ion**
	ven·tril·o·quist	vermuth	**ver·mouth**
veola	**vi·o·la**	vernaculer	**ver·nac·u·lar**
veracious	**vo·ra·cious**	verneer	**ve·neer**
	(greedy)	verrisimilitude	
veracius	**ve·ra·cious**		**ver·i·si·mil·i·tude**
	(truthful)	verses	**ver·sus** *(against)*
verafiable	**ver·i·fi·a·ble**	versitile	**ver·sa·tile**
verafy	**ver·i·fy**	vertabra	**ver·te·bra**
verasimilitude		vertago	**ver·ti·go**
	ver·i·si·mil·i·tude	verticle	**ver·ti·cal**
verasity	**ve·rac·i·ty**	vertually	**vir·tu·al·ly**
veratable	**ver·i·ta·ble**	very	**vary** *(alter)*
verbatem	**ver·ba·tim**	verzion	**ver·sion**
verbeage	**ver·bi·age**	vesa	**vi·sa**

233

WRONG	RIGHT	WRONG	RIGHT
vessal	**ves·sel** *(container)*	vijilance	**vig·i·lance**
vessel	**vas·sal** *(subordinate)*	vilage	**vil·lage**
vestabule	**ves·ti·bule**	vilain	**vil·lain** *(scoundrel)*
vestage	**ves·tige**	vile	**vi·al** *(bottle)*
veteren	**vet·er·an**	vilet	**vi·o·let**
veternarian	**vet·er·i·nar·i·an**	villege	**vil·lage**
		villein	**vil·lain** *(scoundrel)*
vetos	**ve·toes**	villify	**vil·i·fy**
vetran	**vet·er·an**	vindacate	**vin·di·cate**
vetrinarian	**vet·er·i·nar·i·an**	vindictave	**vin·dic·tive**
		vinereal	**ve·ne·re·al**
vial	**vile** *(evil)*	Vinetian	**Ve·ne·tian**
vialate	**vi·o·late**	vineyard	**vine·yard**
vialence	**vi·o·lence**	vinigar	**vin·e·gar**
vialet	**vi·o·let**	vinil	**vi·nyl**
vialin	**vi·o·lin**	vinilla	**va·nil·la**
vibrateing	**vi·brat·ing**	vinnegar	**vin·e·gar**
vibrater	**vi·bra·tor**	vintege	**vin·tage**
vibrent	**vi·brant**	vinyard	**vine·yard**
vicarius	**vi·car·i·ous**	violance	**vi·o·lence**
vice	**vise** *(clamp)*	virchually	**vir·tu·al·ly**
vicissatude	**vicis·si·tude**	virel	**vi·ral** *(of a virus)*
vicius	**vi·cious**	virel	**vir·ile** *(manly)*
vicker	**vic·ar**	vires	**vi·rus**
victem	**vic·tim**	virgenal	**vir·gin·al**
victer	**vic·tor**	virgenity	**vir·gin·i·ty**
victorius	**vic·to·ri·ous**	virtous	**vir·tu·ous**
victry	**vic·to·ry**	virtully	**vir·tu·al·ly**
vidio	**vid·e·o**	virtuossity	**vir·tu·os·i·ty**
vieing	**vy·ing**	virulant	**vir·u·lent**
viel	**veil** *(screen)*	visable	**vis·i·ble**
vigel	**vig·il**	visator	**vis·i·tor**
vigerous	**vig·or·ous**	viscus	**vis·cous** *(adj.)*
vigilence	**vig·i·lance**	vise	**vice** *(wickedness)*
vijil	**vig·il**	visege	**vis·age**

WRONG	RIGHT	WRONG	RIGHT
viser	**vi·sor**	vollatile	**vol·a·tile**
viseral	**vis·cer·al**	vollcano	**vol·ca·no**
vise versa	**vi·ce ver·sa**	volluble	**vol·u·ble**
vishiate	**vi·ti·ate**	vollume	**vol·ume**
vishus	**vi·cious**	volluminous	**volu·mi·nous**
visibillity	**vis·i·bil·i·ty**	volluntary	**vol·un·tary**
visinity	**vi·cin·i·ty**	volluptuous	**volup·tu·ous**
visissitude	**vicis·si·tude**	volly	**vol·ley**
vitallity	**vi·tal·i·ty**		*(discharge; ball return)*
vitamen	**vi·ta·min**	voltege	**volt·age**
vitel	**vi·tal**	volumenous	**volu·mi·nous**
vivacius	**vi·va·cious**	volunter	**vol·un·teer**
vivasection	**viv·i·sec·tion**	voluntery	**vol·un·tary**
vived	**viv·id**	volupchuous	**volup·tu·ous**
viza	**vi·sa**	vommit	**vom·it**
vizage	**vis·age**	voracious	**ve·ra·cious**
viz-a-ve	**vis-à-vis**		*(truthful)*
vizibility	**vis·i·bil·i·ty**	voratious	**vo·ra·cious**
vizible	**vis·i·ble**		*(greedy)*
vizion	**vi·sion**	voteing	**vot·ing**
vizit	**vis·it**	votery	**vo·ta·ry**
vizitor	**vis·i·tor**	vowl	**vow·el**
vizual	**vis·u·al**	voyce	**voice**
vocabulery	**vo·cab·u·lary**	voyd	**void**
vocallize	**vo·cal·ize**	voyege	**voy·age**
vocul	**vo·cal**	voyure	**vo·yeur**
vodeville	**vaude·ville**	vue	**view**
voge	**vogue**	vulcanic	**vol·can·ic**
voise	**voice**	vulcano	**vol·ca·no**
vokabulary	**vo·cab·u·lary**	vulchure	**vul·ture**
volatle	**vol·a·tile**	vulgarety	**vul·gar·i·ty**
volcanick	**vol·can·ic**	vulger	**vul·gar**
voley	**vol·ley**	vulnerible	**vul·ner·a·ble**
	(discharge; ball return)	vurbal	**ver·bal**
volision	**vo·li·tion**	vurbatim	**ver·ba·tim**

WRONG	RIGHT	WRONG	RIGHT
vurdict	**ver·dict**	vurtical	**ver·ti·cal**
vurge	**verge**	vurtigo	**ver·ti·go**
vurginal	**vir·gin·al**	vurtue	**vir·tue**
vurmin	**ver·min**	vurtuous	**vir·tu·ous**
vurse	**verse**	vurve	**verve**
vursus	**ver·sus** *(against)*	vyable	**vi·a·ble**
vurtebra	**ver·te·bra**	vye	**vie**

W

WRONG	RIGHT	WRONG	RIGHT
wabble	**wob·ble**	wajer	**wa·ger**
wach	**watch**	wakeing	**wak·ing**
wack	**whack**	wale	**whale** *(animal)*
wackey	**wacky**	wale	**wail** *(cry)*
wacks	**wax**	walet	**wal·let**
waddle	**wat·tle**	wallbord	**wall·board**
	(fold of skin)	wallnut	**wal·nut**
wadeing	**wad·ing**	wallrus	**wal·rus**
	(walking)	walop	**wal·lop**
wading	**wad·ding**	walow	**wal·low**
	(stuffing)	walris	**wal·rus**
wadle	**wad·dle** *(toddle)*	walz	**waltz**
wafe	**waif**	wan	**won** *(pt. of win)*
waff	**waft** *(float)*	wander	**won·der** *(marvel)*
waffer	**wa·fer**	wandrings	**wan·der·ings**
wafle	**waf·fle**	waneing	**wan·ing**
wagen	**wag·on**	wann	**wan** *(pale; feeble)*
wagish	**wag·gish**	want	**wont** *(accustomed)*
wagle	**wag·gle**	wan ton	**won ton** *(food)*
waigh	**weigh**	warant	**war·rant**
	(measure weight of)	wardon	**war·den**
wail	**wale** *(ridge)*	ware	**wear** *(to dress in)*
wail	**whale** *(animal)*	ware	**where** *(adv.)*
waist	**waste** *(squander)*	warewolf	**were·wolf**
wait	**weight** *(heaviness)*	warey	**wary**
waive	**wave**	warf	**wharf**
	(curving motion)	warhouse	**ware·house**
waje	**wage**	warior	**war·ri·or**

237

WRONG	RIGHT
warmunger	**war·mon·ger**
warn	**worn** (pp. of wear)
warrent	**war·rant**
warrenty	**war·ran·ty**
warrier	**war·ri·or**
warsh	**wash**
waryness	**war·i·ness**
wasail	**was·sail**
wasent	**wasn't**
washible	**wash·a·ble**
wassel	**was·sail**
wastbasket	**waste·bas·ket**
waste	**waist** (middle section)
wastege	**wast·age**
wasteing	**wast·ing**
wat	**watt**
watage	**watt·age**
wate	**wait** (stay)
waterey	**wa·tery**
watermellon	**wa·ter·mel·on**
watle	**wat·tle** (fold of skin)
watress	**wait·ress**
wattege	**watt·age**
watter	**wa·ter**
wattery	**wa·tery**
wattle	**wad·dle** (toddle)
wauk	**walk** (stroll)
wauk	**wok** (pan)
wave	**waive** (give up)
waveing	**wav·ing**
waver	**waiv·er** (a relinquishing)
wavey	**wavy**

WRONG	RIGHT
waxey	**waxy**
way	**weigh** (measure weight of)
way	**whey** (milk product)
wayfer	**wa·fer**
waywerd	**way·ward**
wazn't	**wasn't**
wead	**weed**
weak	**week** (seven days)
weakend	**week·end**
weal	**wheal** (pimple)
weal	**wheel** (disk)
weapen	**weap·on**
wear	**ware** (merchandise)
wearyness	**wea·ri·ness**
weasle	**wea·sel**
weather	**wheth·er** (if)
weaveing	**weav·ing**
weavil	**wee·vil**
webing	**web·bing**
Wedgewood	**Wedg·wood**
weding	**wed·ding**
weedling	**whee·dling**
week	**weak** (not strong)
weekley	**week·ly**
weel	**weal** (ridge)
weel	**wheel** (disk)
weelbarrow	**wheel·bar·row**
ween	**wean**
weener	**wie·ner**
weepey	**weepy**
weesel	**wea·sel**
weeve	**weave**
weevle	**wee·vil**

WRONG	RIGHT
weeze	**wheeze**
wege	**wedge**
wegies	**wedg·ies**
weild	**wield**
weiner	**wie·ner**
wellcome	**wel·come**
wellfare	**wel·fare**
welp	**whelp**
welth	**wealth**
wen	**when** *(adv.)*
wench	**winch** *(mechanical device)*
wendow	**win·dow**
Wensday	**Wednes·day**
wepon	**weap·on**
we're	**were** *(pt. of be)*
were	**we're** *(we are)*
were	**where** *(adv.)*
werever	**wher·ev·er**
werewulf	**were·wolf**
wern't	**weren't**
werth	**worth**
wery	**wea·ry** *(tired)*
wery	**wary** *(careful)*
westerley	**west·er·ly**
westurn	**west·ern**
westwerd	**west·ward**
wet	**whet** *(sharpen)*
wether	**weath·er** *(atmospheric conditions)*
wether	**wheth·er** *(if)*
wey	**weigh** *(measure weight of)*
wey	**whey** *(milk product)*
whale	**wail** *(cry)*

WRONG	RIGHT
whale	**wale** *(ridge)*
whaleing	**whal·ing** *(whale hunting)*
wheather	**wheth·er** *(if)*
wheedeling	**whee·dling**
wheel	**wheal** *(pimple)*
wheel	**weal** *(ridge)*
wheelbarow	**wheel·bar·row**
wheet	**wheat**
wheezey	**wheezy**
wherabouts	**where·a·bouts**
wheras	**where·as**
wherl	**whirl** *(spin)*
whether	**weath·er** *(atmospheric conditions)*
which	**witch** *(sorceress)*
while	**wile** *(trick)*
whimsey	**whim·sy**
whimsicle	**whim·si·cal**
whine	**wine** *(drink)*
whinny	**whiny** *(complaining)*
whiny	**whin·ny** *(neigh)*
whiping	**whip·ping**
whipoorwill	**whip·poor·will**
whirl	**whorl** *(fingerprint design)*
whispring	**whis·per·ing**
whissle	**whis·tle**
whistful	**wist·ful**
whistleing	**whis·tling**
whit	**white** *(color)*

WRONG	RIGHT
whitch	**witch** *(sorceress)*
whither	**with·er** *(wilt)*
whitle	**whit·tle**
whole	**hole** *(cavity)*
wholesell	**whole·sale**
wholesum	**whole·some**
wholistic	**ho·lis·tic**
wholy	**whol·ly** *(totally)*
whoose	**whose** *(poss.)*
whore	**hoar** *(frost)*
whorf	**wharf**
whorl	**whirl** *(spin)*
who's	**whose** *(poss.)*
whose	**who's**
	(who is; who has)
wich	**which** *(pron.)*
wicket	**wick·ed** *(bad)*
wickit	**wick·et** *(arch)*
widdow	**wid·ow**
wierd	**weird**
wiff	**whiff**
wiggley	**wig·gly**
wigle	**wig·gle**
wikker	**wick·er**
wikket	**wick·et** *(arch)*
wile	**while** *(time)*
wiley	**wily**
wilfull	**will·ful**
willderness	**wil·der·ness**
wilow	**wil·low**
wily-nily	**wil·ly-nil·ly**
wimen	**wom·en** *(pl.)*
wimsical	**whim·si·cal**
winch	**wench** *(woman)*
windey	**windy**

WRONG	RIGHT
windless	**wind·lass** *(winch)*
wine	**whine** *(cry)*
winerey	**win·ery**
winfall	**wind·fall**
winlass	**wind·lass** *(winch)*
winner	**win·ter**
	(cold season)
winney	**whin·ny** *(neigh)*
winow	**win·now**
winry	**win·ery**
winse	**wince**
winsum	**win·some**
wintrey	**win·try**
wintur	**win·ter**
	(cold season)
wipeing	**wip·ing**
wippoorwill	
	whip·poor·will
wireing	**wir·ing**
wirey	**wiry**
wirl	**whirl** *(spin)*
wirlpool	**whirl·pool**
wisacre	**wise·acre**
wisdum	**wis·dom**
wishfull	**wish·ful**
wisk	**whisk**
wisker	**whisk·er**
wiskey	**whis·key**
wisper	**whis·per**
wistfull	**wist·ful**
wistle	**whis·tle**
witch	**which** *(pron.)*
wite	**white** *(color)*
withdrawl	**with·draw·al**
wither	**whith·er** *(where)*

WRONG	RIGHT	WRONG	RIGHT
withold	**with·hold**	worble	**war·ble**
witicism	**wit·ti·cism**	worden	**war·den**
witnes	**wit·ness**	wordey	**wordy**
witth	**width**	workible	**work·a·ble**
wittle	**whit·tle**	workoholic	**work·a·holic**
wity	**wit·ty**	worl	**whorl**
wizdom	**wis·dom**		*(fingerprint design)*
wizerd	**wiz·ard**	worldley	**world·ly**
wobbley	**wob·bly**	wormth	**warmth**
woble	**wob·ble**	worn	**warn** *(caution)*
wock	**wok** *(pan)*	worp	**warp**
wodding	**wad·ding**	worrant	**war·rant**
	(stuffing)	worrysome	**wor·ri·some**
woddle	**wad·dle** *(toddle)*	wort	**wart** *(blemish)*
woffel	**waf·fle**	worthey	**wor·thy**
woft	**waft** *(float)*	wort hog	**wart hog**
wok	**walk** *(stroll)*	worthwile	**worth·while**
wolfs	**wolves** *(pl.)*	wosh	**wash**
woll	**wall**	wosp	**wasp**
woman	**wom·en** *(pl.)*	wossel	**was·sail**
women	**wom·an** *(sing.)*	wott	**watt**
won	**one** *(a unit)*	wottle	**wat·tle**
won	**wan** *(pale; feeble)*		*(fold of skin)*
wonder	**wan·der** *(stray)*	woud	**would** *(aux.v.)*
wonderous	**won·drous**	wouden	**wouldn't**
wont	**won't** *(will not)*		*(would not)*
wont	**want** *(lack; desire)*	wrak	**rack** *(framework)*
wonton	**wan·ton** *(reckless)*	wrak	**wrack** *(torment)*
woodden	**wood·en**	wrangel	**wran·gle**
woolf	**wolf**	wraping	**wrap·ping**
wooly	**wool·ly**	wreak	**reek** *(smell)*
woom	**womb**	wreath	**wreathe**
Woosershire			*(to encircle)*
	Worces·ter·shire	wreathe	**wreath** *(a band)*
woozey	**woozy**	wreckedge	**wreck·age**

WRONG	RIGHT	WRONG	RIGHT
wreckless	**reck·less**	wry	**rye** *(grain)*
wreeth	**wreath** *(a band)*	wunce	**once**
wressle	**wres·tle**	wundrous	**won·drous**
wrestleing	**wres·tling**	wurd	**word**
wretch	**retch** *(vomit)*	wurld	**world**
wrigle	**wrig·gle**	wurm	**worm**
wrinkel	**wrin·kle**	wurry	**wor·ry**
write	**right** *(correct)*	wurse	**worse**
writen	**writ·ten**	wurship	**wor·ship**
writting	**writ·ing**	wurst	**worst**
wrote	**rote** *(routine)*	wurth	**worth**
wrung	**rung** *(crossbar)*	wuz	**was**

X-Y-Z

WRONG	RIGHT
X-rey	**X-ray**
xylaphone	**xy·lo·phone**
yack	**yak** *(animal)*
yaht	**yacht**
yaking	**yak·king** *(talking)*
yamaka	**yar·mul·ke**
yamer	**yam·mer**
yander	**yon·der**
Yankie	**Yan·kee**
yardege	**yard·age**
yarmulka	**yar·mul·ke**
yashiva	**ye·shi·va**
yaun	**yawn**
	(open the mouth wide)
yeer	**year**
yeest	**yeast**
yeild	**yield**
yellowey	**yel·lowy**
yesheva	**ye·shi·va**
yestirday	**yes·ter·day**
yew	**ewe** *(female sheep)*
yewe	**yew** *(evergreen)*
Yidish	**Yid·dish**
yodle	**yo·del**
yogert	**yo·gurt**
yogey	**yo·gi**
	(yoga practicer)
yogi	**yo·ga** *(exercises)*

WRONG	RIGHT
yoke	**yolk**
	(part of an egg)
yokle	**yo·kel**
yolk	**yoke** *(harness)*
yoman	**yeo·man**
yon	**yawn**
	(open the mouth wide)
yool	**yule** *(Christmas)*
yore	**your** *(poss.)*
yore	**you're** *(you are)*
you	**ewe** *(female sheep)*
you	**yew** *(evergreen)*
you'l	**you'll** *(you will)*
your	**you're** *(you are)*
you're	**your** *(poss.)*
your's	**yours**
yowel	**yowl**
Yugaslavia	**Yugo·sla·via**
yukka	**yuc·ca**
yull	**you'll** *(you will)*
yull	**yule** *(Christmas)*
yungster	**young·ster**
yuppy	**yup·pie**
yurn	**yearn**
yuth	**youth**
zaney	**za·ny**
Zavier	**Xa·vi·er**
zealet	**zeal·ot**

WRONG	RIGHT	WRONG	RIGHT
zealus	**zeal·ous**	zinfundel	**zin·fan·del**
zeanith	**ze·nith**	zink	**zinc**
zeel	**zeal**	zinnea	**zin·nia**
zefyr	**zeph·yr**	ziper	**zip·per**
zelot	**zeal·ot**	zirkon	**zir·con**
zenia	**zin·nia**	ziro	**ze·ro**
zepelin	**zep·pe·lin**	zithur	**zith·er**
zepher	**zeph·yr**	zoalogy	**zo·ol·o·gy**
zeppalin	**zep·pe·lin**	zodiak	**zo·di·ac**
zercon	**zir·con**	zomby	**zom·bie**
zerconia	**zir·co·nia**	zoneing	**zon·ing**
zeti	**zi·ti**	zonel	**zon·al**
zideco	**zy·deco**	zoologecal	**zo·o·log·i·cal**
zigote	**zy·gote**	zuccini	**zuc·chi·ni**
zigurat	**zig·gu·rat**	Zues	**Zeus**
zigzaged	**zig·zagged**	Zurick	**Zur·ich**
zilion	**zil·lion**	zweeback	**zwie·back**
ziltch	**zilch**	zylophone	**xy·lo·phone**